THE MYTHOLOGY IN OUR LANGUAGE

THE MYTHOLOGY IN OUR LANGUAGE

Remarks on Frazer's Golden Bough

Translated by Stephan Palmié

Edited by Giovanni da Col and Stephan Palmié

With critical reflections by Veena Das,
Wendy James, Heonik Kwon, Michael Lambek,
Sandra Laugier, Knut Christian Myhre,
Rodney Needham, Michael Puett,
Carlo Severi, and Michael Taussig

HAU

Hau Books
Chicago

Cover: "A wicker man, filled with human sacrifices (071937)" © The British Library Board. C.83.k.2, opposite 105.

Cover and layout design: Sheehan Moore

Editorial office: Michelle Beckett, Justin Dyer, Sheehan Moore, Faun Rice, and Ian Tuttle

Typesetting: Prepress Plus (www.prepressplus.in)

ISBN: 978-0-9905050-6-8
LCCN: 2018962822

Hau Books
Chicago Distribution Center
11030 S. Langley
Chicago, IL 60628
www.haubooks.com

Hau Books is printed, marketed, and distributed by The University of Chicago Press.
www.press.uchicago.edu

Printed in the United States of America on acid-free paper.

Table of Contents

Ludwig Josef Johann Wittgenstein 1889–1951

Sir James George Frazer 1854–1941

CONTRIBUTORS

Stephan Palmié is Professor of Anthropology at the University of Chicago. He is the author of *Wizards and Scientists: Explorations in Afro-Cuban Modernity and Tradition* (2002) and *The Cooking of History: How Not to Study Afro-Cuban Religion* (2013) as well as the editor of several volumes on Caribbean and Afro-Atlantic anthropology and history.

Giovanni da Col is Research Associate at SOAS, University of London and Founder and Editor of HAU: Journal of Ethnographic Theory as well several volumes and collections on the anthropology of hospitality; luck and fortune; the anthropology of future; the history of anthropology; animism; and the spirit world in Tibet and Southwest China.

Veena Das is Krieger-Eisenhower Professor of Anthropology at the Johns Hopkins University and author of *Affliction: Health, Disease, Poverty* and *Life and Words: Violence and the Descent into the Ordinary*.

Wendy James recently retired as Professor of Social Anthropology at Oxford and is author of *War and Survival in Sudan's Frontierlands: Voices from the Blue Nile*, *The Ceremonial Animal: A New Portrait of Anthropology* and *The Listening Ebony: Moral Knowledge, Religion and Power among the Uduk of Sudan*.

Heonik Kwon is professorial Senior Research Fellow at Trinity College, University of Cambridge, and an APJ associate. The author of *The Other Cold War*, he co-authored *North Korea: Beyond Charismatic Politics* and is completing a book on intimate histories of the Korean War.

Michael Lambek is Professor of Anthropology at the University of Toronto, Scarborough. The author of *The Ethical Condition: Essays on Action, Person, and Value*, and *The Weight of the Past: Living with History in Mahajanga, Madagascar*, he co-authored *Four Lectures on Ethics: Anthropological Perspectives*.

Sandra Laugier is Professor of Philosophy at Université Paris 1 Panthéon-Sorbonne and author of *Etica e politica dell'ordinario, Recommencer la philosophie*, and *Why We Need Ordinary Language Philosophy*.

Knut Christian Myhre is a researcher at the Department of Ethnography, Numismatics, Classical Archaeology and University History, University of Oslo. He is the author of *Returning Life: Language, Life Force and History in Kilimanjaro* and editor of *Cutting and Connecting: 'Afrinesian' Perspectives on Networks, Relationality, and Exchange*.

Professor Rodney Needham (1923–2006) held the chair of social anthropology at Oxford University from 1976 to 1990 and was author of *Mamboru, history and structure in a domain of Northwestern Sumba*, *Counterpoints*, and *Exemplars*.

Michael Puett is the Walter C. Klein Professor of Chinese History and Anthropology at Harvard University. He is the author of *The Ambivalence of Creation: Debates Concerning Innovation and Artifice in Early China* and *To Become a God: Cosmology, Sacrifice, and Self-Divinization in Early China*.

Carlo Severi is Directeur d'études at the École des Hautes Etudes en Sciences Sociales, Paris. He is author of *L'Objet-Personne: Une anthropologie de la croyance visuelle*, *The Chimera Principle: An Anthropology of Memory and Imagination*, and co-author of *Naven, ou le donner à voir*.

Michael Taussig is Professor of Anthropology at The European Graduate School and author of *What Color is the Sacred?*, *Walter Benjamin's Grave*, and *My Cocaine Museum*.

Preface

Ludwig Wittgenstein's *Remarks on Frazer's Golden Bough* are of profound interest for anthropology. Anthropologists have read and learned from them but have not often put them into the perspective of the anthropological understanding that has been gained through the sustained ethnographic fieldwork that became the hallmark of the discipline since James Frazer and Wittgenstein wrote. Generating such a perspective is the ambitious project that was conceived by Giovanni da Col in 2013. Noting that the *Remarks on Frazer* were out of print and thinking it would be good to have a translation that was carried out by an anthropologist, he commissioned Stephan Palmié to do the job.

Da Col secured the rights for a translation and invited a number of anthropologists to offer their thoughts on the *Remarks*. The original idea was to have contributors think about how—after 83 years of ethnography and reflections—anthropologists can engage with Wittgenstein's forays into their domain (which predated by decades the now so-called 'ontological turn'). The idea was also to draw a balance and consider once again what anthropology has to offer today to philosophy.

Da Col decided to number the remarks in order to facilitate distribution to the contributors, and originally wrote contributors: There are 50 numbered remarks. We expect you to choose about 9 remarks each, just in case there are any overlaps. Each of you will end up commenting on about 6 or 7 remarks, 250–500 words comment on each. . . . Feel free to approach each remark according to your style and preferences. We are just expecting an engagement from the point of view of anthropology: What can anthropology speak to Wittgenstein's reflections? . . . What did anthropology achieve in the last eight decades? How can we significantly engage with Wittgenstein's ideas today?" He also circulated quite a number of published articles on the *Remarks* and on Wittgenstein, including pieces by Veena Das and Wendy James, as well as Michael Taussig's as yet unpublished essay on the corn wolf and published reflections by Rodney Needham, Thomas de Zengotita, Terence Evens, Stanley Tambiah, Godfrey Lienhardt, and several philosophers.

By the summer of 2014, we settled on a title for the volume: *The Mythology in our Language: Remarks on Frazer's Golden Bough.* A number of anthropologists signed on to the project: Veena Das, David Graeber, Wendy James, Heonik Kwon, Michael Lambek, Michael Puett, Carlo Severi, and Michael Taussig. There ensued a fruitful exchange of ideas over email as we circulated our initial individual choices and began "trading" the Remarks among ourselves. On July 17, 2014, Lambek asked, somewhat facetiously, "Do we all pick numbers until the last person left ends up . . . as the corn wolf?" As da Col noted in response, "choosing remarks is quite an entertaining process!"

Several of the contributors also wondered whether addressing the material "Remark by Remark" was the best way forward. The concern was both how each commentator could best make their arguments and also how to be faithful to Wittgenstein's *Remarks* themselves. On July 17, 2014, Lambek wrote da Col: "Your recent instructions . . . still leave open the question: Is it your intention that each of Wittgenstein's remarks will be followed by or paired with an individual commentary? Is this in fact the best way to proceed? If the commentaries each address several of Wittgenstein's remarks, as Wendy [James] and David [Graeber] indicate they would like to do, and if the remarks themselves connect to each other in various ways, then this suggests a bit more flexibility is in order. In any case, one of the things Wittgenstein's text leaves us with is precisely how to read it and I'm not sure we should pre-empt that with a single formula." Das, however, liked "the innovative idea of providing remark by remark," pointing out that it could be "very enlightening to think how one would relate to the specificity of that particular remark from the anthropological archive" (email from Das to contributors July 21, 2014).

Most of the original contributors submitted their essays by the fall of September 2014. However, after this initial spurt of collegial energy, for various reasons, the project languished. It was briefly rekindled in 2015 but soon stalled again. The project was restarted yet once more in 2018 when Palmié rallied many of the original contributors and was also able to get Knut Myhre on board. Much to our regret, David Graeber withdrew at this point. The distinguished philosopher Sandra Laugier joined the project, to comment and provide insight on the book as a whole. Laugier rightly noted that the original *Remarks* were unnumbered and asked us to remove the notation throughout the volume. However, as some of the contributors retained the initial 2014 format and others did not, this proved to be confusing and unwieldy. The result is what we hope is a happy compromise: the German unnumbered text faces the numbered text in English.

Because Rodney Needham was one of the first anthropologists to see the significance of the *Remarks* and of Wittgenstein more generally for anthropology, da Col also secured the rights to the republication of one of Needham's signature contributions, which we are delighted to include here.

We are indebted to the contributors for their patience during what was been a very long journey and trust it has been worth the wait.

—Giovanni da Col and Stephan Palmié
March 2019

CHAPTER I

Translation is Not Explanation
Remarks on the Intellectual History and Context of Wittgenstein's *Remarks on Frazer*

STEPHAN PALMIÉ

The origins of Ludwig Wittgenstein's "Bemerkungen über Frazer's *The Golden Bough*" are as complex and unclear as its checkered editorial and translational history (see Orzechowski and Pichler's [1995], Rothhaupt's [2016], and Westergaard's [2015] systematic assessments and critiques). The way Wittgenstein's literary executor, Rush Rhees (in Wittgenstein 1967: 233) presents the matter, one year after Wittgenstein's return to Cambridge in 1929, he expressed to his student Maurice O'Connor Drury an interest in reading James Frazer. As Rhees reports, Drury appears to have procured the first volume of the 1906–15 third edition (*The Magic Art and the Evolution of Kings I*) and proceeded to read to his mentor from it for the course of one academic term, before the two abandoned their conversations. Despite Drury's mention of the third (12 volume) edition, there is some agreement that Wittgenstein based his occasional lecture remarks during 1930–31 concerning Frazer as well as his notes on *The Golden Bough* on the 1922 abridged edition, which, perhaps not insignificantly, had been purged of most of its reference to Christianity that had caused such public furor upon publication of the second edition in 1900. Again, according to Rhees's version, Wittgenstein commenced writing on Frazer for a few weeks in June 1931, eventually dictating the results as part of what became known as "The Early Big Typescript," but rearranging the materials repeatedly, and eventually dropping practically all of them in what eventually became the so-called "Big Typescript."

As Rhees tells us, there was a second set of notes on *The Golden Bough*, jotted down on "odd bits of paper," not "earlier than 1936 [when Wittgenstein acquired a personal copy of the 1922 abridged edition] and probably after 1948." Elizabeth Anscombe discovered these after Wittgenstein's death. Rhees eventually united the various sets of notes for the 1967 publication in the German journal *Synthese*, though he never gave a clear rationale for his editorial interventions, or for why significant segments of the resulting text were omitted from the eventual translation published in 1979. Based on Rhees's original selection and arrangement for the 1967 *Synthese* publication, the following text is a complete English retranslation of Wittgenstein's *Remarks on Frazer's Golden Bough*.[1]

The following translator's notes need to be prefaced by the disclaimer that I am neither a philosopher nor an intellectual historian, but an anthropologist. Hence the title of this contribution, which aims to gesture toward a set of problems peculiar to my discipline since at least the last decades of the twentieth century. Putting matters in Wittgensteinian terms, the question is this: Is it even possible to translate the language games constitutive of other forms of life into those we find ourselves immersed in? At what cost do we attempt to override their incommensurabilities? And what, for that matter, are the entailments of such attempts at translation? What are its politics, and what are its consequences for both the language of origin and target (Gal 2015)? Like me, Wittgenstein was a native German speaker working in an Anglophone environment. But even though English and German are closely related languages, he chose to think and write in the latter idiom. This fact may seem of trivial consequence at first glance. Surely, all of his work has long been available to Anglophone audiences, and has spawned a vast secondary literature in English. But taking Wittgenstein by his own word, to entertain such a view is to trivialize the

---

1.   The numbering of Wittgenstein's Notes in this new translation has been undertaken solely for ease of reference, and should decidedly *not* be seen as Wittgenstein's own choice. Rhees's *Synthese* publication features them in unnumbered succession, but does not make clear whether the order in which they are presented originated with Wittgenstein, or from Rhees himself. For an editorial procedure comparable to the one presented here, see G. E. M. Anscombe and G. H. von Wright's "Editor's Preface" in Wittgenstein (1981).

difference between the forms of life constitutive of—and recursively constituted by—specific language games, the mutual interintelligibility of which cannot be a foregone conclusion.

In his *Remarks on Frazer*, Wittgenstein opposed a now bygone tendency in my discipline to rationalize—according to metropolitan European standards of reason—what used to be called "ostensibly irrational beliefs" and practices in the non-Western world, or Europe's own peasant periphery. What he opposed was the moment of "explanation" that aimed to reduce other forms of life and their associated language games to—perhaps historically explicable, but nonetheless erroneous—category mistakes. But, of course, Wittgenstein did so intuitively, neither being acquainted with the history of the discipline Frazer stood for, nor understanding the transformations it was undergoing all the while that he penned his *Remarks*.

While I hope that my new translation will be of use to practitioners of other disciplines, my brief in the following is thus to contextualize Wittgenstein's foray—and his *Remarks* really are that just that: disjointed notes, never meant for publication—into a disciplinary domain that Frazer significantly helped to establish (not the least by giving Edward Tylor's chair at Cambridge a new lease on life): Social Anthropology. Of course, by the time Wittgenstein read the abridged edition of Sir James's crowning achievement, Frazer's influence on anthropology (though not the British intelligentsia in a more general sense) was on the wane. It had been eclipsed by what Bronisław Malinowski once self-aggrandizingly called "the events of 1910" (i.e., his own arrival in England) and I. C. Jarvie (1964) famously bemoaned as "the revolution in anthropology."

As has often been noted, Frazer's biographer Robert Ackerman began his—by no means unsympathetic—study of Frazer's life and work with the following remarks:

Frazer is an embarrassment. The man who has had more readers and who was arguably a better writer than any anthropologist writing in English does not appear in any of the professional lineages that anthropologists acknowledge today. The reason for this is plain enough: he wrote vast, assured tomes about primitive religion and mythology without ever leaving the library. He based his comprehensive theories on the often crude and ethnocentric reports of explorers, missionaries, and traders. He lacked the idea of culture as the matrix, both conscious and unconscious, that gives meaning to social behavior and belief, and thus had no qualms about comparing terms of culture from the most disparate times and places. He was a hard-line rationalist who used ethnographic facts to try and knock the last nail in the coffin of religion in the name of objective science. If from time to time he achieved a kind of prophetic power, it is because he was the spokesman for an imperialist confidence that has now been swept away. It is no wonder that no one wants him for a professional ancestor. (Ackerman 1987: 1)

Parts of this assessment could be debated (Frazer certainly provided considerable inspiration to artists critical of "modernity" and may well be regarded as one of the unsung heroes of early twentieth-century modernist "primitivism," cf. Lienhardt 1993). Yet the fact remains that Frazer has been summarily dismissed by practically all of his successors. Different from Tylor's *Primitive Culture* (1871), which retained its status as a foundational (though otherwise increasingly irrelevant) text for Anglophone anthropology, Frazer's *Golden Bough* is now, at best, regarded as a footnote to a phase of the development of the discipline—and an unfortunate one at that. This phase came to an end with the emergence of genuinely fieldwork-based anthropological theorizing under W. H. R. Rivers, Alfred Cort Haddon, Arthur M. Hocart, Malinowski, and others in Great Britain, and with the vigorous attacks launched in the United States by Franz Boas against pseudo-evolutionary speculation from 1896 onward.

If Frazer had been the priest king of the "science of man" that Tylor inaugurated in the Victorian period, soon after Prince Edward assumed the throne, Frazer's eventual successors had begun to prowl the sacred grove at Cambridge, swords in hands.[2] Though Malinowski (himself once a protégé of Frazer) paid tribute to him (Malinowski 1948) toward the end of both of their lives (Frazer predeceased Malinowski by a year in 1941), there was no question that the so-called "comparative method" against which Boas (1896) had begun to rail more than a generation earlier, and which formed the cornerstone of Frazer's

---

2.   Intriguingly, both Frazer and Wittgenstein were Fellows of Trinity College, and technically overlapped there for considerable amounts of time. However, Brian Clack (1999: 177n5) is surely right in arguing that the likelihood that they would ever have interacted is small. Josef Rothhaupt (2016: 76) notes the curious coincidence that Frazer presented his inaugural William Wyse lectures on "The Fear of the Dead in Primitive Religion" during the Michaelmas Term of 1932 and May Term of 1933 on the exact days and at the exact time of day that Wittgenstein was himself lecturing. The one exception was Frazer's lecture on May 8, 1933, which Wittgenstein could have attended (and even though G. E. Moore's lecture notes show that Wittgenstein had mentioned Frazer earlier, he did make reference to him in his own lecture on May 9, 1933).

enterprise, was no longer a subject of debate. By the 1930s, at the latest, it had become irrelevant to the ways in which Anglophone anthropology, on both sides of the Atlantic, conceived of its own tasks and future.

Frazer's grand scheme of deriving universally valid developmental sequences from indiscriminate raids on uncontextualized ethnographica from across the globe now was perceived as the last—however grandiose—instantiation of a "method" that had driven comparative philology as it emerged from the eighteenth century onward, exerted its influence upon Charles Darwin and Lewis Henry Morgan, and received perverse reinforcement from Herbert Spencer's misapplications of evolutionary theory to the social realm. It was the method that Adam Smith's disciple Dugald Stewart had christened "conjectural history," and in the face of a new definition of the discipline's tasks it had not so much run into a dead end than become outright *dégoutant*: as British anthropologists turned to structural functionalism and their American counterparts embarked on similarly synchronic forms of holistic analyses—thus transforming their predecessors' searches for laws of social development into searches for laws of social organization and cultural coherence—Frazer's (and Tylor's) program for anthropology had been given a 90-degree shift.[3]

There is no shortage of autopsies of Frazer's project (e.g., Evans-Pritchard [1933] 1973; 1965: 27–29; Leach 1961, 1966; Smith 1973; Beard 1992; Lienhardt 1993; Stocking 1995: 126–51). And even though Jarvie's (1964) strictures against ethnographic particularism and cultural relativism reverberated through the "rationality debate" (conveniently summed up by Lukes [1982], if in a somewhat partisan spirit), with the significant exception of Mary Douglas (1978), it was not until the aftermath of the *Writing Culture* moment of the mid-1980s that scholars such as Marilyn Strathern (1987) or James Boon (1992) began to appreciate how Frazer's emplotment of humanity's differential "rise to civilization" recurred to narrative forms different in degree, but not so much kind, that were flourishing in the discipline of their day and age. Putting the matter bluntly, what had been the "persuasive fictions" (Strathern 1987) of anthropology in, say 1900, had stopped being persuasive by the 1930s. What is more, they had become unpalatable to the discipline as the kind of "just-so

---

3. As E. E. Evans-Pritchard (1962: 47) put it, "The functionalist critics of both evolutionists and diffusionists should have challenged them, not for writing history, but for writing bad history. As it was, they dropped the history and kept the pursuit of laws, which was often precisely what had made the history bad."

stories" that had once seemed to underwrite the discipline's social function in an age of (however anxious) Victorian liberal progressivism. By the 1980s, however, the affinities between Frazerian styles of exposition, and, say, the no less poetically driven self-referential accounts of the authors of *Argonauts of the Western Pacific* (Malinowski 1922), or *Witchcraft, Oracles, and Magic Among the Azande* (Evans-Pritchard 1937) were rife for exploration and comparison. This, we should note, was not because a resurgence of idiographic inscriptivism—however "thick," in Clifford Geertz's (1973) sense—might have gotten the better of residual nomothetic impulses still lingering in anthropology. On the contrary, perhaps, it was because its last great attempt at positivistic universalism—Claude Lévi-Strauss's positing of elementary structures of the human mind—had given way to a poststructuralist hermeneutics of suspicion to end all hermeneutics of suspicion.

Despite the overwhelming importance of Michel Foucault and Jacques Derrida, this was a moment inspired, at least in some quarters (Needham [1972] being an anticipatory case in point), by Wittgenstein's own thought—though *inspired* must surely be the key word here. However much Wittgenstein polemicized against scientism in his later years, and however much he may have been partisan to Oswald Spengler's gloomy ruminations about Occidental Modernity as a civilization in decline: the author of the *Tractatus Logico-Philosophicus* (Wittgenstein 1922) can only be assimilated to "postmodern" epistemic sensibilities (in our discipline or elsewhere) by a considerable stretch of the imagination.[4] To be sure, Wittgenstein appears to go to considerable length in reprovincializing (Bauman and Briggs 2003) the universalistic pretensions of Frazer's scholarship—such as when he charges that all that Frazer's explanations achieve is to make exotic practices "plausible to people who think like him" in presenting "all these practices, in the end, so to speak, as foolishness" (#1) or based on "false physics, or as the case may be, false medicine, technology, etc." (#15). Or when he accuses Frazer of a "narrowness of spiritual life" that precludes him from "grasping a life different from the English one of his time" and of imagining "a priest who is not basically an English parson of our times, with all his stupidity and shallowness" (#12). Or again, when he calls Frazer "far more savage than most of his savages, for these savages will not be as far removed from an understanding of spiritual matters as an Englishman of the twentieth century" (#19). But these vituperative attacks on Frazer's often smug

---

4.   See the contributions to Beale and Kidd (2017), in particular Coliva (2017).

ethnocentrism, or Wittgenstein's disparagement of Frazer's rationalization of magic and religion as bastard science as simply arising from "the stupid superstition of our time" (#13) hardly amount to a coherent argument.

Nor does Wittgenstein's alighting on Frazer's "tone"—we might say, poetics of exposition—present a sustained critique, such as when he writes that "Frazer begins by telling us the story of the King of the Woods at Nemi" so as to show "that something strange and terrible is happening here" (#2). Wittgenstein eventually does pursue this latter line of inquiry regarding the affective tenor of Frazer's writing in the sections on the Beltane Fire Festival (a much later addition to the text). But, as we shall see, what Wittgenstein has in mind is not at all the kind of vicarious frisson Frazer's reveling in bizarre exotica may well have produced among his contemporary late Victorian and Edwardian lay audiences (cf. Beard 1992; Lienhardt 1993).

***

A different matter is Wittgenstein's dismissal of Frazer's historicizing "explanations" of ostensibly obscure ritual practices "in the form of a hypothesis concerning temporal development" (#20) as inadequate to what Wittgenstein variously calls the "inner nature," "spirit," "depth," or even "mystery" of such practices—and it gets us closer not only to Wittgenstein's apparent concerns in the *Remarks* but also to a set of controversies within anthropology to which they have been often thought to speak. I refer here to the longstanding debate between proponents of what E. E. Evans-Pritchard (1965, 1973) called "intellectualist" approaches toward ritual, and those often labeled "symbolist." The particulars of the theoretical divide marked by these terms—which found its most poignant expression in the "rationality debate" of the 1960s and 1970s (Wilson 1970; Hollis and Lukes 1982) in which a Wittgensteinian (Peter Winch) played a considerable role—are well known, and need not be rehearsed here at any length. Standing in the tradition of Tylor and Frazer, intellectualist approaches found their culmination with Robin Horton's (e.g., 1967, 1982) contributions to a view of "African traditional thought" as a system of "explanation, prediction and control," and John Skorupski's (1976) summary defense of the broadly "theoretical" nature of the beliefs underlying ritual action, and their origin "out of a need to understand and control the natural environment" (Skorupski 1976: 9). It is this type of approach to ritual that appears to bear the brunt of Wittgenstein's critique:

One could begin a book on anthropology in this way: when one observes the life and behavior of humans all over the earth, one sees that apart from the kinds of behavior, one could call animal, the intake of food, etcetera, etcetera, humans also carry out actions that bear a peculiar character, and might be called ritual actions. But then again it is nonsense to go on and say that the characteristic feature of these actions is that they spring from erroneous notions about the physics of things. (#15)

But surely, the "symbolist" alternative, harking back to William Robertson-Smith and Émile Durkheim and largely prevailing in twentieth-century British Social Anthropology, appears alien to Wittgenstein's thinking as well. Characteristic of the tenor of the work of A. R. Radcliffe-Brown, Edmund Leach, Mary Douglas, John Beattie and others, one of the earlier statements of this position occurs in the Introduction to Meyer Fortes and E. E. Evans-Pritchard's collection *African Political Systems*:

> Members of an African society feel their unity and perceive their common interest in symbols, and it is their attachment to these symbols which more than anything else gives their society cohesion and persistence. . . . To explain these symbols sociologically, they have to be translated into terms of social function and the social structure they serve to maintain. Africans have no objective knowledge of the forces determining their social organization and actuating their social behavior. Yet they would be unable to carry on their collective life if they could not think and feel about the interests which actuate them, the institutions by means of which they organize collective action, and the structure of the groups into which they are organized. (Fortes and Evans-Pritchard 1940: 17–18)

Hence the importance of "sacred symbols, which reflect the social system, endow it with mystical values which evoke acceptance of the social order that goes far beyond the obedience exacted by the secular sanction of force" (Fortes and Evans-Pritchard 1940: 17–18). This is so because the "African does not see beyond the symbols; it might well be held that if he understood their objective meaning, they would lose the power they have over him" (1940: 18). Ritual enacts these symbols, puts them into social circulation, so to say, and feeds them back into the collective order they serve to maintain, endowing it with experiential consistency. There is thus nothing right or wrong, truthful or mistaken, about ritual action (or the sets of beliefs associated with it), as long as we subscribe to the Durkheimian move to see "society" as both subject and object of religious behavior, and are willing to accept indigenous justification for such practices as secondary elaborations of systemic—and systemically necessary—forms of *méconnaissance* (a point Karl Marx would have appreciated).[5]

But this clearly is not what Wittgenstein has in mind, either—unless one wanted to expand his elaborations on "language games" in the *Philosophical Investigations* and elsewhere, beyond the rather unclear sociological implications they or the notion of "forms of life" seem to carry. Is religion a language game among others? Is science? And are their "grammars" compatible, as the intellectualist tradition has held? Given how vague Wittgenstein remained on such matters, the exegetical pendulum has swung both ways.[6] Still, even on Wittgenstein's own view, a rigged game, once its rules are revealed to the disadvantaged player, simply turns into a different game, but remains a game nonetheless—and does not reveal the "real state of matters" (i.e., no game at all, whatever that might be taken to mean).[7] "False physics" and "false social theory" may thus merely be two sides of the same coin, and though Wittgenstein never really seems to have bothered about the kind of anthropology bodying forth from Oxford during his lifetime, it is sufficiently clear that he might not have had much sympathy with it.[8] To be sure, there appears

---

5. Regarding Frazer's assertion that "at a certain stage of early society the king or priest is often thought to be endowed with supernatural powers," Wittgenstein notes (#33): "It is of course not the case that the people believe that the ruler has these powers while the ruler himself very well knows that he does not have them, or does not know so only if he is an idiot or fool. Rather, the notion of his powers is of course arranged in a way such that it corresponds with experience—his own and that of the people."

6. Peter Winch (1958) certainly took that stance—two different, incompatible games—in helping to kick off the debate about whether bodies of scholarship concerned with the human condition could align themselves with the epistemic standards of the physical sciences. To put it in a nutshell, for Winch, "the idea of a social science" was deeply paradoxical.

7. *Remarks on the Foundations of Mathematics* II, #77. Here Knut Christian Myhre (2006) provides an astute critique of the perennial anthropological temptation to "explain" ostensibly unverifiable truth claims on the part of our ethnographic interlocutors by translating the terms of statements about, for example, witchcraft or sorcery into the putatively "real" world of reference that we claim for ourselves (such as expressions of social tension that, while projected into the unverifiable mystical spheres, feed back into observable social realities—in the form of witchcraft accusations). Cf. Needham (2014: 549–54).

8. But see Philippe de Lara (2000), who makes a convincing case for Wittgenstein's affinity with Evans-Fritchard's (1937, 1970) struggles to ethnographically address

to be some overlap between Wittgenstein's thinking and the distinction between "instrumental" and "expressive" action, as it came to be elaborated in British Social Anthropology from Malinowski onward, and a good deal of Wittgenstein scholarship has focused on it (e.g., Cook 1983; de Zengotita 1989, but see also the critiques by Clack 1999 and de Lara 2000, 2003). But while Wittgenstein might have agreed with John Beattie (1964)—for example, that the distinction between these two modalities of ritual behavior had long been artificially overdrawn—he would nevertheless have insisted that an explanation of the persistence of magical practices regarded as goal-directed by the actors themselves should *not* be sought in the "latent" functions (in Robert Merton's sense) of such rituals:

> The same savage who, apparently in order to kill his enemy, pierces an image of him, really builds his hut out of wood, and carves his arrows skillfully and not in effigy. (#10)

Thus, instrumental orientations in magical behavior are not to be confused with inadequate knowledge of natural phenomena:

> Frazer says it is very hard to discover the error in magic—and this is why it persists for so long—because, for example, a conjuration intended to bring rain will sooner or later appear as effective. But then it is strange that, after all, the people would not hit upon the fact that it will rain sooner or later anyway. (#2, cf. #31)

Although A. J. Ayer (1986) dealt a blow to this argument by suggesting that if rain ceremonies were to be performed faithfully before the start of each and every rainy season, no one could be presumed to know the difference, Wittgenstein wants to take the argument in a different direction:

> Burning in effigy. Kissing the picture of a loved one. This is *obviously not* based on a belief that it will have a definite effect on the object which the picture represents. It aims at some satisfaction, and does achieve it, too. Or rather, it does not *aim* at anything, we act in this way and then feel satisfied. (#9)

---

what de Lara calls Lucien Lévy-Bruhl's problem; that is, "how to make sense of mystical thought, once we refuse both intellectualist reduction and dualism" (de Lara 2000: 124–25). By "dualism," de Lara means a strict separation between "mystical and empirical" idioms of thought (empirically illusory, as it is).

More sharply:

> How misleading Frazer's explanations are becomes clear, I think, from the fact
> that one could very well invent primitive practices oneself, and it would only be
> by chance if they were not actually to be found elsewhere. That is, the principle
> according to which these practices are ordered is a much more general one than
> [it appears] in Frazer's explanation, and it exists in our own soul, so that we could
> think up all the possibilities ourselves. (#13)

And so he does throughout much of the *Remarks*, confronting Frazer's casu-
istry with rites that one might just as well "make up" oneself—and then might
find confirmed in the ethnographic literature on some or the other corner
of the world (or not—which, in fact, would not matter as long as such practices *could* be imagined; and imagined as persisting *because* they "correspond to
a general inclination among the people" [#45] who would continue to enact
them):

> We can thus readily imagine that, for instance, the king of a tribe becomes vis-
> ible for no one, but also that every member of the tribe is obliged to see him.
> The latter will then certainly not occur in a manner more or less left to chance;
> instead, he will be *shown* to the people. Perhaps no one will be allowed to touch
> him, or perhaps they will be *compelled* to touch him. Think how after Schubert's
> death his brother cut Schubert's scores into small pieces and gave to his favorite
> pupils these pieces of a few bars. As a gesture of piety, this action is *just* as com-
> prehensible as that of preserving the scores untouched and accessible to no one.
> And if Schubert's brother had burned the scores, this could still be understood
> as a gesture of piety. The ceremonial (hot or cold) as opposed to the haphazard
> (lukewarm) is what characterizes piety. (#13)

In all of this, Wittgenstein refuses "explanation," and not just of the historicizing kind that he finds so objectionable in Frazer's work on the *rex nemorenis*:

> If one sets the phrase "majesty of death" next to the story of the priest king of
> Nemi, one sees that they are one and the same. The life of the priest king repre-
> sents what is meant by that phrase. Whoever is gripped by the [idea of] majesty of
> death can express this through just such a life. —Of course, this is also not an ex-
> planation, it just puts one symbol for another. Or one ceremony for another. (#5)

The "majesty of death"—just like fire, sex and procreation, the change of seasons, the anthropomorphic shape of our shadow, political power, and so forth—ultimately is a matter that continues to arouse human affect, though it does so in locally and historically variable cultural forms. In the end: "One can only resort to description here, and say: such is human life" (#3), thus recurring to the multiplicity of language-mediated "life forms" natural to what Wittgenstein calls the existential (i.e., cultural) condition of a "ceremonial animal."

Here, at the latest, it ought to be clear that ideological criticism was not the "game" Wittgenstein was after. He rejected Frazerian intellectualism, and certainly would have rejected later anthropological symbolist or expressivist explanations. Instead, he appears to be opting for a resolutely nonreductionist account of humanity as an inescapably "ritualizing" species (whether it be the "instinct" to hit the ground with a stick upon a mishap, kissing the picture of a loved one, devising rituals such as the rites of succession at the sacred grove of Nemi, or routinized courses of action that insinuate their association with human sacrifice [see below]). This notion of an essential human propensity to ritualize is one that Wittgenstein undergirds by a characteristic call for a methodology that he opposes to "explanation" (in the case at hand, he means genetic explanations à la Frazer, but the case is easily extendable to "symbolist" ones as well), and that may have meant to constitute part and parcel of what is often called his "therapeutic" project to cure thought of the maladies—that is, philosophical problems—inflicted upon it by a "bewitchment of language" (*Philosophical Investigations* §109). This methodology is associated with one of the most vexingly untranslatable terms in Wittgenstein's lexicon, to which I now turn: übersichtliche *Darstellung*.

***

Although this concept recurs again and again in Wittgenstein's later writings, the *locus classicus* is often taken to be §122 in the *Philosophical Investigations* (4th edition), and its translation already indicates the problems of glossing Wittgenstein's language in English:

> A main source of our failure to understand is that we don't have an *overview* of the use of our words. —Our grammar is deficient in surveyability. A surveyable representation produces precisely that kind of understanding which consists in "seeing connections." Hence the importance of finding and inventing intermediate links.

> The concept of a surveyable representation is of fundamental significance
> for us. It characterizes the way we represent things, how we look at matters.
> (Is this a "Weltanschauung"?)

Not incidentally, these remarks are followed by one of Wittgenstein's most
celebrated sayings, §123: "A philosophical problem has the form: 'I don't know
my way about'" ("*Ich kenne mich nicht aus*"). Of course, the German original
is open to all kinds of interpretations—from the one chosen by G. E. M.
Anscombe, P. M. S. Hacker, and Joachim Schulte (2009) that implies un-
familiarity with a terrain, to a much broader spectrum of states of unknow-
ing (I am not familiar with the subject or problem, its origin, history, and so
forth)—and it is perhaps not surprising that A. C. Miles and Rhees chose
the admittedly fanciful adjective "perspicuous" for the kind of presentation
(or representation—terminology in the secondary literature varies wildly in
regard to the prefix) for the quality that Wittgenstein intended to designate
by *übersichtlich* (cf. footnote to #22). This is not the place to "survey," provide
a "synopsis," or give a "bird's eye view," let alone to "perspicuously represent"
the various interpretations that *übersichtliche Darstellung* has received in the
secondary literature.[9] Instead, and since the concept is elaborated in a somewhat different direction in the *Remarks on Frazer's Golden Bough* than in either
the *Philosophical Investigations* or *Remarks on the Foundations of Mathematics*,
it might be best to turn to what, arguably, are a number of key passages in the
text itself:

> An historical explanation, an explanation in the form of a hypothesis of develop-
> ment is only *one* kind of summary arrangement of the data—of their synopsis. It
> is equally possible to see the data in their relation to one another and to gather
> them into a general picture without doing so in the form of a hypothesis con-
> cerning temporal development. (#20)

Alluding to (in fact, quoting) Goethe's notion of an ideal *Urpflanze* as a key to
an understanding of the morphology of floral life, he continues:

---

9.   All these are terms variously applied to translate the phrase. I have found Peter
      Hacker (1992) and Brian Clack (1999: 53–78) to provide useful discussions of the
      possible semantic range of Wittgenstein's usage of *übersichtliche Darstellung*. Phil
      Hutchinson and Rupert Read (2008) provide a broader perspective on the debate
      between proponents of "elucidative" and "therapeutic" interpretations.

"And so the chorus points to a secret law" is what one might want to say about Frazer's collection of facts. Now, I *can* represent this law, this idea, in the form of a hypothesis of development, but also in analogy to the schema of a plant, I can represent it as the schema of a religious ceremony, or again by grouping the facts alone in a "perspicuous" presentation.

For us the concept of perspicuous presentation is of fundamental importance. It designates our form of presentation, the way we see things (A kind of "Weltanschaung" as it is apparently typical of our time. Spengler).

The perspicuous presentation transmits an understanding of the kind that what we see are "just the connections." Hence the importance of finding *intermediate links*.

However, in this case, a hypothetical link is not meant to do anything other than draw attention to the similarity, the connections between the *facts*. Just as one might illustrate an inner relation between a circle and an ellipse by gradually transforming an ellipse into a circle; *but not to claim that a given ellipse in fact, historically, emerged from a circle* (developmental hypothesis), rather only to sharpen our eye for a formal connection.

But I also cannot see the developmental hypothesis as anything but the investiture [clothing] of a formal connection. (#22)

Such formal connections, of course, are the ones that Wittgenstein elaborates on at great length under the conceptual rubric of "family resemblances" in §§66–77 of the *Philosophical Investigations*. There, his cases in point are games, numbers, plants, and colors; here, he extends the method—with its characteristic antireductive implications to ritual practices that, once "intermediate links" have been identified, may likewise be shown to "transform into each other" without implying genetic devolution (or, although Wittgenstein does not consider this, without imputing diffusionary relationships across social space). What he does not do, however, is elaborate *rules of transformation*, such as would, under the impact of Saussurean linguistics, become the touchstone of a very different, but similarly ahistorical (if not antihistorical) kind of comparativist anthropology, Leví-Straussian structuralism.[10] The relationships Wittgenstein is after are on a morphological plane, not one of deep structure and surface manifestation,

---

10. That the most Wittgensteinian of British social anthropologists, Rodney Needham (e.g., 1972, 1985), was also a partisan of French Structuralism underscores these affinities.

paradigm, and syntagma. Rather, we are dealing with what Wittgenstein, in *Remarks on the Philosophy of Psychology* (1980), calls "aspect seeing" or "aspect change," as when our perception of "the duck rabbit" (§70) oscillates between two modalities of cognitively organizing sensory data, once we "see things differently" (cf. Redding 1987; Hutchinson and Read 2008).

At first glance, Wittgenstein thus seems to be aiming to force an aspect change upon Frazer's "method" of short-circuiting widely (if not to say wildly) disparate ethnographical and historical data so as to construct a narrative about dying gods and priest kings along an "evolutionary" line of derivation and "survival." Frazer's conceit, Wittgenstein seems to say, is to submerse an entirely different set of relations under the organizing rubric of—shall we say?—descent with modification.[11] As a result, Frazer remains beholden to the thought-constraining blindness of a developmental hypothesis as the primary aspect of organizing his materials, which, looked at from a different angle, might reveal an entirely different (conceptual) shape and form. What a concrete alternative to this might look like, what aspect might "light up," once we abandon Frazer's "explanations" is spelled out most clearly in Wittgenstein's (later, even decades later) comments on the Beltane Fire Festival. Speaking of Frazer's chapter LXII, "The Fire Festivals of Europe" in the 1922 abridged edition of the *Golden Bough*, Wittgenstein notes:

> What is most striking are not merely the similarities but also the differences between all these rites. There is a manifold of faces with common features that keep surfacing here and there. And what one would like to do is draw lines that connect the components in common. (#39)

---

11. This includes forgetting the original rationale for certain ritual practices, and the investment of what has come to be misunderstood, with novel meanings, decipherable by historicizing comparison. Here, it may be apt to recall Evans-Pritchard's ([1933] 1973: 140) important earlier critique of Frazer's "intellectualist" reductions. Regarding Frazer's example of the "homeopathic" connection between jaundice and gold in Greek folk medicine, Evans-Pritchard similarly rejects Frazer's grounding of such "connections" in a psychological logic: "We must not say that a Greek peasant sees that gold and jaundice have the same colour and that therefore he can use the one to cure the other. Rather we must say that because gold is used to cure jaundice colour associations between them become established in the mind of a Greek peasant." Wittgenstein's sociology, implicit as it is, squarely comes down on the fact that to acquire a language is to acquire a conceptual scheme or *Weltbild*.

This, of course, sounds very much like the program of übersichtliche *Darstellung* as elaborated in the *Philosophical Investigations*. Yet in the sentence immediately following this passage, Wittgenstein continues with an ostensibly astonishing step beyond the mere establishment of "family resemblances":

> What would still be lacking then is a part of our contemplation, and it is the one that connects this picture with our own feelings and thoughts. This part gives such contemplation its depth. (#39)

What he means becomes clear when he turns to Frazer's account of the eighteenth-century Beltane Fire Festival, in which a cake in which a button had been baked was ceremonially consumed by the celebrants, and the person who got the piece with the button was mockingly threatened with being thrown into the fire. Frazer sees this as an attenuated "survival" of past rituals of human sacrifice.

> It is thus clear that what gives this practice depth is its connection with the burning of a human being. If it were custom at some festival for men to ride on one another (as in horse-and-rider games), we would see nothing more in this than a way of carrying someone, which reminds us of people riding horses; however, if we knew that it had been custom among many people to, for example, use slaves as mounts and to celebrate certain festivals mounted in this way, then we should see in the harmless practice of our times something deeper and less harmless. (#42)

This is immediately followed by these crucial remarks:

> The question is: Does this—shall we say—sinister character adhere to the custom of the Beltane fire in itself as it was practiced a hundred years ago, or only if the hypothesis of its origin were to be confirmed? (#42)

Clearly, this "now you see it, now you don't" question strikes to the heart of the matter. "The life of the priest king" and "the majesty of death" may be aspects of the same figuration. But would mock threats of burning or horse-and-rider games impress us if we had no idea of their origins in a past of truly "deep and sinister business" (#43)? Here we should remember Wittgenstein's earlier remarks on Frazer's "tone":

When Frazer begins by telling us the story of the King of the Woods at Nemi, he does so in a tone that shows that something strange and terrible is happening here. However, the question "Why is this happening" is essentially answered by just this: because it is terrible. In other words, it is what to us appears as terrible, impressive, horrible, tragic, etcetera that gave birth to this event. (#2)

If so, the allegation of Frazer's "blindness to the life of the spirit" thus may be a bit of sloganeering on Wittgenstein's part (cf. Clack 1999). And yet, consider this:

Here [in the Beltane Fire Festival] one sees something like the remnants [*sic*] of a casting of lots. And through this aspect it suddenly gains depth. Should we learn that the cake with the buttons was originally baked in a determinate case, say, in honor of a button-maker on the occasion of his birthday, and that the practice had then merely persisted on the local level, it would in fact lose all its "depth," unless this were to lie in its present form as such. (#43)

Attacking Frazer's method rather than expository aims, he continues:

In this case it is often said: "this custom is obviously ancient." How does one know that? Is it merely because historical evidence for ancient practices of this sort is at hand? Or is there another reason, one that we can attain through interpretation? But even if its prehistoric origin and its descent from an earlier practice is historically established, then it is still possible that there is *nothing at all* sinister about the practice anymore, that nothing of the ancient horror still adheres to it. Perhaps it is only performed by children today who have contests in baking cakes and decorating them with buttons. (#43)

Or consider yet another imaginative nail to drive into the coffin of Frazer's enterprise: what if Frazer's method were just a way of establishing *aspectivally* "persuasive fictions" at a suitably safe remove (ethnologically and historically) from what Frazer himself might well regard as "deep" and "terrible" but then takes pains to project onto "ruder stages of civilization"?

Above all: whence the certainty that such a practice must be ancient (what are the data, what is the verification)? But have we any certainty, could we not be mistaken and proven to be in error by historical means? Certainly, but there remains something of which we are sure. . . . For when I say: what is deep about this lies in its origin *if it did* come about in this way, then such deepness lies either in the thought of [its derivation from] such origins, or else the deepness is in itself hypothetical—in which case one can only say: if that is how it went, then this was a deep and sinister business. What I want to say is this: what is sinister, deep [about all this] does not lie in how the history of this practice actually went, for perhaps it did not go that way at all; nor that it maybe or [even] probably went that way, but in what gives me reason to assume so. (#43)

What gives me reason to assume so, indeed. Clearly, "the solution is not anymore disquieting than the riddle" (#45). "The correct and interesting thing is not to say, 'this has come from that,' but 'it could have come from that'" (#47). If we accept these premises, then we are—perhaps surprisingly—thrown back on a set of questions that guided enterprises such as Tylor's and Frazer's right from the start but that the latter only spelled out in the matter of an afterthought, late in his life: Why would Frazer's—increasingly impossibly massive—compendia of savage rites and customs even have attained the (civilized) readership they did? Frazer (1927: 218–19) himself tells us in no uncertain terms:

> Among the ignorant and superstitious classes of modern Europe it is very much like it was thousands of years ago in Egypt and in India, and what it now is amongst the lower savages surviving in the remotest corners of the world. . . . It is not our business here to consider what bearing the permanent existence of such a solid layer of savagery beneath the surface of society, and unaffected by the superficial changes of religion and culture, has upon the future of humanity. The dispassionate observer, whose studies have led him to plumb its depths, can hardly regard it otherwise than as a standing menace to civilization. We seem to move on a thin crust which may at any one moment be rent by the subterranean forces slumbering below.

Note here the change from Tylor's mid-Victorian optimism about anthropology as a "reformer's science" to Frazer's doubts about the "thin crust" of "civilization" precariously resting on a slumbering volcano of irrational energy[12]—so reminiscent of Sigmund Freud, or indeed the skepticism characterizing much

---

12. Cf. George Stocking (1995: 146–48) on Frazer's ambivalent vacillation between chauvinism and gloomy prophecy.

of European literary modernity during the period Wittgenstein read and re-marked upon the *Golden Bough*. In all fairness to Frazer, might we not read this passage as effecting something very much like the aspect change Wittgenstein is trying to induce?

Perhaps Frazer's preoccupation with the resonances of the "deep and sin-ister business" in the midst of modern civilization could not but have struck a responsive chord with a philosopher who sympathized with Spengler's deeply pessimistic views of an impending Decline of the West. But will it make do to book off the *Remarks on Frazer's Golden Bough* as an essay in (however un-conventionally "modernistic") cultural critique? To be sure, Wittgenstein lived through the horrors of two World Wars—enough perhaps to dissuade anyone from optimistic assessments of the progress of civilization, and make him or her inclined to see their own world as marked by a recurrence of "deep and sinister business," ever ready to irrupt into our own experience. After all, "Frazer's ex-planations would not be explanations at all if they did not, in the end, appeal to an inclination in ourselves" (#13) because "there is something in us, too, that speaks in support of such observances" (#18). Regarding the Beltane Fire Festi-val, Wittgenstein thus writes:

> I believe that what appears to us as sinister is [not the history, real or imputed, but] the inner nature of the practice as performed in recent times, and the facts of human sacrifice as we know them only indicate the direction in which we ought to look at it. When I speak of the inner nature of the practice, I mean all of those circumstances in which it is carried out and that are not included in the report on such a festival, because they consist not so much in particular actions that characterize the festival than in what one might call the spirit of the festival that would be described, for example, if one were to describe the kind of people that take part in it, their usual way of behaving [on other occasions]—that is, their character—and the kind of games they play at other times. And then one would see that what is sinister lies in the character of these people themselves. (#42)

Perhaps the very shudder at the thought that eating an arbitrarily selected piece of cake might be our sentence to an awful, violent, and (as opposed to illness) nonarbitrary death reveals what Wittgenstein's übersichtliche *Darstellung* aims to drive at: a moment of self-reflection, perhaps mediated by, but certainly not contingent upon, the adducement of ethnographic or historical data. For no doubt about it: Even though Wittgenstein never once seems to have remarked about it, plenty of "deep and sinister business" was afoot in the midst of the very "civilization" he took as his point of departure. After all, the horrors of European fascism mark the period during which he commenced—and ended—his writings on the subject. At the very least, we might say that Wittgenstein's refusal of historicization has more to do with Ernst Bloch's (1977) disquieting 1932 meditations on the "synchronicity of the nonsynchronous" than with the apollonian spirit of Bruno Latour's (1993) proclamation that "we have never been modern."

***

Be that as it may, a final note on the method (if we can call it that) of übersichtliche *Darstellung* is in order here, and it draws inspiration from another expositor of "family resemblances," Carlo Ginzburg (1991, 2004). In an earlier monograph on how the selective uptake of elements of an (however putative) ancient pan-Eurasian shamanistic tradition into the demonological discourses of an inquisitorial elite in the fourteenth and fifteenth centuries gave rise to the idea (and persecutorial reality) of the "witches Sabbath," Ginzburg (1991: 15) noted that his own methodology paralleled and received belated reinforcement when he came across Wittgenstein's writings on *übersichtliche Darstellung*. In the later essay, and with characteristic erudition, Ginzburg (2004) "connects the lines" between Wittgenstein's project and a number of roughly contemporaneous but at first glance seemingly unrelated intellectual pursuits. These include, for example, Francis Galton's "composite photographs" designed to draw out what one might well call physiognomic "Urformen." But what I want to alight on in closing are the connections Ginzburg draws between Wittgenstein's methodological aim of *übersichtliche Darstellung* and the expository experiments of a contemporary anthropologist—and one as un-Frazerian as they come: Gregory Bateson. Ginzburg merely mentions this in passing. But, in a rather unusual move for the time, Bateson prefaced his 1936 monograph on the Iatmul Naven ceremony with a lengthy reflection on "Methods of Presentation" (Bateson 1958) that aimed to highlight the experimental character of his study, but that also can be seen as bearing strong "family resemblances" to Wittgenstein's program. It is to these reflections of Bateson's that I now turn.[13]

---

13. Gregory Bateson, too, had an important Cambridge connection, not the least through his famous biologist father William Bateson, a former student of Francis

As Bateson wrote in 1936, he wanted to clarify from the outset that his main analytical categories (ritual, structure, pragmatic functioning, and ethos) are not to be regarded as "individual entities but as fundamentally inseparable *aspects* of culture" (Bateson 1958: 3; emphasis mine). However, since it is

> impossible to present the whole of a culture simultaneously in a single flash, I must begin at some arbitrarily chosen point in the analysis; and since words must necessarily be arranged in lines, I must present the culture, which like all other cultures is really an elaborate reticulum of interlocking cause and effect, not with a network of words, but with words in linear series. (Bateson 1958: 3)

No doubt that Wittgenstein would have approved of such attempts at *übersichtliche Darstellung*. But there is more: conceding that the resulting order or presentation cannot be other than "arbitrary and artificial," Bateson goes on to explain that "I shall first present the ceremonial behavior, torn from its context, so that it appears bizarre and nonsensical" only to then redescribe the same data to "indicate how the ceremonial can be related to the various aspects of the culture" (1958: 3). And then he adds a crucial antihistorical disclaimer—again very much in Wittgenstein's sense:

> I shall not inquire what either the ceremonies or their cultural setting may have been like in the past. In my use of causal terminology I shall be referring to *conditional* rather than to *precipitating* causes. Thus in a synchronic study of a fire I should say that the fire burns because there is oxygen in the room, etc., but I should not inquire into how the fire was first ignited. (Bateson 1958: 3)

In Bateson's view, Iatmul culture (like any other culture) formed a "reticulated system" of mutually reinforcing input and output values that could not be ethnographically captured in linear fashion. But, or so Bateson thought, its operation could be analytically approximated by refracting the ethnography itself through the prism of the Naven ceremony. Consider here the following passage from Bateson's "Epilogue 1936," worth quoting at some length:

Galton's, who had been involved in the rediscovery of Gregor Mendel's writings. More intriguingly, Gregory Bateson returned to Cambridge from New Guinea in the 1930s. But as in the case of Frazer, there are no indications that Bateson and Wittgenstein ever met (Ginzburg 2004: 546–47).

I began to doubt the validity of my own categories, and performed an experiment. I chose three bits of culture: (a) the *wau* [kin classified with the mother's brother] giving food to the *laua* [kin classified with the sister's son]; a pragmatic bit, (b) a man scolding his wife; an ethological bit, and (c) a man marrying his father's sister's daughter; a structural bit. Then I drew a lattice of nine squares on a large piece of paper, three rows of squares with three squares in each row. I labeled the horizontal lines with my bits of culture and the vertical columns with my categories. Then I forced myself to see each bit as conceivably belonging to each category. I found that it could be done.

I found that I could think of each bit of culture structurally; I could see it in accordance with a consistent set of rules or formulations. Equally, I could see each bit as "pragmatic," either as satisfying the needs of individuals or as contributing to the integration of society. Again, I could see each bit ethologically, as an expression of emotion.

This experiment may seem puerile, but to me it was very important, and I have recounted it at length because there may be some among my readers who tend to regard such concepts as "structure" as concrete parts which "interact" in culture, and who find, as I did, a difficulty in thinking of these concepts as labels merely for points of view adopted either by the scientist or by the natives. (Bateson 1958: 262)

And then he concludes with the following remarks:

It is instructive too to perform the same experiment with such concepts as economics, kinship and land tenure, and even religion, language, and "sexual life" do not stand too surely as categories of behavior, but tend to resolve themselves into labels for points of view from which all behavior may be seen. (Bateson 1958: 262)

Bateson's specific concern was to undercut the tendency toward Alfred North Whitehead's fallacy of misplaced concreteness that had begun to flourish in anthropology, not the least under the influence of the legalistic focus on institutions propagated by Radcliffe-Brown. What he was after, instead, were what Marilyn Strathern (1985), in a perhaps unwittingly Wittgensteinian turn of phrase, called "constitutive orders of a provisional kind"—the sort of second-order language artifices by which both anthropologists and natives seek to render their social world (including shared ethnographic worlds) comprehensible.

Of course, by then Bateson had come under the influence of American configurationism (as ahistorical a mode of ethnographic exposition as any of its British structural functionalist counterparts), and he would soon veer in the direction of yet another master-trope for the organization of ethnographic data: cybernetics (Bateson 1958: 280–303). In any event, it is probably safe to say that he would not have had much truck with Wittgenstein's program of *philosophical* self-elucidation through experimentation with ethnographica—real or invented. Still, the fact that *Naven* can hardly be profitably read in any other way than as an attempt to use the description of a concrete ethnographic case to turn the then-reigning epistemological orientation (positivistic, to be sure) on the discipline's own methods of analysis reveals a striking affinity to Wittgenstein's therapeutic endeavors. In other words, perhaps Wittgenstein's ruminations on Frazer were not just in tune with a general theoretical shift in anthropology but were not far, either, from what some of the discipline's future concerns would eventually become.

To be sure, one of the outcomes of the impact of poststructuralist philosophy on our discipline has been the "Historic Turn in the Social Sciences" (MacDonald 1996), revaluating "developmental explanations" in a fashion attentive to both the "endogenous historicity of local worlds" (Comaroff and Comaroff 1992), and that of the descriptive second order languages in which they are ethnographically and analytically rendered (e.g., Palmié 2013, 2018). This, certainly, is not the place to explore this moment, "therapeutic" (in Wittgenstein's sense) though its goals may be. Nor does it seem apposite to go into any detail about even more recent developments in regard to the mobilization of ethnographica to the end of disciplinary self-elucidation and the relativization of "Western" epistemology in favor of plural ontologies. But it strikes me that a good deal of what currently sails under labels such as "perspectivism" and "ontological turn" (Holbraad 2012; Viveiros de Castro 2012; Holbraad and Pedersen 2017) might not have surprised Wittgenstein one single bit.

REFERENCES

Ackerman, Robert. 1987. *J. G. Frazer: His Life and Work*. Cambridge: Cambridge University Press.

Ayer, A. J. 1986. *Wittgenstein*. Chicago: University of Chicago Press.

Bateson, Gregory. 1958. *Naven: The Culture of the Iatmul People of New Guinea as Revealed Through a Study of the "Naven" Ceremonial*. Stanford, CA: Stanford University Press.

Bauman, Richard, and Charles Briggs. 2003. *Voices of Modernity: Language Ideologies and the Politics of Inequality*. Cambridge: Cambridge University Press.

Beale, Jonathan, and Ian James Kidd, eds. 2017. *Wittgenstein and Scientism*. New York: Routledge.

Beard, Mary. 1992. "Frazer, Leach, and Virgil: The Popularity (and Unpopularity) of the Golden Bough." *Comparative Studies in Society and History* 34 (2): 203–24.

Beattie, John H. M. 1964. *Other Cultures*. London: Routledge and Kegan Paul.

Bloch, Ernst. 1977. "Nonsynchronism and the Obligation to Its Dialectics." *New German Critique*, no. 11 (Spring): 22–38.

Boas, Franz. 1896. "The Limitations of the Comparative Method of Anthropology." *Science* 4 (103): 901–08.

Boon, James. 1992. *Other Tribes, Other Scribes: Symbolic Anthropology in the Comparative Study of Cultures, Histories, Religions, and Texts*. Cambridge: Cambridge University Press.

Clack, Brian R. 1999. *Wittgenstein, Frazer and Religion*. New York: St. Martin's Press.

Coliva, Annalisa. 2017. "Rituals, Philosophy, Science, and Progress." In *Wittgenstein and Scientism*, edited by Jonathan Beale and Ian James Kidd, 38–51. New York: Routledge.

Comaroff, John, and Jean Comaroff. 1992. *Ethnography and the Historical Imagination*. Boulder, CO: Westview Press.

Cook, John W. 1983. "Magic, Science and Religion." *Philosophical Investigations* 6 (10): 2–36.

De Lara, Philippe. 2000. "Wittgenstein and Evans-Pritchard on Ritual: Twenty-Two Reasons to Think that Wittgenstein was an Anthropologist." *JASO* 21 (2): 119–32.

———. 2003. "Wittgenstein as Anthropologist: The Concept of Ritual Instinct." *Philosophical Investigations* 26 (2): 109–24.

De Zengotita, Thomas. 1989. "On Wittgenstein's *Remarks on Frazer's Golden Bough*." *Cultural Anthropology* 4 (4): 390–98.

Douglas, Mary. 1978. "Judgments on James Frazer." *Daedalus* 107 (4): 151–64.

Evans-Pritchard, E. E. (1933) 1973. "The Intellectualist (English) Interpretation of Magic." *JASO* 4 (3): 123–42.

———. 1937. *Witchcraft, Magic, and Oracles among the Azande*. Oxford: Clarendon Press.

———. 1962. *Essays in Social Anthropology*. London: Faber and Faber.

———. 1965. *Theories of Primitive Religion*. Oxford: Oxford University Press.

Fortes, Meyer, and E. E. Evans-Pritchard. 1940. "Introduction." In *African Political Systems*, edited by Meyer Fortes and E. E. Evans-Pritchard, 1–23. Oxford: Oxford University Press.

Frazer, James G. 1927. *Man, God, and Immortality: Thoughts on Human Progress*. New York: Macmillan.

Gal, Susan. 2015. "Politics of Translation." *Annual Reviews of Anthropology* 44: 225–40.

Geertz, Clifford. 1973. *The Interpretation of Cultures*. New York: Basic Books.

Ginzburg, Carlo. 1991. *Ecstasies: Deciphering the Witches' Sabbath*. Chicago: University of Chicago Press.

———. 2004. "Family Resemblances and Family Trees: Two Cognitive Metaphors." *Critical Inquiry* 30 (3): 537–56.

Hacker, Peter M. S. 1992. "Developmental Hypotheses and Perspicuous Representation." *Iyyun: The Jerusalem Philosophical Quarterly* 41: 277–99.

Holbraad, Martin. 2012. *Truth in Motion: The Recursive Anthropology of Cuban Divination*. Chicago: University of Chicago Press.

Holbraad, Martin, and Axel Morton Pedersen. 2017. *The Ontological Turn: An Anthropological Exposition*. Cambridge: Cambridge University Press.

Hollis, Martin, and Steven Lukes, eds. 1982. *Rationality and Relativism*. Cambridge, MA: MIT Press.

Horton, Robin. 1967. "African Traditional Thought and Western Science." *Africa* 37 (1): 50–71; 37 (2): 155–87.

———. 1982. "Tradition and Modernity Revisited." In *Rationality and Relativism*, edited by Martin Hollis and Steven Lukes, 201–60. Cambridge, MA: MIT Press.

Hutchinson, Phil, and Rupert Read. 2008. "Toward a Perspicuous Presentation of 'Perspicuous Presentation.'" *Philosophical Investigations* 31 (2): 141–60.

Jarvie, I. C. 1964. *The Revolution in Anthropology*. London: Routledge and Kegan Paul.

Latour, Bruno. 1993. *We Have Never Been Modern*. Cambridge, MA: MIT Press.

Leach, Edmund. 1961. "Golden Bough or Gilded Twig?" *Daedalus* 90 (2): 317–87.

———. 1966. "On the 'Founding Fathers.'" *Current Anthropology* 7 (5): 560–67.

Lienhardt, Godfrey. 1993. "Frazer's Anthropology: Science and Sentiment." *JASO* 24 (1): 1–12.

Lukes, Steven. 1982. "Relativism in Its Place." In *Rationality and Relativism*, edited by Martin Hollis and Steven Lukes, 261–305. Cambridge, MA: MIT Press.

MacDonald, Terence J., ed. 1996. *The Historic Turn in the Social Sciences*. Ann Arbor: University of Michigan Press.

Malinowski, Bronislaw. 1922. *Argonauts of the Western Pacific*. London: Routledge and Kegan Paul.

———. 1948. "Dedication to Sir James Frazer." In *Magic, Science, and Religion and Other Essays*, edited by Robert Redfield, 93–95. Glencoe, IL: The Free Press.

Myhre, Knut Christian. 2006. "The Truth of Anthropology: Epistemology, Meaning and Residual Positivism." *Anthropology Today* 22 (6): 16–19.

Needham, Rodney. 1972. *Belief, Language, and Experience*. Oxford: Blackwell.

———. 1985. *Exemplars*. Berkeley: University of California Press.

———. 2014. "Synthetic Images." *HAU: Journal of Ethnographic Theory* 4 (1): 549–64.

Orzechowski, Andrzej, and Alois Pichler. 1995. "A Critical Note on the Editions of Wittgenstein's Remarks on Frazer's Golden Bough." *Wittgenstein Studien* 2: 1–17.

Palmié, Stephan. 2013. *The Cooking of History: How Not to Study Afro-Cuban Religion*. Chicago: University of Chicago Press.

———. 2018. "When is a Thing? Transduction and Immediacy in Afro-Cuban Ritual; or, ANT in Matanzas, Summer of 1948." *Comparative Studies in Society and History* 60 (4): 1–24.

Redding, Paul. 1987. "Anthropology as Ritual: Wittgenstein's Reading of Frazer's *The Golden Bough*." *Metaphilosophy* 18 (3–4): 253–69.

Rhees, Rush. 1967. "Introductory Note to Ludwig Wittgenstein 'Bemerkungen Über Frazer's *The Golden Bough*.'" *Synthese* 17 (3): 233–53.

Rothhaupt, Josef G. F. 2016. "Wittgenstein's 'Bemerkungen über Frazers *The Golden Bough*': Verortung im Gesamtnachlass—Einbindung in die Philosophietradition—Editions- und Publikationsgeschichte." In *Wittgenstein's Remarks on Frazer: The Text and the Matter*, edited by Lars Albinus, Josef G. F. Rothhaupt, and Aidan Seery, 11–83. Berlin: de Gruyter.

Skorupski, John. 1976. *Symbol and Theory: A Philosophical Study of Theories of Religion in Anthropology*. Cambridge: Cambridge University Press.

Smith, Jonathan Z. 1973. "When the Bough Breaks." *History of Religions* 12 (4): 342–71.

Stocking, George. 1995. *After Tylor: British Social Anthropology, 1888–1951*. Madison: University of Wisconsin Press.

Strathern, Marilyn. 1985. "Kinship and Economy: Constitutive Orders of a Provisional Kind." *American Ethnologist* 12 (2): 191–209.

———. 1987. "Out of Context: The Persuasive Fictions of Anthropology." *Current Anthropology* 28 (3): 251–81.

Tylor, Edward B. 1871. *Primitive Culture*. London: John Murray.

Viveiros de Castro, Eduardo. 2012. *Cosmological Perspectivism in Amazonia and Elsewhere*. Masterclass Series 1. Manchester: HAU Network of Ethnographic Theory.

Westergaard, Peter K. 2015. "On the 'Ketner and Eigsti Edition' of Wittgenstein's *Remarks on Frazer's 'The Golden Bough.'*" *Nordic Wittgenstein Review* 4 (2): 117–42.

Wilson, Brian, ed. 1970. *Rationality*. Oxford: Blackwell.

Winch, Peter. 1958. *The Idea of a Social Science*. London: Routledge and Kegan Paul.

Wittgenstein, Ludwig. 1922. *Tractatus Logico-Philosophicus*. London: Kegan Paul.

———. 1956. *Remarks on the Foundations of Mathematics*. Edited by G. H. von Wright, R. Rhees, and G. E. M. Anscombe, translated by G. E. M. Anscombe. Oxford: Blackwell.

———. 1967. "Remarks on James Frazer's *The Golden Bough*." *Synthese* 17 (3): 233–53.

———. 1980. *Remarks on the Philosophy of Psychology*. Edited by G. E. M. Anscombe and G. H. von Wright, translated by G. E. M. Anscombe. Oxford: Blackwell.

———. 1981. *Zettel*. 2nd ed. Edited by G. E. M. Anscombe and G.H. von Wright, translated by G. E. M. Anscombe. Oxford: Blackwell.

———. 2009. *Philosophical Investigations*. Revised 4th edition. Edited by Peter M. S. Hacker and Joachim Schulte, translated by G. E. M. Anscombe, Peter M. S. Hacker, and Joachim Schulte. Oxford: Wiley-Blackwell.

CHAPTER 2

Remarks on Frazer's *The Golden Bough*

Ludwig Wittgenstein

INTRODUCTORY NOTE*

Dr. M. O'C. Drury writes: "I think it would have been in 1930 that Wittgenstein said to me that he had always wanted to read Frazer but hadn't done so, and would I get hold of a copy and read some of it out loud to him. I borrowed from the Union Library the first volume of the multivolume edition and we only got a little way through this because he talked at considerable length about it, and the next term we didn't start it again." —Wittgenstein began writing on Frazer in his manuscript book on June 19, 1931, and he added remarks during the next two or three weeks—although he was writing more about other things (such as Verstehen eines Satzes, Bedeutung, Komplex und Tatsache, Intention . . .). He may have made earlier notes in a pocket notebook, but I have found none.

---

*   This translation is based on Rush Rhees's publication of the entire German text of Ludwig Wittgenstein's "Bemerkungen Über Frazers *The Golden Bough*" in *Synthese* 17: 233–53, 1967. Notes added in the first (abridged) translation by A. C. Miles and Rush Rhees, *Ludwig Wittgenstein: Remarks on Frazer's The Golden Bough*, Atlantic Highlands, NJ: Humanities Press, 1979, are marked [Miles/Rhees]; my own notes are marked [SP]. Numbers in square brackets indicate the original page breaks in the *Synthese* edition. Wittgenstein's remarks feature numbers in neither the *Synthese* version nor the first translation. They have been numbered in my translation purely for ease of reference. In the *Synthese* publication, Rhees's Introductory Note appeared in English, with the exception of the short passage in German (translated here for legibility).

It was probably in 1931 that he dictated to a typist the greater part of the manuscript books written since July 1930; often changing the order of remarks, and
details of the phrasing, but leaving large blocks as they stood. (He rearranged the
material again and again later on.) This particular typescript runs to 771 pages. It
has a section, just under 10 pages long, of the remarks on Frazer, with a few changes
in order and phrasing. Others are in different contexts, and a few are left out.

The typed section on Frazer begins with three remarks which are not connected with them in the manuscript. He had begun there with remarks which
he later marked S (= "schlecht") and did not have typed. I think we can see why.
The earlier version was:

"Ich glaube jetzt, daß es richtig wäre, mein Buch mit Bemerkungen über die
Metaphysik als eine Art von Magie zu beginnen.

Worin ich aber weder der Magie das Wort reden noch mich über sie
lustig machen darf.

[234] Von der Magie müßte die Tiefe behalten werden. —

Ja, das Ausschalten der Magie hat hier den Charakter der Magie selbst.

Denn, wenn ich damals anfing von der 'Welt' zu reden (und nicht von
diesem Baum oder Tisch), was wollte ich anderes als etwas Höheres in
meine Worte bannen."

("I now believe that it would be right to begin my book with remarks on
metaphysics as a kind of magic.

Where, in doing so, however, I must neither speak out for magic, nor
ridicule it.

The depth of magic ought to be preserved. —

Yes, here canceling out magic has the character of magic itself.

For when I began earlier [i.e., in a prior work] to speak about the 'world'
(and not of this tree or table), what else was I attempting than to conjure up
something higher in my words.")

He wrote the second set of remarks—and they are only rough notes—years
later; not earlier than 1936 and probably after 1948. They are written in pencil
on odd bits of paper; probably he meant to insert the smaller ones in the copy of
the one volume edition of *The Golden Bough* that he was using. Miss Anscombe
found them among some of his things after his death.

RUSH RHEES

I

1. One must begin with error and transform it into truth.

That is, one must uncover the source of the error, otherwise hearing the truth won't help us. It cannot penetrate when something else is taking its place.

To convince someone of what is true, it is not enough to state the truth; one must find the *way* from error to truth.

Again and again I must submerge myself in the water of doubt.

Frazer's representation of human magical and religious notions is unsatisfactory: it makes these notions appear as *mistakes*.

Was Augustine mistaken, then, when he called on God on every page of the *Confessions*?

But—one might say—if he was not in error, then surely was the Buddhist saint—or whoever else—whose religion expresses entirely different notions. But none of them was in error except where he was putting forth a theory.

Already the idea of explaining the practice—say the killing of the priest king—[235] seems to me wrong-headed. All that Frazer does is to make the practice plausible to those who think like him. It is very strange to present all these practices, in the end, so to speak, as foolishness.

But it never does become plausible that people do all this out of sheer stupidity.

When he explains to us, for example, that the king would have to be killed in his prime because, according to the notions of the savages, his soul would otherwise not be kept fresh, then one can only say: where that practice and these notions go together, there the practice does not spring from the notion; instead they are simply both present.

It could well be, and often occurs today, that someone gives up a practice after having realized an error that this practice depended on. But then again, this case holds only when it is enough to make someone aware of his error so as to dissuade him from his mode of action. But surely, this is not the case with the religious practices of a people, and that is why we are *not* dealing with an error here.[1]

---

1.   [Miles/Rhees]: Cf. *The Golden Bough*, p. 264: "But reflection and enquiry should satisfy us that to our predecessors we are indebted for much of what we thought most our own, and that their errors were not willful extravagances or the ravings

I

Man muß beim Irrtum ansetzen und ihm die Wahrheit überführen.

D.h., man muß die Quelle des Irrtums aufdecken, sonst nützt uns das Hören der Wahrheit nichts. Sie kann nicht eindringen, wenn etwas anderes ihren Platz einnimmt.

Einen von der Wahrheit zu überzeugen, genügt es nicht, die Wahrheit zu konstatieren, sondern man muß den *Weg* von Irrtum zur Wahrheit finden.

Ich muß immer wieder im Wasser des Zweifels untertauchen.

Frazers Darstellung der magischen und religiösen Anschauungen der Menschen ist unbefriedigend: sie läßt diese Anschauungen als *Irrtümer* erscheinen.

So war also Augustinus im Irrtum, wenn er Gott auf jeder Seite der *Confessionen* anruft?

Aber—kann man sagen—wenn er nicht im Irrtum war, so war es doch der Buddhistische Heilige—oder welcher immer—dessen Religion ganz andere Anschauungen zum Ausdruck bringt. Aber *keiner* von ihnen war im Irrtum, außer wo er eine Theorie aufstellte.

Schon die Idee, den Gebrauch—etwa die Tötung des Priesterkönigs—erklären zu wollen, scheint mir verfehlt. Alles was Frazer tut ist, sie Menschen, die so ähnlich denken wie er, plausibel zu machen. Es ist sehr merkwürdig, daß alle diese Gebräuche endlich so zu sagen als Dummheiten dargestellt werden.

Nie wird es aber plausibel, daß die Menschen aus purer Dummheit all das tun.

Wenn er uns z.B. erklärt, der König müsse in seiner Blüte getötet werden, weil nach den Anschauungen der Wilden sonst seine Seele nicht frisch erhalten würde, so kann man doch nur sagen: wo jener Gebrauch und diese Anschauungen zusammengehn, dort entspringt nicht der Gebrauch der Anschauung, sondern sie sind eben beide da.

Es kann schon sein, und kommt heute oft vor, daß ein Mensch einen Gebrauch aufgibt, nachdem er einen Irrtum erkannt hat, auf den sich dieser Gebrauch stützte. Aber dieser Fall besteht eben nur dort, wo es genügt den Menschen auf seinen Irrtum aufmerksam zu machen, um ihn von seiner Handlungsweise abzubringen. Aber das ist doch bei den religiösen Gebräuchen eines Volkes nicht der Fall und *darum* handelt es sich eben um *keinen* Irrtum.

2. Frazer says it is very hard to discover the error in magic—and this is why it persists for so long—because, for example, a conjuration intended to bring about rain will sooner or later appear as effective.[2] But then it is strange that, after all, the people would not hit upon the fact that it will rain sooner or later anyway.

I believe that the enterprise of explanation is already wrong because we only have to correctly put together what one already *knows*, without adding anything, and the kind of satisfaction that one attempts to attain through explanation comes of itself.

And here it isn't the explanation at all that satisfies us. When Frazer begins by telling us the story of the King of the Woods at Nemi, he does so in a tone that shows that something strange and terrible is happening here. However, the question "Why is this happening?" is essentially answered by just this [mode of exposition]: because it is terrible. In other words, it is what appears to us a terrible, impressive, horrible, tragic, etcetera that gave birth to this event [or process].

3. [236] One can only resort to *description* here, and say: such is human life.

Compared to the impression that what is so described to us, explanation is too uncertain.

Every explanation is a hypothesis.

But someone who, for example, is unsettled by love will be ill-assisted by a hypothetical explanation. It won't calm him or her.

---

of insanity, but simple hypotheses, justifiable as such at the time when they were propounded, but which fuller experience has proved to be inadequate. It is only by the successive testing of hypotheses and rejection of the false that the truth is at last elicited. After all, what we call truth is only the hypothesis that is found to work best. Therefore in reviewing the opinions and practices of ruder ages and races shall we do well to look with leniency upon their errors as inevitable slips made in the search for truth, and to give them the benefit of that indulgence that we ourselves may one day stand in need of: *cum excusatione itaque veteres audiendi sunt*."

2.   [Miles/Rhees]: Cf. *The Golden Bough*, p. 59: "A ceremony intended to make the wind blow or the rain fall, or to work the death of an enemy, will always be followed, sooner or later, by the occurrence it is meant to bring to pass; and primitive man may be excused for regarding the occurrence as a direct result of the ceremony, and the best possible proof of its efficacy."

Frazer sagt, es sei sehr schwer, den Irrtum in der Magie zu entdecken—und darum halte sie sich so lange—weil z.B. eine Beschwörung, die Regen herbeiführen soll, früher oder später gewiß als wirksam erscheint. Aber dann ist es eben merkwürdig, daß die Menschen nicht früher daraufkommen, daß es ohnehin früher oder später regnet.

Ich glaube, daß das Unternehmen einer Erklärung schon darum verfehlt ist, weil man nur richtig zusammenstellen muß, was man *weiß*, und nichts dazusetzen, und die Befriedigung, die durch die Erklärung angestrebt wird, ergibt sich von selbst.

Und die Erklärung ist es hier gar nicht, die befriedigt. Wenn Frazer anfängt und uns die Geschichte von dem Waldkönig von Nemi erzählt, so tut er dies in einem Ton, der zeigt, daß hier etwas Merkwürdiges und Furchtbares geschieht. Die Frage aber "warum geschieht dies?" wird eigentlich dadurch beantwortet: Weil es furchtbar ist. Das heißt, dasselbe, was uns bei diesem Vorgang furchtbar, großartig, schaurig, tragisch, etc., nichts weniger als trivial und bedeutungslos vorkommt, *das* hat diesen Vorgang ins Leben gerufen.

Nur *beschreiben* kann man hier und sagen: so ist das menschliche Leben.

Die Erklärung ist im Vergleich mit dem Eindruck, den uns das Beschriebene macht, zu unsicher.

Jede Erklärung ist eine Hypothese.

Wer aber, etwa, von der Liebe beunruhigt ist, dem wird eine hypothetische Erklärung wenig helfen. —Sie wird ihn nicht beruhigen.

4. The crowding of thoughts that will not come out because they all try to push ahead and are wedged at the door.

5. If one sets the phrase "majesty of death" next to the story of the priest king of Nemi, one sees that they are one and the same.

The life of the priest king represents what is meant by that phrase.

Whoever is gripped by the [idea of] majesty of death can express this through just such a life. —Of course, this is also not an explanation, it just puts one symbol for another. Or one ceremony in place of another.

6. A religious symbol is not grounded in an *opinion*.

Error only corresponds to opinion.

7. One would like to say: This or the other event took place here; laugh if you can.

8. The religious actions or the religious life of the priest king are not different in kind from any genuinely religious action today, say, a confession of sins. This, too, can be "explained" and cannot be explained.

9. Burning in effigy. Kissing the picture of a loved one. This is *obviously not* based on a belief that it will have a definite effect on the object [237] that the picture represents. It aims at some satisfaction, and does achieve it, too. Or rather, it does not *aim* at anything; we act in this way and then feel satisfied.

One could also kiss the name of the loved one, and here the representation through the name [as a place-holder] would be clear.

10. The same savage who, apparently in order to kill his enemy, pierces an image of him, really builds his hut out of wood, and carves his arrow skillfully and not in effigy.

The idea that one could beckon a lifeless object to come, just as one would beckon a person. Here the principle is that of personification.

Das Gedränge der Gedanken, die nicht herauskommen, weil sich alle vordrängen wollen und so am Ausgang verkeilen.

Wenn man mit jener Erzählung vom Priesterkönig von Nemi das Wort "die Majestät des Todes" zusammenstellt, so sieht man, daß die beiden Eins sind.
    Das Leben des Priesterkönigs stellt das dar, was mit jenem Wort gemeint ist.

Wer von der Majestät des Todes ergriffen ist, kann dies durch so ein Leben zum Ausdruck bringen. —Dies ist natürlich auch keine Erklärung, sondern setzt nur ein Symbol für ein anderes. Oder: eine Zeremonie für eine andere.

Einem religiösen Symbol liegt keine *Meinung* zu Grunde.
    Und nur der Meinung entspricht der Irrtum.

Man möchte sagen: Dieser und dieser Vorgang hat stattgefunden; lach', wenn Du kannst.

Die religiöse Handlungen, oder das religiöse Leben des Priesterkönigs ist von keiner andern Art, als jede echt religiöse Handlung heute, etwa ein Geständnis der Sünden. Auch dieses läßt sich "*erklären*" und läßt sich nicht erklären.

In Effigie verbrennen. Das Bild des Geliebten küssen. Das basiert *natürlich nicht* auf einem Glauben an eine bestimmte Wirkung auf den Gegenstand, den das Bild darstellt. Es bezweckt eine Befriedigung und erreicht sie auch. Oder vielmehr, es *bezweckt* gar nichts; wir handeln so und fühlen uns dann befriedigt.

Man könnte auch den Namen der Geliebten küssen, und hier wäre die Stellvertretung durch den Namen klar.

Der selbe Wilde, der, anscheinend um seinen Feind zu töten, dessen Bild durchsticht, baut seine Hütte aus Holz wirklich und schnitzt seinen Pfeil kunstgerecht und nicht in Effigie.

Die Idee, daß man einen leblosen Gegenstand zu sich herwinken kann, wie man einen Menschen zu sich herwinkt. Hier ist das Prinzip das, der Personifikation.

11.   And magic always rests on the idea of symbolism and of language.

The representation of a wish is, eo ipso, the representation of its fulfillment.
    But magic gives representation to a wish; it expresses a wish.

Baptism as washing.—An error arises only when magic is interpreted
scientifically.
    When the adoption of a child is carried out in a way that the mother pulls
the child through her clothes, then is it not crazy to think that there is an *error*,
and that she believes to have born the child.[3]

We should distinguish between magical operations and those operations that
rest on false, oversimplified notions of things and processes. For instance, if one
says that the illness is moving from one part of the body into another, or if one
takes measures to draw off the illness as though it were a liquid or a state of heat,
then one is entertaining a false, inappropriate image.

12.   What narrowness of spiritual life we find in Frazer! Hence the impossibil-
    ity of grasping a life different from the English one of his time!

[238] Frazer cannot imagine a priest who is not basically an English parson of
our times, with all his stupidity and shallowness.

13.   Why should it not be possible for someone's own name to be sacred to
    himself? On the one hand, it surely is the most important instrument
    given to him, and, on the other, it is like a jewel hung around his neck at
    birth.

How misleading Frazer's explanations are becomes clear, I think, from the fact
that one could very well invent primitive practices oneself, and it would only
be by chance if they were not actually found somewhere. That is, the principle

3.   [Miles/Rhees] "The same principle of make-believe, so dear to children, has led
    other peoples to employ a simulation of birth as a form of adoption. . . . A woman
    will take a boy whom she intends to adopt and push or pull him through her clothes;
    ever afterward he is regarded as her very son, and inherits the whole property of his
    adoptive parents" (*The Golden Bough*, pp. 14, 15)

Und immer beruht die Magie auf der Idee des Symbolismus und der Sprache.

Die Darstellung eines Wunsches ist, eo ipso, die Darstellung seiner Erfüllung.
    Die Magie aber bringt einen Wunsch zur Darstellung; sie äußert einen Wunsch.

Die Taufe als Waschung. —Ein Irrtum entsteht erst, wenn die Magie wissenschaftlich ausgelegt wird.
    Wenn die Adoption eines Kindes so vor sich geht, daß die Mutter es durch ihre Kleider zieht, so ist es doch verrückt zu glauben, daß hier ein *Irrtum* vorliegt und sie glaubt, das Kind geboren zu haben.
    Von den magischen Operationen sind die zu unterscheiden, die auf einer falschen, zu einfachen, Vorstellung der Dinge und Vorgänge beruhen. Wenn man etwa sagt, die Krankheit ziehe von einem Teil des Körpers in den andern, oder Vorkehrungen trifft, die Krankheit abzuleiten, als wäre sie eine Flüssigkeit oder ein Wärmezustand. Man macht sich dann also ein falsches, das heißt hier, unzutreffendes Bild.

Welche Enge des seelischen Lebens bei Frazer! Daher: Welche Unmöglichkeit, ein anderes Leben zu begreifen, als das englische seiner Zeit!

Frazer kann sich keinen Priester vorstellen, der nicht im Grunde ein englischer Parson unserer Zeit ist, mit seiner ganzen Dummheit und Flauheit.

Warum sollte dem Menschen sein Name nicht heilig sein können. Ist er doch einerseits das wichtigste Instrument, das ihm gegeben wird, anderseits wie ein Schmuckstück, das ihm bei der Geburt umgehangen wird.

Wie irreführend die Erklärungen Frazers sind, sieht man—glaube ich—daraus, daß man primitive Gebräuche sehr wohl selbst erdichten könnte und es müßte ein Zufall sein, wenn sie nicht irgendwo wirklich gefunden würden. Das heißt, das Prinzip,

according to which these practices are ordered[4] is a much more general one than [it appears] in Frazer's explanation, and it exists in our own soul, so that we could think up all the possibilities ourselves. —We can thus readily imagine that, for instance, the king of a tribe becomes visible for no one, but also that every member of the tribe is obliged to see him. The latter will then certainly not occur in a manner more or less left to chance; instead, he will be *shown* to the people. Perhaps no one will be allowed to touch him, or perhaps they will be *compelled* to touch him. Think how after Schubert's death his brother cut Schubert's scores into small pieces and gave to his favorite pupils these pieces of a few bars. As a gesture of piety, this action is *just* as comprehensible as that of preserving the scores untouched and accessible to no one. And if Schubert's brother had burned the scores, this could still be understood as a gesture of piety.

The ceremonial (hot or cold) as opposed to the haphazard (lukewarm) is what characterizes piety.

Yes, Frazer's explanations would not be explanations at all if they did not, in the end, appeal to an inclination in ourselves.

Eating and drinking have their dangers, not only for the savage but also for us; nothing more natural than wanting to protect oneself against them; and we could think up such protective measures ourselves. —But what principle do we follow in confabulating them? Clearly that of formally reducing all dangers to a few very simple ones that are ready to see for everyone. In other words, according to the same principle that leads uneducated people in our society to say that the illness is moving from the head to the chest, etcetera, etcetera. [239] In these simple images personification will, of course, play a great role, for everyone knows that people (hence [also] spirits) can become dangerous to others.

That a human shadow, which looks like a human being, or one's mirror image, that rain, thunderstorms, the phases of the moon, the change of seasons, the likeness or difference of animals to one another and to human beings, the phenomenon of death, of birth, and of sexual life, in short, everything that a human being senses around himself, year in, year out, in manifold mutual connection—that all this should play a role in the thought of human beings (their

---

4.   [Miles/Rhees] That is, how they stand related to one another and what this depends on.

nach welchem diese Gebräuche geordnet sind, ist ein viel allgemeineres als Frazer es erklärt und in unserer eigenen Seele vorhanden, so daß wir uns alle Möglichkeiten selbst ausdenken könnten. —Daß etwa der König eines Stammes für niemanden sichtbar wird, können wir uns wohl vorstellen, aber auch, daß jeder Mann des Stammes ihn sehen soll. Das letztere wird dann gewiß nicht in irgendeiner mehr oder weniger zufälligen Weise geschehen dürfen, sondern er wird den Leuten *gezeigt* werden. Vielleicht wird ihn niemand berühren dürfen, vielleicht aber berühren *müssen*. Denken wir daran, daß nach Schuberts Tod sein Bruder Partituren Schuberts in kleine Stücke zerschnitt und seinen Lieblingsschülern solche Stücke von einigen Takten gab. Diese Handlung, als Zeichen der Pietät, ist uns *ebenso* verständlich, wie die andere, die Partituren unberührt, niemandem zugänglich, aufzubewahren. Und hätte Schuberts Bruder die Partituren verbrannt, so wäre auch das als Zeichen der Pietät verständlich.

Das Zeremonielle (heiße oder kalte) im Gegensatz zum Zufälligen (lauen) charakterisiert die Pietät.

Ja, Frazers Erklärungen wären überhaupt keine Erklärungen, wenn sie nicht letzten Endes an eine Neigung in uns selbst appellierten.

Das Essen und Trinken ist mit Gefahren verbunden, nicht nur für den Wilden, sondern auch für uns; nichts natürlicher, als daß man sich vor diesen schützen will; und nun könnten wir uns selbst solche Schutzmaßnahmen ausdenken. —Aber nach welchem Prinzip erdichten wir sie? Offenbar danach, daß alle Gefahren der Form nach auf einige sehr einfache reduziert werden, die dem Menschen ohne weiteres sichtbar sind. Also nach dem selben Prinzip, nach dem die ungebildete Leute unter uns sagen, die Krankheit ziehe sich vom Kopf in die Brust etc., etc. In diesen einfachen Bildern wird natürlich die Personifikation eine große Rolle spielen, denn, daß Menschen (also Geister) dem Menschen gefärlich werden können, ist jedem bekannt.

Daß der Schatten des Menschen, der wie ein Mensch ausschaut, oder sein Spiegelbild, daß Regen, Gewitter, die Mondphasen, der Jahreszeitwechsel, die Ähnlichkeit und Verschiedenheit der Tiere unter einander und zum Menschen, die Erscheinungen des Todes, der Geburt und des Geschlechtslebens, kurz alles, was der Mensch jahraus jahrein um sich wahrnimmt, in mannigfaltigster Weise mit einander verknüpft, in seinem Denken (seiner Philosophie) und seinen Gebräuchen eine Rolle spielen wird, ist selbstverständlich, oder ist eben das, was wir wirklich wissen und interessant ist.

philosophy) and in their practices is self-evident; or, in other words, it is what we really know and find interesting.[5]

How could the fire or the fire's resemblance to the sun have failed to make an impression on the awakening mind of man? But not perhaps "because he can't explain it to himself" (the stupid superstition of our time)—for does an "explanation" make it less impressive?—

The magic in *Alice in Wonderland*, trying to dry out by reading the driest thing there is.[6]

14.   In magical healing one *indicates* to the illness that it should leave the patient.

After the description of such a magical cure one wants to say, If the illness doesn't understand *that*, then I don't know *how* else to tell it [to do so].

15.   I do not mean that it is especially *fire* that must make an impression on anyone. Fire no more than any other phenomenon, and one will impress this person and another that. For no phenomenon is particularly mysterious in itself, but any of them can become so to us, and it is precisely the characteristic feature of the awakening human mind that a phenomenon acquires significance for it. One could almost say that man is a ceremonial animal. This is probably partly false, partly nonsensical, but there is also some truth to it.

In other words, one could begin a book on anthropology in this way: when one observes the life and behavior of humans all over the earth, one sees that apart from the kinds of behavior one could call animal [240], the intake of food, etcetera, etcetera, etcetera, humans also carry out actions that bear a peculiar character, and might be called ritual actions.

But then again, it is nonsense to go on and say that the characteristic feature of these actions is that they spring from erroneous notions about the physics of things. (As Frazer does when he says that magic is really false physics, or as the case may be, false medicine, technology, etc.)

---

5.   [Miles/Rhees, both in German and English] In another part of the manuscript, Wittgenstein wrote: "It never occurs to humans on what foundations their inquiries really rest. Unless, that is, *this* has, at some point, occurred to them (Frazer, etc., etc.)."

6.   [Miles/Rhees] Chapter III, the remark of the mouse.

Wie hätte das Feuer oder die Ähnlichkeit des Feuers mit der Sonne verfehlen können auf den erwachenden Menschengeist einen Eindruck zu machen. Aber nicht vielleicht "weil er sich's nicht erklären kann" (der dumme Aberglaube unserer Zeit)—denn wird es durch eine "Erklärung" weniger eindrucksvoll?—

Die Magie in "Alice in Wonderland" beim Trocknen durch Vorlesen des Trockensten was es gibt.[1]

Bei der magischen Heilung einer Krankheit *bedeutet* man ihr, sie möge den Patienten verlassen.

Man möchte nach der Beschreibung so einer magischen Kur immer sagen: Wenn *das* die Krankheit nicht versteht, so weiß ich nicht, *wie* man es ihr sagen soll.

Ich meine nicht, daß gerade das *Feuer* jedem einen Eindruck machen muß. Das Feuer nicht mehr, wie jede andere Erscheinung, und die eine Erscheinung Dem, die andere Jenem. Denn keine Erscheinung ist an sich besonders geheimnisvoll, aber jede kann es uns werden, und das ist eben das Charakteristische am erwachenden Geist des Menschen, daß ihm eine Erscheinung bedeutend wird. Man könnte fast sagen, der Mensch sei ein zeremonielles Tier. Das ist wohl teils falsch, teils unsinnig, aber es ist auch etwas Richtiges daran.

Das heißt, man könnte ein Buch über Anthropologie so anfangen: Wenn man das Leben und Benehmen der Menschen auf der Erde betrachtet, so sieht man, daß sie außer den Handlungen, die man tierische nennen könnte, der Nahrungsaufnahme, etc., etc., etc., auch solche ausführen, die einen eigentümlichen Charakter tragen und die man rituelle Handlungen nennen könnte.

Nun aber ist es Unsinn, so fortzufahren, daß man als das Charakteristische *dieser* Handlungen sagt, sie seien solche, die aus fehlerhaften Anschauungen über die Physik der Dinge entsprängen. (So tut es Frazer, wenn er sagt, Magie sei wesentlich falsche Physik, bzw. falsche Heilkunst, Technik, etc.)

---

1   Lewis Carroll, *Alice in Wonderland*, Chapter III.

Rather, what is characteristic of ritual action is not at all any view, opinion, be it right or wrong, although an opinion—a belief—can itself be of ritual nature, or belong to a rite.

16. If one takes it to be self-evident that people take pleasure in their own imaginations, then one should remember that such imagination is not like a picture or a three-dimensional model, but a complicated pattern of heterogeneous components: words and images. [Once one does so] one will then no longer oppose operating with written or acoustic signs to operating with "mental images" of events.

17. We must plow over language in its entirety.

18. Frazer: ". . . That these operations are dictated by fear of the ghost of the slain seems certain . . ." [p.212]. But why does Frazer use the word "ghost"?[7] He thus evidently understands this superstition only too well, since he explains it with a superstitious term familiar to him. Or rather, he could have seen from this that there is something in us, too, that speaks in support of such observances on the part of the savages. —When I, who do not believe that there exist, anywhere, human-superhuman beings whom one can call gods—when I say: "I fear the wrath of the gods," then this shows that I can mean something with this [utterance], or can express a sentiment that is not necessarily connected with such belief.

19. Frazer seems capable of believing that a savage dies out of error. In the elementary school primers it says that Attila undertook his great campaigns because he believed he possessed the sword of the god of thunder.

[241] Frazer is far more savage than most of his savages, for these savages will not be as far removed from an understanding of spiritual matters as an Englishman of the twentieth century.[8] His explanations of primitive practices are much cruder than the meaning of these practices themselves.

---

7. [SP] "Ghost" appears in English in the original.
8. [SP] "Savage" appears in English in the original.

Vielmehr ist das Charakteristische der rituellen Handlung gar keine Ansicht, Meinung, ob sie nun richtig oder falsch ist, obgleich eine Meinung— ein Glaube—selbst auch rituell sein kann, zum Ritus gehören kann.

Wenn man es für selbstverständlich hält, daß sich der Mensch an seiner Phantasie vergnügt, so bedenke man, daß diese Phantasie nicht wie ein gemaltes Bild oder ein plastisches Modell ist, sondern ein kompliziertes Gebilde aus heterogenen Bestandteilen: Wörtern und Bilder. Man wird dann das Operieren mit Schrift- und Lautzeichen nicht mehr in Gegensatz stellen zu dem Operieren mit "Vorstellungsbildern" der Ereignisse.

Wir müssen die ganze Sprache durchpflügen.

Frazer: ". . . That these observances are dictated by fear of the gost [*sic*] of the slain seems certain; . . ." Aber warum gebraucht Frazer denn das Wort "ghost"? Er versteht also sehr wohl diesen Aberglauben, da er ihn uns mit einem ihm geläufigen abergläubischen Wort erklärt. Oder vielmehr, er hätte daraus sehen können, daß auch in uns etwas für jene Handlungsweisen der Wilden spricht. —Wenn ich, der ich nicht glaube, daß es irgendwo menschlich-übermenschliche Wesen gibt, die man Götter nennen kann—wenn ich sage: "ich fürchte die Rache der Götter," so zeigt das, daß ich damit etwas meinen kann, oder einer Empfindung Ausdruck geben kann, die nicht notwendig mit jenem Glauben verbunden ist.

Frazer wäre im Stande zu glauben, daß ein Wilder aus Irrtum stirbt. In den Volksschullesebüchern steht, daß Attilla seine großen Kriegszüge unternommen hat, weil er glaubte, das Schwert des Donnergottes zu besitzen.

Frazer ist viel mehr savage, als die meisten seiner savages, denn diese werden nicht so weit vom Verständnis einer geistigen Angelegenheit entfernt sein, wie ein Engländer des 20sten Jahrhunderts. *Seine* Erklärungen der primitiven Gebräuche sind viel roher, als der Sinn dieser Gebräuche selbst.

20.   A historical explanation, an explanation in the form of a hypothesis of development is only *one* kind of summary arrangement of the data—of their synopsis. It is equally possible to see the data in their relation to one another and to gather them into a general picture without doing so in the form of a hypothesis concerning temporal development.

21.   Identification of one's own gods with the gods of other peoples. One convinces oneself that the names have the same meaning.

22.   "And so the chorus points to a secret law" is what one might want to say about Frazer's collection of facts. Now, I *can* represent this law, this idea, in the form of a hypothesis of development,[9] but also in analogy to the schema of a plant, I can represent it as the schema of a religious ceremony, or again by grouping the facts alone in a "perspicuous" presentation.

For us the concept of perspicuous presentation is of fundamental importance.[10] It designates our form of presentation, the way we see things. (A kind of "Weltanschauung" as it is apparently typical of our time. Spengler.)

This perspicuous presentation transmits an understanding of the kind that what we see are "just the connections." Hence the importance of finding *intermediate links*.

However, in this case, a hypothetical link is not meant to do anything other than draw attention to the similarity, the connection between the *facts*. Just as one

---

9.   [Miles/Rhees] Or evolution.

10.   [SP] In their translation, Miles and Rhees add a parenthesis in the English text at this point. It reads as follows: "A way of setting out the whole field together by making easy the passage from one part of it to another." "Introduced in translation, not in Wittgenstein's text. His word is 'übersichtlich.' He uses this constantly in writing of logical notation and of mathematical proof, and it is clear what he means. So we ought to have an English word. We have put "perspicuous" here, too. But no one uses this in English either. Perhaps a reader with more flexible wrists will hit on something." In fact, "übersichtlich" is a term that has notoriously vexed Anglophone commentators on the *Remarks on Frazer's Golden Bough*, since it not only has no lexical equivalent in English but also because Wittgenstein's use of the term in German remains open to interpretation (as his own quotation marks already indicate).

Die historische Erklärung, die Erklärung als eine Hypothese der Entwicklung ist nur *eine* Art der Zusammenfassung der Daten—ihrer Synopsis. Es ist ebensowohl möglich, die Daten in ihrer Beziehung zu einander zu sehen und in ein allgemeines Bild zusammenzufassen, ohne es in Form einer Hypothese über die zeitliche Entwicklung zu machen.

Identifizierung der eigenen Götter mit Göttern andrer Völker. Man überzeugt sich davon, daß die Namen die gleiche Bedeutung haben.

"Und so deutet das Chor auf ein geheimes Gesetz" möchte man zu der Frazer'schen Tatsachensammlung sagen. Dieses Gesetz, diese Idee, *kann* ich nun durch eine Entwicklungshypothese darstellen oder auch, analog dem Schema einer Pflanze, durch das Schema einer religiösen Zeremonie, oder aber durch die Gruppierung des Tatsachenmaterials allein, in einer "*übersichtlichen*" Darstellung.

Der Begriff der übersichtlichen Darstellung ist für uns von grundlegender Bedeutung. Er bezeichnet unsere Darstellungsform, die Art wie wir die Dinge sehen. (Eine Art der "Weltanschauung" wie sie scheinbar für unsere Zeit typisch ist. Spengler.)

Diese übersichtliche Darstellung vermittelt das Verständnis, welches eben darin besteht, daß wir die "Zusammenhänge sehen." Daher die Wichtigkeit des Findens von *Zwischengliedern*.

Ein hypothetisches Zwischenglied aber soll in diesem Falle nichts tun, als die Aufmerksamkeit auf die Ähnlichkeit, den Zusammenhang, der *Tatsachen* lenken. Wie man eine interne Beziehung der Kreisform zur Ellipse dadurch illustrierte,

might illustrate an inner relation between a circle and an ellipse by gradually transforming an ellipse into a circle; *but not to claim that a given ellipse in fact, historically, emerged from a circle* (developmental [242] hypothesis[11]), rather only to sharpen our eye for a formal connection.

But I also cannot see the developmental hypothesis as anything but the investiture [clothing] of a formal connection.

***

23.   [In the manuscript, the following remarks are not grouped with the ones above:][12]

I would like to say: nothing shows our kinship to those savages better than the fact that Frazer has at hand a word as familiar to us as "ghost" or "shade"[13] to describe the views of these people.

(For this surely is something different from what it would be if he were to describe, say, how the savages imagined that their heads would fall off when they have slain an enemy; in this case, *our description* would have nothing superstitious or magical about it.)

Yes, the strangeness of this relates not only to the expressions "ghost" and "shade,"[14] and far too little is made of the fact that we count the words "soul" [*Seele*] and "spirit" [*Geist*] into our own civilized vocabulary. Compared to this, it is a minor detail that we do not believe that our soul eats and drinks.

24.   A whole mythology is deposited in our language.

25.   Casting out death or slaying death; but on the other hand he is also represented as a skeleton, as if he were in some sense dead himself. "As dead

11.   [Miles/Rhees] Or evolution.

12.   [SP] This bracketed remark appears in Wittgenstein's *Remarks*. Miles and Rhees add the following in the translation: "[The remarks up to this point form the 'selection' Wittgenstein had typed as though forming a separate essay. The passages that follow now were not included in this, although they come—at various points— in the same large manuscript and in the revision and typing of it]."

13.   [SP] Both "ghost" and "shade" appear in English in the original.

14.   [SP] Both "ghost" and "shade" appear in English in the original.

daß man eine Ellipse allmählich in einen Kreis überführt; *aber nicht um zu behaupten, daß eine gewiße Ellipse tatsächlich, historisch, aus einem Kreis entstanden wäre* (Entwicklungshypothese), sondern nur um unser Auge für einen formalen Zusammenhang zu schärfen.

Aber auch die Entwicklungshypothese kann ich als weiter nichts sehen, als eine Einkleidung eines formalen Zusammenhangs.

***

[Die folgenden Bemerkungen stehen im Maschineskript nicht mit den obigen zusammen:]

Ich möchte sagen: nichts zeigt unsere Verwandtschaft mit jenen Wilden besser, als daß Frazer ein ihm und uns so geläufiges Wort wie "ghost" oder "shade" bei der Hand hat, um die Ansichten dieser Leute zu beschreiben.

(Das ist ja doch etwas anderes, als wenn er etwa beschriebe, die Wilden bilden sich ein, daß ihnen ihr Kopf herunter fällt, wenn sie einen Feind erschlagen haben. Hier hätte *unsere Beschreibung* nichts Abergläubisches oder Magisches an sich.)

Ja, diese Sonderbarkeit sich nicht nur auf die Ausdrücke "ghost" und "shade," und es wird viel zu wenig Aufhebens davon gemacht, daß wir das Wort "Seele, " "Geist" ("spirit") zu unserem eigenen gebildeten Vokabular zählen. Dagegen ist es eine Kleinigkeit, daß wir nicht glauben, daß unsere Seele ißt und trinkt.

In unserer Sprache ist eine ganze Mythologie niedergelegt.

Austreiben des Todes oder Umbringen des Todes; aber anderseits wird er als Geripppe dargestellt, als selbst in gewissem Sinne tot. "As dead as death."

as death."[15] "Nothing is so dead as death; nothing is so beautiful as beauty herself."[16] Here the image used in thinking of reality is that beauty, death, etcetera are the pure (concentrated) substances, and that they are present in a beautiful object as an admixture. —And do I not recognize here my own observations on "object" and "complex"?[17]

26.   What we have in the ancient rites is the use of a highly cultivated gestural language.

And when I read Frazer, I keep wanting to say at every step: All these processes, these changes of meaning [243] are still present to us in our word language. If what is called the "corn-wolf" is what is hidden in the last sheaf, but [if this name applies] also to the last sheaf itself and the man who binds it, then we recognize in this a linguistic process with which we are perfectly familiar.[18]

* * * * * * * * * *

27.   I could imagine that I might have had to choose some being on earth as my soul's dwelling place, and that my spirit had chosen this unsightly creature as its seat and vantage point. Perhaps because the exception of a beautiful dwelling would repel him. Of course, for the spirit to do so, he would have to be very sure of himself.[19]

28.   One could say "every view has its charm," but that would be wrong. What is correct is that every view is significant for whoever sees it so (but that

---

15. [SP] English in the original.
16. [SP] "Death" (*der Tod*) takes masculine grammatical gender in German, "beauty" (*die Schönheit*), feminine.
17. [Miles/Rhees] In *Tractatus Logico-Philosophicus* (*Logisch-Philosophische Abhandlung*), first published 1921.
18. [Miles/Rhees] "In various parts of Mecklenburg, where the belief in the Corn-Wolf is particularly prevalent, everyone fears to cut the last corn, because they say the Wolf is sitting in it; . . . the last bunch of corn is itself commonly called the Wolf, and the man who reaps it . . . is himself called Wolf" (*The Golden Bough*, p. 449).
19. [SP] Miles and Rhees vacillate here between masculine and neutral grammatical gender, variously referring to *spirit* as both "he" and "it."

"Nichts ist so tot wie der Tod, nichts ist so schön wie die Schönheit selbst." Das Bild, worunter man sich hier die Realität denkt ist, daß die Schönheit, der Tod, etc. die reinen (konzentrierten) Substanzen sind, während sie in einem schönen Gegenstand als Beimischung vorhanden sind. —Und erkenne ich hier nicht meine eigenen Betrachtungen über "Gegenstand" und "Komplex"?

In den alten Riten haben wir den Gebrauch einer äußerst ausgebildeten Gebärdensprache.

Und wenn ich in Frazer lese, so möchte ich auf Schritt und Tritt sagen: Alle diese Prozesse, diese Wandlungen der Bedeutung, haben wir noch in unserer Wortsprache vor uns. Wenn das, was sich in der letzten Garbe verbirgt, der "Kornwolf" genannt wird, aber auch diese Garbe selbst, und auch der Mann der sie bindet, so erkennen wir hierin einen uns wohlbekannten sprachlichen Vorgang.

* * * * * * * * *

Ich könnte mir denken, daß ich die Wahl gehabt hätte, ein Wesen der Erde als die Wohnung für meine Seele zu wählen, und daß mein Geist dieses unansehnliche Geschöpf als seinen Sitz und Aussichtspunkt gewählt hätte. Etwa, weil ihm die Ausnahme eines schönen Sitzes zuwider wäre. Dazu müsste freilich der Geist seiner selbst sehr sicher sein.

Man könnte sagen "jeder Aussicht ist ein Reiz abzugewinnen," aber das wäre falsch. Richtig ist, zu sagen, jede Aussicht ist bedeutsam für den, der sie

does not mean one sees it as something other than it is). Indeed, in this sense every view is equally significant.

Yes, it is important that I must make my own even anyone's contempt for me, as an essential and significant part of the world seen from my vantage point.

29.   If a human being were free to choose to be born in a tree in the forest, then there would be some who would seek out the most beautiful or highest tree for themselves, some who would choose the smallest, and some who would choose an average or below-average tree, and I do not mean out of philistinism, but for just the reason, or the kind of reason for which some-one else chose the highest. That the feeling we have for our life is compa-rable to that of a being that could choose its standpoint in the world has, I believe, its basis in the myth—or belief—that we choose our bodies before birth.

* * * * * * * * *

30.   I believe the characteristic feature of primitive man is that he does not act on the basis of opinions (as Frazer thinks).

31.   I read, among many similar examples, of a rain-king in Africa to whom the people appeal for rain *when the rainy season comes.*[20] [244] But surely this does not mean that they actually think he can make rain, for other-wise they would do it in the dry periods of the year when the land is "a parched and arid desert."[21] For if one assumes that the people originally

---

20. [Miles/Rhees—possibly Wittgenstein himself] "The Kings of the Rain, *Mata Kodou*, who are credited with the power of giving rain at the proper time; that is, in the rainy season. Before the rain begins to fall at the end of March, the country is a parched and arid desert; and the cattle, which form the people's chief wealth, perish for lack of grass. So, when the end of March draws on, each householder betakes himself to the King of Rain and offers him a cow so that he can make the blessed waters of heaven drip on the brown and withered pastures" (*The Golden Bough*, p. 107).

21. [SP] English in the original.

bedeutsam sieht (das heißt aber nicht, sie anders sieht als sie ist). Ja, in diesem Sinne ist jede Aussicht gleich bedeutsam.

Ja, es ist wichtig, daß ich auch die Verachtung jedes Andern für mich mir zu eigen machen muß, als einen wesentlichen und bedeutsamen Teil der Welt von meinem Ort gesehen.

Wenn es einem Menschen freigestellt wäre, sich in einen Baum eines Waldes gebären zu lassen: so gäbe es Solche, die sich den schönsten oder höchsten Baum aussuchen würden, solche die sich den kleinsten wählten und solche die sich einen Durchschnitts- oder minderen Durchschnittsbaum wählen würden, und zwar meine ich nicht aus Philostrosität, sondern aus eben dem Grund, oder der Art von Grund, warum der Andre den höchsten gewählt hat. Daß das Gefühl, welches wir für unser Leben haben, mit dem eines solchen Wesens, das sich seinen Standpunkt in der Welt wählen konnte, vergleichbar ist, liegt, glaube ich, dem Mythus—oder dem Glauben—zu Grunde, wir hätten uns unsern Körper vor der Geburt gewählt.

* * * * * * * * *

Ich glaube, das Charakteristische des primitiven Menschen ist es, daß er nicht aus *Meinungen* handelt (dagegen Frazer).

Ich lese, unter vielen ähnlichen Beispielen, von einem Regenkönig in Afrika, zu dem die Leute um Regen bitten *wenn die Regenperiode kommt*. Aber das heißt doch, daß sie nicht eigentlich meinen, er könne Regen machen, sonst würden sie es in den trockenen Perioden des Jahres, in der das Land "a parched and arid desert" ist, machen. Denn wenn man annimmt, daß die Leute einmal aus Dummheit dieses Amt des Regenkönigs eingesetzt haben, so ist es doch

instituted the office of the rain-king out of stupidity, it certainly still is
clear that they would have previously made the experience that the rains
commence in March, and they could have let the rain-king perform his
work during the other parts of the year. Or again: toward morning, when
the sun is about to rise, people celebrate rites of daybreak, but not at night,
for then they simply burn lamps.

When I am angry about something, I sometimes hit the ground or a tree with
my cane. But surely, I do not believe that the ground is at fault or that the hitting would help matters. "I vent my anger." And all rites are of this kind. One
can call such practices instinctual behavior. —And a historical explanation, for
instance that I or my ancestors earlier believed that hitting the ground would
help, is mere shadow-boxing, for these [sic] are superfluous assumptions that
explain *nothing*. What is important is the semblance of the practice to an act of
punishment, but more than this semblance cannot be stated.

Once such a phenomenon is brought into relation with an instinct that I
possess myself, it thus constitutes the desired explanation; that is, one that resolves this particular difficulty. And further investigation of the history of my
instinct now proceeds along different tracks.

32.   It could have been no insignificant reason—that is, no *reason* at all—for
      which certain races of man came to venerate the oak tree other than that
      they and the oak were united in a community of life, so that they came
      into being not by choice, but jointly, like the dog and the flea (were fleas
      to develop a ritual, it would relate to the dog).

One might say, it was not their union (of oak trees and humans) that occasioned
these rites, but, in a certain sense, their separation.

[245] For the awakening of intellect goes along with the separation from the
original *soil*, the original ground of life. (The origin of *choice*.)

(The form of the awakening mind is veneration.)

gewiß klar, daß sie schon vorher die Erfahrung hatten, daß im März der Regen beginnt und sie hätten dann den Regenkönig für den übrigen Teil des Jahres funktionieren lassen. Oder auch so: Gegen morgen, wenn die Sonne aufgehen will, werden von den Menschen Riten des Tagwerdens zelebriert aber nicht in der Nacht, sondern da brennen sie einfach Lampen.

Wenn ich über etwas wütend bin, so schlage ich manchmal mit meinem Stock auf die Erde oder an einen Baum etc. Aber ich glaube doch nicht, daß die Erde schuld ist oder das Schlagen etwas helfen kann. "Ich lasse meinen Zorn aus." Und dieser Art sind alle Riten. Solche Handlungen kann man Instinkt-Handlungen nennen. —Und eine historische Erklärung, etwa daß ich früher oder meine Vorfahren früher geglaubt haben, das Schlagen der Erde helfe etwas, sind Spiegelfechtereien, denn sie sind überflüssige Annahmen, die *nichts* erklären. Wichtig ist die Ähnlichkeit des Aktes mit einem Akt der Züchtigung, aber mehr als diese Ähnlichkeit ist nicht zu konstatieren.

Ist ein solches Phänomen einmal mit einem Instinkt, den ich selber besitze, in Verbindung gebracht, so ist eben dies die gewünschte Erklärung; d.h. die, welche diese besondere Schwierigkeit löst. Und eine weitere Forschung über die Geschichte meines Instinkts bewegt sich nun auf andern Bahnen.

Kein geringer Grund, d.h. überhaupt kein *Grund* kann es gewesen sein, was gewisse Menschenrassen den Eichbaum verehren ließe, sondern nur das, daß sie und die Eiche in einer Lebensgemeinschaft vereinigt waren, also nicht aus Wahl, sondern, wie der Floh und der Hund, mit einander entstanden (Entwickelten die Flöhe einen Ritus, er würde sich auf den Hund beziehen.)

Man könnte sagen, nicht ihre Vereinigung (von Eiche und Mensch) hat zu diesen Riten die Veranlassung gegeben, sondern, in gewissem Sinne, ihre Trennung.

Denn das Erwachen des Intellekts geht mit einer Trennung von dem ursprünglichen *Boden*, der ursprünglichen Grundlage des Lebens vor sich. (Die Entstehung der *Wahl*.)

(Die Form des erwachenden Geistes ist die Verehrung.)

II

33.   P. 168.[22] (At a certain stage of early society the king or priest is often
       thought to be endowed with supernatural powers or to be an incarnation
       of a deity, and consistently with this belief the course of nature is supposed
       to be more or less under his control . . .)

It is of course not the case that the people believe that the ruler has these powers
while the ruler himself very well knows that he does not have them, or does not
know so only if he is an idiot or fool. Rather, the notion of his power is of course
arranged in a way such that it corresponds with experience—his own and that
of the people. That any kind of hypocrisy plays a role in this is only true to the
extent that it suggests itself in most of what humans do anyway.

34.   P. 169. (In ancient times he was obliged to sit on the throne for some
       hours every morning, with the imperial crown on his head, but to sit alto-
       gether like a statue, without stirring either hands or feet, head or eyes, nor
       indeed any part of his body, because, by this means, it was thought that he
       could preserve peace and tranquility in his empire . . .)

When someone in our (or at least my) society laughs too much, I press my lips
together in an almost involuntary fashion, as if I believed I could thereby keep
his lips closed.

35.   P. 170. (The power of giving or withholding rain is ascribed to him, and he
       is lord of the winds . . .)

What is nonsensical here is that Frazer presents it as if these people had an
entirely wrong (indeed, insane) notion of the course of nature, while they really
only entertain a somewhat peculiar interpretation of the phenomena. That is, if
they wrote it down, their knowledge of nature would not be *fundamentally* different from ours. Only their *magic* is different.

---

22. [SP] The paragraphs beginning with page numbers are quotations (in English)
     from the 1922 one-volume edition of the *Golden Bough*.

II

S. 168.[2] (At a certain stage of early society the king or priest is often thought to be endowed with supernatural powers or to be an incarnation of a deity, and consistently with this belief the course of nature is supposed to be more or less under his control . . .)

Dies ist natürlich nicht so, daß das Volk glaubt, der Herrscher habe diese Kräfte, der Herrscher aber sehr wohl weiß, daß er sie nicht hat, oder es nur dann nicht weiß, wenn er ein Schwachkopf oder ein Narr ist. Sondern die Notion von seiner Kraft ist natürlich so eingerichtet, daß sie mit der Erfahrung—des Volkes und seiner—übereinstimmen kann. Daß dabei irgendeine Heuchelei eine Rolle spielt, ist nur wahr, sofern sie überhaupt bei dem meisten was Menschen tun nahe liegt.

S. 169. (In ancient times he was obliged to sit on the throne for some hours every morning, with the imperial crown on his head, but to sit altogether like a statue, without stirring either hands or feet, head or eyes, nor indeed any part of his body, because, by this means, it was thought that he could preserve peace and tranquility in his empire . . .) Wenn ein Mensch in unserer (oder doch meiner) Gesellschaft zu viel lacht, so presse ich halb unwillkürlich die Lippen zusammen, als glaubte ich die seinen dadurch zusammen halten zu können.

S. 170. (The power of giving or withholding rain is ascribed to him, and he is lord of the winds . . .)

Der Unsinn ist hier, daß Frazer es so darstellt, als hätten diese Völker eine vollkommen falsche (ja wahnsinnige) Vorstellung vom Laufe der Natur, während sie nur eine merkwürdige Interpretation der Phänomene besitzen. D.h., ihre Naturkenntnis, wenn sie sie niederschrieben, würde von der unsern sich nicht *fundamental* unterscheiden. Nur ihre *Magie* ist anders.

---

2   Page-numbers refer to the one-volume edition of *The Golden Bough*.

36.   [246] P. 171. ". . . a network of prohibitions and observances, of which the
       intention is not to contribute to his dignity . . ." This is both true and false.
       Of course not the dignity of the protection of the person but rather—as it
       were—the natural sacredness of the divinity in him.

37.   Simple though it may sound: The difference between magic and science
       can be expressed in the way that there is progress in science, but not in
       magic. Magic possesses no direction of development internal to itself.

38.   P. 179. (The Malays conceive the human soul as a little man . . . who cor-
       responds exactly in shape, proportion, and even in complexion to the man
       in whose body he resides . . .)

How much more truth in granting the soul the same multiplicity as the body
than in a watered-down modern theory.
     Frazer does not realize that what we are facing here are the teachings of
Plato and Schopenhauer.

We re-encounter all childish (infantile) theories in contemporary philosophy;
only without the charm of childishness.

39.   P. 614.[23] (In Chapter LXII, "The Fire Festivals of Europe")

What is most striking are not merely the similarities but also the differences
between all these rites. There is a manifold of faces with common features that
keep surfacing here and there. And what one would like to do is draw lines that
connect the components in common. What would still be lacking then is a part
of our contemplation, and it is the one that connects this picture with our own
feelings and thoughts. This part gives such contemplation its depth.

40.   In all these practices, however, one sees something related or akin to the
       association of ideas. One could speak of an association of practices.

---

23.   [SP] The Miles/Rhees edition gives this reference as p. 617ff.

S. 171. ". . . a network of prohibitions and observances, of which the intention is not to contribute to his dignity, . . ." Das ist wahr und falsch. Freilich nicht die Würde des Schutz der Person, wohl aber die—sozusagen—natürliche Heiligkeit der Gottheit in ihm.

So einfach es klingt: der Unterschied zwischen Magie und Wissenschaft kann dahin ausgedrückt werden, daß es in der Wissenschaft einen Fortschritt gibt, aber nicht in der Magie. Die Magie hat keine Richtung der Entwicklung, die in ihr selbst liegt.

S. 179. (The Malays conceive the human soul as a little man . . . who corresponds exactly in shape, proportion, and even in complexion to the man in whose body he resides . . .)

Wievielmehr Wahrheit darin, daß der Seele dieselbe Multiplizität gegeben wird, wie dem Leib, als in einer modernen verwässerten Theorie.

Frazer merkt nicht, daß wir da Platos und Schopenhauers Lehre vor uns haben.

Alle kindliche (infantile) Theorien finden wir in der heutigen Philosophie wieder; nur nicht mit dem Gewinnenden des Kindlichen.

S. 614. (In Chapter LXII: The Fire Festivals of Europe.)

Das Auffallendste scheint mir außer den Ähnlichkeiten die Verschiedenheit aller diesen Riten zu sein. Es ist eine Mannigfaltigkeit von Gesichtern mit gemeinsamen Zügen, die da und dort immer wieder auftauchen. Und was man tun möchte ist, Linien ziehen, die die gemeinsamen Bestandteile verbinden. Es fehlt dann noch ein Teil der Betrachtung und es ist der, welcher dieses Bild mit unsern eigenen Gefühlen und Gedanken in Verbindung bringt. Dieser Teil gibt der Betrachtung ihre Tiefe.

In allen diesen Gebräuchen sieht man allerdings etwas, der Ideen-assoziation ähnliches und mit ihr verwandtes. Man könnte von einer Assoziation der Gebräuche reden.

P. 618. (. . . So soon as any sparks were emitted by means of the violent [247] friction, they applied a species of agaric, which grows on old birch trees and is very combustible. This fire had the appearance of being immediately derived from heaven, and manifold were the virtues ascribed to it . . .)

41.   Nothing speaks for why fire should be surrounded with such a nimbus. And what an odd thing [to say], "it had the appearance of being derived from heaven." What does this actually mean? From what heaven? No, it is not at all self-evident that fire is regarded in this way—but that is how it is regarded.[24]

The person who officiated as master of the feast produced a large cake baked with eggs and scalloped round the edge, called *am bonnach bealtine*—that is, the Beltane cake. It was divided into a number of pieces, and distributed in great form to the company. There was one particular piece that whoever got was called *cailleach beal-tine*—that is, the Beltane *carline*, a term of great reproach. Upon this being known, part of the company laid hold of him and made a show of putting him in the fire. . . . And while the feast was fresh in people's memory, they affected to speak of the *cailleach beal-tine* as dead. (*The Golden Bough*, p. 618)

42.   Here it appears as though it were only the hypothesis that gives the matter depth. And then one may remember the explanation of the strange relationship between Siegfried and Brunhild in our *Nibelungenlied*. Namely, that Siegfried seems to have seen Brunhilde [*sic*] some time before. It is thus clear that what gives this practice depth is its *connection* with the burning of a human being. If it were custom at some festival for men to ride on one another (as in horse-and-ride games), we would see nothing more in this than a way of carrying someone, which reminds us of people riding horses; —however, if we knew that it had been custom among many peoples to, for example, use slaves as mounts and to celebrate certain festivals mounted in this way, then we should see in the harmless practice of our times something deeper and less harmless. The question is: Does this—shall we say—sinister character adhere to the custom of the Beltane

---

24.   The following quotation from Frazer is omitted in the *Synthese* edition, but appears in the Miles/Rhees edition.

S. 618. (. . . So soon as any sparks were emitted by means of the violent friction, they applied a species of agaric which grows on old birch-trees, and is very
combustible. This fire had the appearance of being immediately derived from
heaven, and manifold were the virtues ascribed to it . . .)

Nichts spricht dafür, warum das Feuer mit solchem Nimbus umgeben sein sollte. Und, wie seltsam, was heißt es eigentlich, "es schien vom Himmel gekommen zu sein"? von welchem Himmel? Nein es ist gar nicht selbstverständlich,
daß das Feuer so betrachtet wird—aber es wird eben so betrachtet.

Hier scheint die Hypothese erst der Sache Tiefe zu geben. Und man kann sich
an die Erklärung des seltsamen Verhältnisses von Siegfried und Brunhild im
unsren Nibelungenlied erinnern. Nämlich, daß Siegfried Brunhilde schon früher einmal gesehen zu haben scheint. Es ist nun klar, daß, was diesem Gebrauch
Tiefe gibt, sein *Zusammenhang* mit dem Verbrennen eines Menschen ist. Wenn
es bei irgendeinem Fest Sitte wäre, daß Menschen (wie beim Roß-und-Reiter-
Spiel) auf einander reiten, so würden wir darin nichts sehen als eine Form des
Tragens, die an das Reiten des Menschen auf einem Pferd erinnert; —wüßten
wir aber, daß es unter vielen Völkern Sitte gewesen wäre, etwa Sklaven als Reit-
tiere zu benützen, und so beritten gewisse Feste zu feiern, so würden wir jetzt in
dem harmlosen Gebrauch unserer Zeit etwas Tieferes und weniger Harmloses
sehen. Die Frage ist: haftet dieses—sagen wir—Finstere dem Gebrauch des
Beltane Feuers, wie er vor 100 Jahren geübt wurde, an sich an, oder nur dann,
wenn die Hypothese seiner Entstehung sich bewahrheiten sollte. Ich glaube es
ist offenbar die innere Natur des neuzeitlichen Gebrauchs selbst, die uns finster
anmutet, und die uns bekannten Tatsachen von Menschenopfern weisen nur die

fire in itself as it was practiced a hundred years ago, or only if the hypothesis of its origin were to be confirmed? I believe that what appears to us as sinister is the inner nature of the practice as performed in recent times, and the facts of human sacrifice as we know them only indicate the direction in which we ought to look at it. When I speak of the inner nature of the practice, I mean all of those circumstances in which it is carried out and that are not included in the report on such a festival, because they consist not so much in particular actions that characterize the festival than in what one might call the spirit of the festival that would be described, for example, if one were to describe the kind of people that take part in it, their usual way of behaving [on other occasions]—that is, their character—and the kind of games they play at other times. And then one would see that what is sinister lies in the character of these people themselves.[25]

In . . . western Perthshire, the Beltane custom was still en vogue toward the end of the eighteenth century. It has been described as follows by the parish minister of the time [248]: "They put all the bits of the cake into a bonnet. Every one, blindfold, draws out a portion. . . . Whoever draws the black bit is the *devoted* person who is to be sacrificed to *Baal* . . ."

Thomas Pennant, who traveled in northern Perthshire in the year 1769, tells us that "everyone takes a cake of oatmeal upon which are raised nine square knobs, each dedicated to some particular being . . ."

Another writer of the eighteenth century has described the Beltane festival as it was held in the parish of Logierait in Perthshire. He says: "These dishes they eat with a sort of cake baked for the occasion, and having small lumps in the form of *nipples*, raised all over the surface." We may conjecture that the cake with knobs was formerly used for the purpose of determining who should be the "Beltane carline" or victim doomed to the flames (*The Golden Bough*, pp. 618, 619).

43.   Here one sees something like the remnants of a casting of lots. And through this aspect it suddenly gains depth. Should we learn that the cake with the buttons [i.e., "knobs," a mistranslation on Wittgenstein's part] was originally baked in a determinate case, say, in honor of a button-maker

---

25. [SP] The following three quotes from Frazer's *Golden Bough* do not appear in the *Synthese* edition of the German original, but only in the Miles/Rhees translation.

Richtung in der wir den Gebrauch ansehen sollen. Wenn ich von der inneren Natur des Gebrauchs rede, meine ich alle Umstände, in denen er geübt wird und die in dem Bericht von so einem Fest nicht enthalten sind, da sie nicht sowohl in bestimmten Handlungen bestehen, die das Fest charakterisieren, als in dem was man den Geist des Festes nennen könnte, welcher beschrieben würde indem man z.B. die Art von Leuten beschriebe, die daran teilnehmen, ihre übrige Handlungsweise, d.h. ihren Charakter, die Art der Spiele, die sie sonst spielen. Und man würde dann sehen, daß das Finstere im Charakter dieser Menschen selbst liegt.

S. 619. (. . . They all put the bits of cake into a bonnet. Everyone, blindfold, draws out a portion. He who holds the bonnet is entitled to the last bit. Whoever draws the black bit is the *devoted* person who is to be sacrificed to *Baal* . . .)

Hier sieht etwas aus wie die Überreste eines Losens. Und durch diesen Aspekt gewinnt es plötzlich Tiefe. Würden wir erfahren, daß der Kuchen mit den Knöpfen in einem bestimmten Fall etwa ursprünglich zu Ehren eines Knopfmachers zu seinem Geburtstag gebacken worden sei, und sich der Gebrauch

on the occasion of his birthday, and that the practice had then merely persisted on a local level, it would in fact lose all its "depth," unless this were
to lie in its present form as such. But in this case, it is often said: "this custom is obviously ancient." How does one know that? Is it merely because
historical evidence for ancient practices of this sort is at hand? Or is there
another reason, one that we can attain through interpretation? But even
if its prehistoric origin and its descent from an earlier practice is historically established, then it is still possible that today there is *nothing at all*
sinister about the practice anymore, that nothing of the ancient horror
still adheres to it. Perhaps it is only performed by children today who have
contests in baking cakes and decorating them with buttons. If so, then the
depth would thus only lie in the thought of such ancestry. Yet this can very
well be uncertain and one feels like saying: "Why worry about something
so uncertain" (like a backward-looking Kluge Else).[26] But worries of that
kind are not involved here. —Above all: whence the certainty that such
a practice must be ancient (what are the data, what is the verification)?
But have we any certainty, could we not be mistaken and proven to be in
error by historical means? Certainly, but there still remains something of
which we are sure. We would then say: "Very well, in this case the origin
may be different, but in general it is surely ancient." What constitutes
evidence for us of this must entail the depth of this assumption. And this
evidence, again, is nonhypothetical, psychological. For when I say: what is
deep about this lies in its origin *if it did* come about in this way, then such
deepness lies either in the thought of [its derivation from] such origins,
or else the deepness is in itself hypothetical—in which case one can only
say: if that is how it went, then this was a deep and sinister [249] business.
What I want to say is this: what is sinister, deep [about all this] does not
lie in how the history of this practice actually went, for perhaps it did not
go that way at all; nor that it maybe or [even] probably went that way, but
in what gives me reason to assume so. What makes human sacrifice so
deep and sinister in the first place? For is it only the suffering of the victim
that impresses us thus? All manners of illnesses bring about just as much
suffering, and yet do not evoke this impression. No, this deep and sinister
aspect does not become self-evident just from our knowledge of the history of the external actions; rather, we impute it to them [reintroduce it
into them] on the basis of an inner experience of our own.

---

26. [SP] Wittgenstein is referring to a character in one of the Grimm brothers' tales.

dann in der Gegend erhalten habe, so würde dieser Gebrauch tatsächlich alles "Tiefe" verlieren, es sei denn daß es in seiner gegenwärtigen Form an sich
liegt. Aber man sagt in so einem Fall oft: "dieser Gebrauch ist offenbar uralt."
Woher weiß man das? Ist es nur, weil man historisches Zeugnis über derar-
tige alte Gebräuche hat? Oder hat es noch einen andern Grund, einen, den
man durch Interpretation gewinnt? Aber auch wenn die vorzeitliche Herkunft
des Gebrauchs und die Abstammung von einem früheren Gebrauch historisch
erwiesen ist, so ist es doch möglich, daß der Gebrauch heute *gar nichts* mehr
Finsteres an sich hat, daß nichts von dem vorzeitlichen Grauen an ihm hangen
geblieben ist. Vielleicht wird er heute nur mehr von Kindern geübt, die im
Kuchenbacken und Verzehren mit Knopfen wetteifern. Dann liegt das Tiefe
also nur im Gedanken an jene Abstammung. Aber diese kann doch ganz unsicher sein und man möchte sagen: "Wozu sich über eine so unsichere Sache
sorgen" (wie eine rückwärts schauende Kluge Else). Aber solche Sorgen sind es
nicht. —Vor allem: woher die Sicherheit, daß ein solcher Gebrauch uralt sein
muß (was sind unsere Daten, was ist die Verifikation)? Aber haben wir denn
eine Sicherheit, können wir uns nicht darin irren und des Irrtums historisch
überführt werden? Gewiß, aber es bleibt dann noch immer etwas, dessen wir
sicher sind. Wir würden dann sagen: "Gut, in diesem Fall mag die Herkunft
anders sein, aber im allgemeinen ist sie sicher die Vorzeitliche." Was uns dafür
Evidenz ist, das muß die Tiefe dieser Annahme enthalten. Und diese Evidenz
ist wieder eine nicht-hypothetische, psychologische. Wenn ich nämlich sage:
das Tiefe in diesem Gebrauch liegt in seiner Herkunft *wenn* sie sich so zugetragen hat. So liegt also entweder das Tiefe in dem Gedanken an so eine Herkunft,
oder das Tiefe ist selbst hypothetisch und man kann nur sagen: *Wenn* es sich
so zugetragen hat, so war das eine finstere tiefe Geschichte. Ich will sagen: Das
Finstere, Tiefe liegt nicht darin, daß es sich mit der Geschichte dieses Gebrauchs so verhalten hat, denn vielleicht hat es sich gar nicht so verhalten; auch
nicht darin, daß es sich vielleicht oder wahrscheinlich so verhalten hat, sondern
in dem, was mir Grund gibt, das anzunehmen. Ja, woher überhaupt das Tiefe
und Finstere im Menschenopfer? Denn sind es nur die Leiden des Opfers, die
uns den Eindruck machen? Krankheiten aller Art, die mit ebensoviel Leiden
verbunden sind, rufen diesen Eindruck *doch* nicht hervor. Nein, dies Tiefe und
Finstere versteht sich nicht von selbst wenn wir nur die Geschichte der äußeren
Handlung erfahren, sondern *wir* tragen es wieder hinein aus einer Erfahrung
in unserm Innern.

The fact that a cake is utilized in drawing the lots does have something especially horrible (almost like betrayal through a kiss), and that this would impress
us as so horrible is, again, of essential importance for the investigation of such
practices.

When I see such a practice, or hear of it, it is like seeing a man who speaks
sternly to another for trivial reasons, and noticing from the tone of his voice and
his demeanor that on a given occasion this man can be scary. The impression I
get from this can be a very deep and extraordinarily sinister one.

44.   The *environment* of a way of acting.

45.   A conviction, at any rate, underlies the speculations about the origins of,
       for example, the Beltane festival; namely that such festivals were not, as it
       were, haphazardly invented, but would have to have an infinitely broader
       basis in order to persist. If I were to invent a festival, it would die out very
       soon, or else be so modified that it would correspond to a general inclina-
       tion among the people.

However, what is it that militates against assuming that the Beltane would have
always been celebrated in its present (or very recent) form? One feels like saying: it is too senseless to have been invented in this way. Is it not like when I see
a ruin and say: that must have been a house once, for no one would erect a heap
like that [250] of hewn and irregular stones? And if it be asked: How do you
know that? Then I could only say: it is what my experience of humans teaches
me. Indeed, even when they build ruins, they derive the form from collapsed
houses.

One might put it this way: Anyone who wanted to impress us with the story of
the Beltane festival would not have to express the hypothesis of its origin; he
would only have to show us the material (which led to the hypothesis) and say
nothing more. Here one might perhaps want to say, "Of course, this is so because the listeners or readers will draw the conclusion for themselves!" But must
they draw the conclusion explicitly? That is, draw it at all? And what conclusion
is it [anyway]? That this or that is *probable*? And if they can draw the conclusions themselves, how should the conclusions impress them? What makes for
the impression must surely be what they have *not* done! Is what causes the

Die Tatsache, daß das Los durch einen Kuchen gezogen wird, hat auch etwas besonders schreckliches (beinahe wie der Verrat durch einen Kuß), und daß uns das besonders schrecklich anmutet, hat wieder eine wesentliche Bedeutung für die Untersuchung solcher Gebräuche.

Es ist, wenn ich so einen Gebrauch sehe, von ihm höre, wie wenn ich einen Mann sehe wie er bei geringfügigem Anlaß streng mit einem Andern spricht, und aus dem Ton der Stimme und dem Gesicht merke, daß dieser Mann bei gegebenem Anlaß furchtbar sein kann. Der Eindruck, den ich hier erhalte, kann ein sehr tiefer und außerordentlich ernster sein.

Die *Umgebung* einer Handlungsweise.

Eine Überzeugung liegt jedenfalls den Annahmen über den Ursprung des Beltanefestes—z.B.—zu Grunde; die ist, daß solche Feste nicht von einem Menschen, sozusagen aufs Geratewohl erfunden werden, sondern eine unendlichviel breitere Basis brauchen, um sich zu erhalten. Wollte ich ein Fest erfinden, so würde es baldigst aussterben oder aber solcherweise modifiziert werden, daß es einem allgemeinen Hang der Leute entspricht.

Was aber wehrt sich dagegen anzunehmen, das Beltanefest sei immer in der gegenwärtigen (oder jüngstvergangenen) Form gefeiert worden? Man möchte sagen: Es ist zu sinnlos um so erfunden worden zu sein. Ist es nicht, wie wenn ich eine Ruine sehe und sage: das muß einmal ein Haus gewesen sein, denn niemand würde einen so beschaffenen Haufen behauener und unregelmäßiger Steine errichten? Und wenn gefragt würde: Woher weißt du das? so könnte ich nur sagen: meine Erfahrung mit den Menschen lehrt es mich. Ja, selbst da wo sie wirklich Ruine bauen, nehmen sie die Formen von eingestürzten Häusern her.

Man könnte auch so sagen: Wer uns mit der Erzählung vom Beltanefest einen Eindruck machen wollte, brauchte jedenfalls die Hypothese von seiner Herkunft nicht zu äußern, sondern er brauchte uns nur das Material (das zu dieser Hypothese führt) vorlegen und nichts weiter dazu sagen. Nun möchte man vielleicht sagen: "Freilich, weil der Hörer oder Leser den Schluß selber ziehen wird!" Aber muß er diesen Schluß explizite ziehen? also, überhaupt, ziehen? Und was ist es denn für ein Schluß? Daß das oder jenes *wahrscheinlich* ist?! Und wenn er den Schluß selber ziehen kann, wie soll ihm der Schluß einen Eindruck machen? was ihm den Eindruck macht muß doch das sein, was *er*

impression the hypothesis once expressed (by them or whomever) or already the material itself? But could I not just as well ask in this case: When I see someone being killed, is it simply what I see that impresses me, or does this impression [only] arise from the hypothesis that someone is being killed here?

But it is obviously not just the idea of the possible origins of the Beltane festival that conveys the impression, but what one calls the immense probability of this idea. All that is derived from the material [itself].

The Beltane festival as it has come down to us is indeed a play, and as such it is similar to children playing at robbers. But then again, it is not like this. For even if it is prearranged that the side that saves the victims wins, there is still, in what eventuates, an affective addition that a mere theatrical performance does not have. But even if it merely were a rather cool performance, would we not anxiously ask ourselves: What is this performance aiming at, what is its *meaning*? And apart from any interpretation, its strange pointlessness could unsettle us (which shows what the reason behind such uneasiness can be). Suppose some harmless interpretation were to be given: perhaps the lot is cast for reasons of the entertainment derived from being able to threaten someone to be thrown into the fire, which would be disagreeable; then the Beltane festival becomes far more like [251] those practical jests in which a member of the company has to endure certain cruelties that, such as they are, satisfy a certain need, in just this form. Through such an explanation, the Beltane festival would lose all mystery, were it not for the fact that it deviates in action and mood from such common games of robbers, etcetera.

Just so, the fact that children may, on certain days, burn a straw man could make us uneasy, even if no explanation were to come forth. How strange that a *man* should be burned by them in celebration! What I want to say is this: The solution is not anymore disquieting than the riddle.

But why should it not really be (partly, anyway) just the *idea* that makes the impression on me? Aren't ideas frightening? Can I not feel horror at the thought that the cake with the buttons once served to select the victim of [human] sacrifice? Hasn't that [very] *thought* something terrible to it? —Yes, but what I see in these stories is something that they acquire, after all, from the evidence, including such evidence as does not seem to be directly connected to them—[they acquire it] through the thought of humans and their past, through

nicht gemacht hat! Impressioniert ihn also erst die geäußerte Hypothese (ob von ihm oder andern geäußert), oder schon das Material zu ihr? Aber könnte ich da nicht ebensogut fragen: Wenn ich sehe wie Einer umgebracht wird, — impressioniert mich da einfach was ich sehe oder erst die Hypothese, daß hier ein Mensch umgebracht wird?

Aber es ist ja nicht einfach der Gedanke an die mögliche Herkunft des Beltanefestes welche den Eindruck mit sich führt sondern, was man die ungeheuere Wahrscheinlichkeit dieses Gedankens nennt. Als das was vom Material hergenommen ist.

So wie das Beltanefest auf uns gekommen ist, ist es ja ein Schauspiel und ähnlich wie wenn Kinder Räuber spielen. Aber doch nicht so. Denn wenn es auch abgekartet ist, daß die Partei die das Opfer rettet gewinnt, so hat doch, was geschieht, noch immer einen Temperamentszusatz, den die bloße schauspielerische Darstellung nicht hat. Aber auch wenn es sich bloß um eine ganz kühle Darstellung handelte, würden wir uns doch beunruhigt fragen: Was soll diese Darstellung, was ist ihr *Sinn*?! Und sie könnte uns abgesehen von jeder Deutung dann durch ihre eigentümliche Sinnlosigkeit beunruhigen. (Was zeigt, welcher Art der Grund so einer Beunruhigung sein kann.) Würde nun etwa eine harmlose Deutung gegeben: Das Los werde einfach geworfen, damit man das Vergnügen hätte, jemanden damit drohen zu können ins Feuer geworfen zu werden, was nicht angenehm sei; so wird das Beltanefest viel ähnlicher einem jener Belustigungen wo einer der Gesellschaft gewisse Grausamkeiten zu erdulden hat und die so wie sie sind ein Bedürfnis befriedigen. Und das Beltanefest würde durch so eine Erklärung auch jedes Geheimnisvolle verlieren, wenn es eben nicht selbst in der Handlung wie in der Stimmung von solchen gewöhnlichen Räuberspielen etc. abwiche.

Ebenso, daß Kinder an gewissen Tagen einen Strohmann verbrennen, auch wenn dafür keine Erklärung gegeben würde, könnte uns beunruhigen. Seltsam, daß *ein Mensch* festlich von ihnen verbrannt werden sollte! Ich will sagen: die Lösung ist nicht beunruhigender als das Rätsel.

Warum soll es aber nicht wirklich nur (oder doch zum Teil) der *Gedanke* sein, der mir den Eindruck gibt? Sind denn Vorstellungen nicht furchtbar? Kann mir bei dem Gedanken, daß der Kuchen mit den Knöpfen einmal dazu gedient hat das Todesopfer auszulosen, nicht schaurig zumut werden? Hat nicht der *Gedanke* etwas Furchtbares? —Ja, aber das was ich in jenen Erzählungen sehe gewinnen sie doch durch die Evidenz, auch durch solche, die damit nicht unmittelbar verbunden zu sein scheint, —durch den Gedanken an den

all the strangeness of what I see in myself and in others, and what I have seen
and heard about it.[27]

46.   P. 640. (?) One can very well imagine this—and the reason might have
      been given that the patron saints would otherwise be at cross-purposes,
      and that only one of them could direct the matter. But this, too, would
      only be a belated extension of the instinct.

All these *various* practices show that we are not dealing with the descent of
one from the other, but with a commonality of spirit. And one could invent
(confabulate) all of these ceremonies on one's own. And the spirit in which one
would invent them is their common one.

47.   P. 641. (. . . as soon as the fire on the domestic hearth had been rekindled
      from the need-fire, a pot full of water was set on it, and water thus heated
      was afterward sprinkled upon the people infected with the plague or upon
      the cattle that were tainted by the murrain.)

[252] The connection of illness and dirt. "The cleansing of a disease."

It is a simple, childlike theory of disease that it is the dirt that could be washed
off.

Just like there are "infantile theories of sexuality," there are infantile theories
more generally. However, this does not mean that everything that a child does
has come *from* an infantile theory as its reason.

The correct and interesting thing is not to say, "this has come from that," but "it
could have come from that."

P. 643. (. . . Dr. Westermark has argued powerfully in favor of the purificatory
theory alone. . . . However, the case is not so clear as to justify us in dismissing
the solar theory without discussion.)

---

27. [SP] The following paragraphs only appear in the *Synthese* edition. They were
     omitted in the Miles/Rhees translation.

Menschen und seine Vergangenheit, durch all das Seltsame, das ich in mir und in den Andern sehe, gesehen und gehört habe.

S. 640. (?)

Das kann man sich sehr gut denken—und als Grund wäre etwa angegeben worden, daß die Schutzheiligen sonst gegeneinander ziehen würden, und daß nur einer die Sache dirigieren könne. Aber auch das wäre nur eine nachträgliche Ausdehnung des Instinkts.

Alle diese *verschiedene* Gebräuche zeigen, daß es sich hier nicht um die Abstammung des einen vom andern handelt, sondern um einen gemeinsamen Geist. Und man könnte alle diese Zeremonien selber erfinden (erdichten). Und der Geist aus dem man sie erfände wäre eben ihr gemeinsamer Geist.

S. 641. (. . . as soon as the fire on the domestic hearth had been rekindled from the need-fire, a pot full of water was set on it, and water thus heated was afterwards sprinkled upon the people infected with the plague or upon the cattle that were tainted by the murrain.)

Die Verbindung von Krankheit und Schmutz. "Von einer Krankheit reinigen."

Es liefert eine einfache, kindliche Theorie der Krankheit, daß sie Schmutz ist, der abgewaschen werden kann.

Wie es "infantile Sexualtheorien" gibt, so überhaupt infantile Theorien. Das heißt aber nicht, daß alles, was ein Kind tut, *aus* einer infantilen Theorie als seinen Grund hervorgegangen ist.

Das Richtige und Interessante ist nicht zu sagen: das ist aus dem hervorgegangen, sondern: es könnte so hervorgegangen sein.

S. 643. (. . . Dr. Westermark has argued powerfully in favour of the purificatory theory alone. . . . However, the case is not so clear as to justify us in dismissing the solar theory without discussion.)

That fire was used for cleansing is clear. But nothing can be more likely than that thoughtful people would have eventually associated cleansing ceremonies with the sun, even when they were originally conceived just as such. When a thought suggests itself to a person (fire-cleansing) and another to someone else (fire-sun) then what can be more likely than that both thoughts will suggest themselves to one person. The scholars who always want to have a theory!!!

The *total* destruction through fire, different from smashing or tearing up, must have been noticed by people.

Even if one didn't know anything of such a connection between the thought of cleansing and the sun, one could assume that it would have occurred somewhere.

48. P. 680. (. . . in New Britain there is a secret society. . . . On his entrance into it every man receives a stone in the shape either of a human being or of an animal, and henceforth his soul is believed to be knit up in a manner with the stone.)

[253] "Soul-stone."[28] Here one sees how such a hypothesis works.

49. P. 681. ([680 infra, 681] . . . it used to be thought that the maleficent powers of witches and wizards resided in their hair, and that nothing could make any impression on these miscreants so long as they kept their hair on. Hence in France it was customary to shave the whole bodies of persons charged with sorcery before handing them over to the torturer.)

This would indicate that this is grounded in a truth rather than in superstition. (Of course it is easy to fall into a spirit of contestation [contradiction] when facing the stupid scholar). But it can very well be that the body entirely shorn of hair leads us in some sense to lose self-respect. (Brothers Karamazoff.) There is no doubt whatsoever that a mutilation that makes us look undignified, ludicrous in our own eyes can rob us of all will to defend ourselves. How embarrassed we are sometimes—or at least many people (I)—by our physical or aesthetic inferiority.

---

28. English in the original.

Daß das Feuer zur Reinigung gebraucht wurde, ist klar. Aber nichts kann wahrscheinlicher sein, als daß die denkenden Menschen Reinigungszeremonien, auch wo sie ursprünglich nur als solche gedacht gewesen wären, später mit der Sonne in Zusammenhang gebracht haben. Wenn sich einem Menschen ein Gedanke aufdrängt (Feuer–Reinigung) und einem ein anderer (Feuer–Sonne) was kann wahrscheinlicher sein, als daß sich einem Menschen beide Gedanken aufdrängen werden. Die Gelehrten die immer eine Theorie haben möchten!!!

Die *gänzliche* Zerstörung durch das Feuer, anders als durch Zerschlagen, Zerreißen etc., muß den Menschen aufgefallen sein.

Auch wenn man nichts von einer solchen Verbindung des Reinigung und Sonne Gedankens wüßte, könnte man annehmen, daß er irgendwo wird aufgetreten sein.

S. 680. (. . . in New Britain there is a secret society. . . . On his entrance into it every man receives a stone in the shape either of a human being or of an animal, and henceforth his soul is believed to be knit up in a manner with the stone.)

"Soul–stone." Da sieht man wie eine solche Hypothese arbeitet.

S. 681. ([680 infra, 681] . . . it used to be thought that the maleficent powers of witches and wizards resided in their hair, and that nothing could make any impression on these miscreants so long as they kept their hair on. Hence in France it was customary to shave the whole bodies of persons charged with sorcery before handing them over to the torturer.)

Das würde darauf deuten, daß hier eine Wahrheit zu Grunde liegt und kein Aberglaube. (Freilich ist es dem dummen Wissenschaftler gegenüber leicht in den Geist des Widerspruchs zu verfallen.) Aber es kann sehr wohl sein, daß der völlig enthaarte Leib uns in irgendeinem Sinne den Selbstrespekt zu verlieren verleitet. (Brüder Karamazoff.) Es ist gar kein Zweifel, daß eine Verstümmelung, die uns in unseren Augen unwürdig, lächerlich, aussehen macht, uns allen Willen rauben kann uns zu verteidigen. Wie verlegen werden wir manchmal—oder doch viele Menschen (ich)—durch unsere physische oder ästhetische Inferiorität.

CHAPTER 3

On Wittgenstein's Remarks on Frazer's *Golden Bough*

Carlo Severi

PART I: INTRODUCTION

Ludwig Wittgenstein wrote the *Remarks on Frazer's Golden Bough* between 1931 and 1948. Like many other writings that he had no intention to publish, they were left unfinished. Splendid intuitions alternate with very short, sometimes rudimentary remarks. Many of these observations are unsystematic, elliptic, and fragmentary. Some of them are so cryptic that they defy interpretation. To understand this text, one feels the need to refer to a more accomplished work, where the many questions alluded to in the *Remarks* can be made clearer. In Wittgenstein's oeuvre, the closest text to the *Remarks* is, obviously, the *Philosophical Investigations*, a masterwork he worked on from 1929 to 1945. Almost all commentators have thus been tempted to read the *Remarks* with reference to the *Investigations*. When one reads in the *Remarks on Frazer*, for instance, that "a whole mythology is deposited in our language" (#24), one quite naturally finds connected thoughts in the *Investigations*, as for instance: "*A picture* held us captive. And we could not get outside it, for it lay in our language and language seemed to repeat it to us inexorably" (Wittgenstein 1958: §115). In a similar vein, Jacques Bouveresse (1977) has used the *Remarks* to uncover the "implicit anthropology" that, according to him, gives to the *Investigations*—and perhaps to all Wittgenstein's philosophy—their real meaning.[1]

This kind of interpretation is useful but insufficient. The *Remarks* are only partially explained by reference to the *Investigations*. When Wittgenstein writes, for instance, that "we must plough over language in its entirety" (#17), or when he remarks that "I now believe that it would be right to begin my book with remarks on metaphysics as a kind of magic" (Rhees 1987: 1), one hears persistent echoes still coming from the *Tractatus*—a very different book, stemming from a radically different approach.

In these comments, I would argue, thus, that to understand the way Wittgenstein read Frazer, one needs not one but two backgrounds. In my view, when Wittgenstein tries to understand the cognitive import, and the kind of theoretical bets that an understanding of "culture" implies, he mobilizes both his major works. If this is true, it might be useful to draw here a brief sketch of these two very different epistemologies.

The *Tractatus* aims to formulate a perfect, modern version of Platonism. Its epistemology, though not explicitly declared in the book, can be summarized in a brief sequence of statements:

The world is made of events.[2]
The same laws that preside over thought rule events.
These laws have a mathematical, or grammar-like, nature.[3]
Thus, to understand the world, as well as the logical picture of it, one has to uncover its secret grammar.[4]

---

1. For instance, Bouveresse writes, "Même s'il n'a écrit qu'un seul texte consacré à l'anthropologie, en fait il n'a jamais écrit d'autre chose" (1977: 46).

2. "1.2: The world divides into facts. 1.13: The facts in logical space are the world" (Wittgenstein [1922] 2010: 25). "The same laws that preside over thought rule events. The logical picture of the facts is the thought" (Wittgenstein [1922] 2010: 30).

3. "6.3: Logical research means the investigation of all regularity. And outside logic all is accident" (Wittgenstein [1922] 2010: 83).

4. "4.04: In the proposition there must be exactly as many things distinguishable as there are in the state of affairs, which it represents. They must both possess the same logical (mathematical) multiplicity." "4.121: The propositions show the logical form of reality. They exhibit it" (Wittgenstein [1922] 2010: 45).

However, the *Tractatus* is far from being only a treatise of Logic. What is unforgettable about it, what makes it unique, is that the theory exposed in the book, which applies to a mathematics-inspired knowledge of the world, is seen as inseparable from what one could call an ethics of the subject of thought. Epistemological remarks cohabit with an anxious and constantly re-elaborated definition of the universe that an *individual* (an abstract notion that obviously does not coincide with—but certainly includes—Wittgenstein himself), *as subject of thought* may inhabit. More exactly, Wittgenstein tries to appreciate, in the most precise way, how far human thought can go. For instance, Wittgenstein writes: "5.6: The limits of my language mean the limits of my world" (Wittgenstein [1922] 2010: 74). And he adds: "6.4311: If by eternity is understood not endless temporal duration but timelessness, then he lives eternally who lives in the present. Our life is endless in the way that our visual field is without limit" (Wittgenstein [1922] 2010: 88–89).

So this thin book, so important for Philosophy and Logic (Wittgenstein wrote once that he thought he "had solved virtually all the problems of philosophy" in the *Tractatus*) also narrates the story of a self-reflexive meditation about what a subject can possibly think—and about how she/he can experience the world. This is why the conclusion of the *Tractatus* resembles more the description of the end of an initiation than the conclusion of a book about philosophy: "6.54: He who understands me finally recognizes [my statements] as senseless, when he has climbed out through them, on them, over them. (He must so to speak throw away the ladder, after he has climbed up on it.) He must surmount these propositions; then he sees the world rightly" (Wittgenstein [1922] 2010: 90).

In the *Philosophical Investigations*, published twenty-three years later, this perspective is reversed. One finds in this book the perfect overcoming of any Platonism. World and language's laws are anything but secret. If there is a secret, it lies not in an invisible general form but in the infinite multiplicity of possible games that the use of a language constantly generates. Coming very close to some remarks in the *Remarks*, Wittgenstein writes, for instance, that "a great deal of stage-setting in the language is presupposed if the mere act of naming is to make sense" (1958: §92). So, in order to understand the world, it would be useless to look for secret laws of mathematical nature. Far from reflecting a sort of mysterious order of reality, mathematics is only to be seen as "an episode in the history of human thought." Language is no more an image of the world, instead: "Language is a labyrinth of paths. You approach from *one* side and know your way about; you approach the same place from another side and no longer know your way about"

(1958: §203). Consequently, one has to work on an entirely different perspective, and pose altogether different questions: Is a private language conceivable? Do those grammatical laws that the study of language uncovers ultimately refer to any totality? Is there any general truth about human thought? Could we at least identify a sort of possible common ground, a *form of life*, where we could identify a sort of unity that would connect together our findings about language and thought? Wittgenstein formulates this problem, for instance, in these terms: "It is what human beings *say* that is true and false; and they agree in the *language* they use. That is not agreement in opinions but in form of life" (1958: §88).

Wittgenstein's interest in Frazer, and in the possible definition of a general concept of culture, comes from questions of this kind that appeared at the end of the *Investigations*. We have seen that in the *Remarks on Frazer*, one finds echoes of *both* of Wittgenstein's antagonistic epistemologies. When he states that the philosopher "must plough over language in its entirety" (#17), it is the young logician, the author of the *Tractatus* who speaks. When he affirms that "a historical explanation, an explanation in the form of a hypothesis of development is only *one* kind of summary arrangement of the data—of their synopsis" (#20), or when he adds that "it is equally possible to see the data in their relation to one another and to gather them into a general picture without doing so in the form of a hypothesis concerning temporal development" (#20), one hears the philosopher of the language games. This is why the *Remarks* do not contain a single philosophical doctrine of culture, nor solutions to the problems posed by Frazer. The *Remarks*, focusing on the *forms* of cultural problems—and on the implications these forms might generate—nonetheless identify a number of interesting problems, and explore possible interpretations. In order to show this "plurality of voices" that one hears in this text, I shall focus now on ritual, and I shall comment on the introductory remarks, and remarks 1, 9, 10, 15, 16, 22, and 37.

PART II: NOTES AND COMMENTS

1. One must begin with error and transform it into truth.

That is, one must uncover the source of the error, otherwise hearing the truth won't help us. It cannot penetrate when something else is taking its place.

To convince someone of what is true, it is not enough to state the truth; one must find the *way* from error to truth.

Commentary: For an anthropologist, this statement contains an obvious truth: the mere description of cultural differences implies the critique of the errors lying in ethnocentrism. The truth of what we describe in ethnography has always a retrospective effect on previous prejudices. However, there is in this remark also a far less obvious idea: general issues concerning thought—going beyond the area of our discipline—are inherent to the anthropological enterprise. Social Anthropology always implies significant consequences for Philosophy.

9. Burning in effigy. Kissing the picture of a loved one. This is *obviously not* based on a belief that it will have a definite effect on the object that the picture represents. It aims at some satisfaction, and does achieve it, too. Or rather, it does not *aim* at anything; we act in this way and then feel satisfied.

Commentary: Ritual fosters a paradoxical relationship with belief. On the one hand, rituals, in that they are made up of sequences of symbolic actions, have frequently been described as attempts to create belief in the supernatural world. Pierre Smith is convincing when he suggests that the establishment of a belief is a good criterion for distinguishing "true rituals" from other, vaguer contexts of social interaction that merely resemble them: for example, festivals, dances, and other profane celebrations (Smith 1979). At the same time, it is quite clear that the kind of beliefs that a ritual seems able to instill is never really dissociated from doubt and uncertainty. Rituals never fail to provoke commentaries on what kind of action they are or on what they may achieve. This means not only that traditional societies, both in Europe and elsewhere, are far from being societies of believers but also that a reflexive attitude, linked to the very nature of the ceremonial action, is seldom absent from the performance of a ritual.

10. The same savage who, apparently in order to kill his enemy, pierces an image of him, really builds his hut out of wood, and carves his arrow skillfully and not in effigy. The idea that one could beckon a lifeless object to come, just as one would beckon a person. Here the principle is that of personification.

Commentary: Virtually everywhere, such formal contexts of the expression of meaning as ritual action, play, and other forms of performance generate their specific "ontologies." Things, artifacts, and living beings may then crucially change their nature, as in the famous "qualitative analogy" that transforms a cucumber into an ox in E. E. Evans-Pritchard's analysis of the Nuer sacrifice (1956). In these cases, the anthropological interpretation of such formal contexts of cultural representation requires translating "worlds" (defined as "oriented contexts for the apprehension of reality" coexisting within single societies), not just words, or other ways to express meaning.

15. I do not mean that it is especially *fire* that must make an impression on anyone. Fire no more than any other phenomenon, and one will impress this person and another that. For no phenomenon is particularly mysterious in itself, but any of them can become so to us, and it is precisely the characteristic feature of the awakening human mind that a phenomenon acquires significance for it. One could almost say that man is a ceremonial animal. This is probably partly false, partly nonsensical, but there is also some truth to it.

In other words, one could begin a book on anthropology in this way: when one observes the life and behavior of humans all over the earth, one sees that apart from the kinds of behavior one could call animal, the intake of food, etcetera, etcetera, etcetera, humans also carry out actions that bear a peculiar character, and might be called ritual actions.

But then again it is nonsense to go on and say that the characteristic feature of these actions is that they spring from erroneous notions about the physics of things. (As Frazer does when he says that magic is really false physics, or as the case may be, false medicine, technology, etc.)

Rather, what is characteristic of ritual action is not at all any view, opinion, be it right or wrong, although an opinion—a belief—can itself be of ritual nature, or belong to a rite.

Commentary: I have learned much from this page. It made me understand that the complexity of ritual action cannot be fully accounted for by reference to meaning and function. Such concerns are indeed always directed toward the premises or the consequences of ritual, and not to the way in which ritual action itself is organized. However, the identification of this latter organizational level is essential if we are to understand how ritual fits in with tradition: in other words, how a sequence of actions may become a medium of symbolization and an instrument of social strategy. The analysis that Michael Houseman and I (Houseman and Severi 1998) proposed in order to grasp the structuring of ritual action in the case of Naven led us to the definition of a relational form of action: a characteristic linkage between relationships involving a constant interactive dynamic. It is by understanding this enacted form, not by referring to any specific belief, that we have been able to recognize the unity of this ritual as an object of study. It is also, we suggest, this particular dynamic—a complex form of reciprocal caricature—that allows the Iatmul to recognize an apparently very wide range of behaviors as parts of a ritual.

16.   If one takes it to be self-evident that people take pleasure in their own imaginations, then one should remember that such imagination is not like a picture or a three-dimensional model, but a complicated pattern of heterogeneous components: words and images. [Once one does so] one will then no longer oppose operating with written or acoustic signs to operating with "mental images" of events.

Commentary: Two points are relevant to this remark. One concerns the nature of ethnography. Despite the tendency—rather common in our discipline—of describing "culture" in the form of a discourse, nonlinguistic forms of representation are constantly present in cultural traditions (Severi 2012). Words are translated into images, music into words, and gestures into objects. Furthermore, even within a single culture, translation processes enable the passage from one context of communication to another.

The second point concerns the possibility of anthropology of imagination. From Lucien Lévy-Bruhl's considerations on "pre-logical mentality" (1949) up to Dan Sperber's arguments on apparently irrational beliefs (1982), a great part of the anthropological literature devoted to this topic does not really concern the study of thought as a general human activity. It concerns rationality and irrationality. In this perspective, anthropologists usually compare an abstract definition of "rationality" with an empirical counterpart, mostly founded on the analysis of some forms of categorization and theories of causality. It is obvious, however, that there is much more about human thought than categorization, or propositional rationality. Ideas about space, language, and communication, for instance, are constantly present in ethnography. It would be hard to qualify them as "rational" or "nonrational" (or "symbolic"). As we know at least since J. L. Austin (1975), these kinds of concepts would be better qualified as "appropriate" or "inappropriate," "felicitous" or not in a certain context, than rational or nonrational. In sum, when approaching the idea of an anthropology of thought, there is a preliminary choice to make. Either one chooses what we may call a Piagetian model of thought-as-rationality, seen in its various manifestations but defined in only one form, rational or non rational (Piaget [1923] 2001, [1926] 2007); or one refers to a more extensive and more realistic definition of thought. One of the classic authors that have worked in this direction (and whom we could, in this respect, oppose to Piaget) is Lev Vygotsky (1978), the great Russian psychologist. Not unaware of the problems posed by cultural differences, Vygotsky has elaborated a multifaceted conception of the exercise of thought, which includes not only rational inference, but also metalinguistic, metacommunicational, aesthetic, and narrative thought. Imagination is one of these forms of thought. To study it, one must take a Vygotskyan approach, and combine it with a reading of Wittgenstein.

22.   "And so the chorus points to a secret law" is what one might want to say about Frazer's collection of facts. Now, I *can* represent this law, this idea, in the form of a hypothesis of development, but also in analogy to the schema of a plant, I can represent it as the schema of a religious ceremony, or again by grouping the facts alone in a "perspicuous" presentation.

Commentary: Indeed, as the translator remarks here, übersichtlich (translated here as "perspicuous") is a strange word. One has to make decisions about its meaning. To me, when he uses this word, Wittgenstein means "seen from different points of view," prismatic, "multidimensional." Wittgenstein sees this "perspicuous" presentation of cultural facts, as the result of a general order, a way—among other possible ways—of generalizing data. Actually, this is why he opposes it here to historical reconstruction. How is it possible to make generalizations from multidimensional phenomena? At first sight, this seems an impossible task. By definition, multidimensionality (since it introduces several criteria in the definition of a phenomenon) seems to make generalization difficult. But this is precisely the task of Social Anthropology. Again, here Wittgenstein gives a neat description of a problem, without proposing a solution.

37.   Simple though it may sound: The difference between magic and science can be expressed in the way that there is progress in science, but not in magic. Magic possesses no direction of development internal to itself.

Commentary: Simple thought it seems indeed. I am not sure that magic could be said to have no "direction of development." But I am sure that science does not achieve the kind of cumulative and unproblematic "progress in knowledge" Wittgenstein had in mind.

REFERENCES

Austin, J. L. 1975. *How to Do Things with Words*. Oxford: Oxford University Press.

Bouveresse, Jacques. 1977. "L'animal cérémoniel: Wittgenstein et l'anthropologie." *Actes de la recherche en sciences sociales* 16 (1): 43–54.

Evans-Pritchard, E. E. 1956. *Nuer Religion*. Oxford: Oxford University Press.

Houseman, Michael, and Carlo Severi. 1998. *Naven; or, The Other Self: A Relational Approach to Ritual Action*. Numen Book Series. Leiden: J. Brill.

Lévy-Bruhl, Lucien. 1949. *Les carnets*. Paris: Presses Universitaires de France.

Piaget, Jean. (1923) 2001. *The Language and Thought of the Child*. Translated by Marjorie Gabain and Ruth Gabain. London: Routledge.

———. (1926) 2007. *The Child's Conception of the World*. Translated by Joan Tomlinson and Andrew Tomlinson. Lanham, MD: Rowman & Littlefield.

Rhees, Rush. 1967. "Introductory Note to Bemerkungen Über Frazers *The Golden Bough*." *Synthese* 17 (3): 233–53.

Severi, Carlo. 2012. "The Arts of Memory: Comparative Perspectives on a Mental Artifact." *HAU: Journal of Ethnographic Theory* 2 (2): 451–85.

Smith, Pierre. 1979. "Aspects de l'organisation des rites." In *La fonction symbolique: Essais d'anthropologie*, edited by Michel Izard and Pierre Smith, 139–70. Paris: Gallimard.

Sperber, Dan. 1982. "Apparently Irrational Beliefs." In *Rationality and Relativism*, edited by Martin Hellis and Steven Lukes, 149–80. Cambridge, MA: MIT Press.

Vygotsky, Lev S. 1978. *Mind in Society*. Cambridge, MA: Harvard University Press.

Wittgenstein, Ludwig. (1922) 2010. *Tractatus Logico-Philosophicus*. Translated by C. K. Ogden. Project Gutenberg. http://www.gutenberg.org/files/5740/5740-pdf.pdf?session_id=ad3e3aed1eed455e8fc6877848f7ed6741568b5f.

———. 1958. *Philosophical Investigations*. Oxford: Basil Blackwell.

———. 1987. *Remarks on Frazer's Golden Bough*. Atlantic Highlands, NJ: Humanities Press.

CHAPTER 4

Wittgenstein's Spirit, Frazer's Ghost

HEONIK KWON

Some of my senior colleagues at Trinity College, Cambridge, still remember James Frazer and Ludwig Wittgenstein (or what they heard of them, especially in the case of Frazer, who died before the end of the Second World War). But their recollections seldom include the main concern of this collection—why the giant of modern philosophy disagreed so violently with one of the founders of modern anthropology. They recall Wittgenstein as a rather reclusive figure and something of a maverick philosopher, especially in contrast to Bertrand Russell, another Trinity fellow and eminent philosopher, who was gregarious and whose work was largely within a mainstream philosophical tradition. Frazer also had a philosophy background; he started his academic career with a thesis on Plato. At Trinity, however, Frazer is remembered primarily as an anthropologist and, by a few, as a classicist. Those who remember Frazer as a specialist in classical studies regard him as an unorthodox scholar, interested in non-European cultural worlds and a variety of magical customs drawn from these worlds—that is, rather than squarely in the literary and cultural achievements of the old Hellenic world, as was usually expected of scholars of classics. Among my colleagues who think of Frazer as an anthropologist, some find it rather challenging to reconcile what they know of anthropology through Frazer's career with the kind of anthropology I say I do. When I discuss my early fieldwork experience in a small-scale indigenous community in Siberia, or my relatively recent work on ghost beliefs in Vietnam, my colleagues will nod and recognize without difficulty that I am an anthropologist. When I add that I also worked on broad historical questions, such as a comparative study of global Cold War politics and history, there is sometimes an awkward moment between us. I can hear them asking, in unspoken words, whether this kind of investigation really belongs to anthropology.

There is nothing unusual about being both a classicist and an anthropologist; other such polyglot scholars exist in the history of modern anthropology. Although what Frazer experimented with in *Golden Bough* (1890) was unfamiliar to the discipline of classics at the turn of the twentieth century, the book's sweeping comparative interests in diverse human cultural worlds—moving uninhibitedly from totemic emblems in indigenous Australia to pagan beliefs in Europe, and from disappearing folkloric customs in rural England to nature spirit beliefs in Africa and South Asia—was far from strange to the literary elite and middlebrow readership of his time. As Mary Beard (1992) argues, the structure of *Golden Bough* was highly attractive to the educated public in the late imperial age. The book brought together an interest in the relics of rural England with an interest in exotic cultural customs collected from England's broad imperial realm, and it combined these interests with a revived quest to discover the classical world. This fitted perfectly, according to Beard, with the public culture of the late Victorian age and the pattern of knowledge consumption in the empire's metropolis. *Golden Bough* embraced the dazzling multitude of religious customs within the empire while, at the same time, opening and ending the oeuvre with a single enigmatic symbol drawn from the classical world—Virgil's golden bough. It allowed late Victorian readers to undertake an imaginary voyage to distant corners of their empire, whereas at the end of a long journey, the readers were securely returned to their familiar cultural home. This narrative strategy was not intended to place Europe's key religious symbols as part of the plurality of human religious ideas and magical customs. It was rather to reaffirm the centrality of these symbols and their properties amid and despite the rich variety of human magical ideas. The strategy generated imperial self-assurance, according to Beard, in which an encounter with diversity strengthens (rather than unsettles) the self's sense of being at the center of the world.

Golden Bough's approach to human diversity deeply frustrated Wittgenstein. By the time Wittgenstein discovered the book, some forty years after its original publication, he was immersed in issues concerning what commentators later referred to as philosophical pluralism or perspectivism—a set of ideas that apparently have a strong affinity with the premises of contemporary anthropology. Wittgenstein's frustration with Frazer and his disappointment with the kind of anthropology he discovered in Frazer's writing are understandable, given the kind of philosophy Wittgenstein was looking out for by the time he started making notes on *Golden Bough* in 1931. The spirit of this philosophy was post-Victorian and postimperial in the sense that it celebrates the sovereignty and integrity of other forms of life and other language worlds. This philosophical orientation resonated strongly with the zeitgeist of the mid-twentieth century, especially the powerful drive for decolonization during the era. Decolonization made the question of political sovereignty and self-determination a firmly legitimate agenda; equally important, it also involved conceptualizing human cultural diversity differently from the previous era. Peter Mandler's new biography of Margaret Mead delves into the question of "how to make the world safe for differences," a central concern for Mead in the 1940s and 1950s (Mandler 2013). The question involves an important move with regard to the concept of culture. The new concept holds that human groups all have authentic and distinct cultural systems, just like languages. It follows that these unique cultures, and variations found among them, need to be understood as *differences* rather than as lower or higher civilizational achievements. This reasoning about cultural integrity and sovereignty accorded with the imperative of decolonization. The translation of civilizational hierarchy to cultural difference was also more broadly relevant. It was meaningful for the United States, which, emerging as a new (and sole) imperial power after the destruction of the Second World War, and confronting the Soviet power while doing so, had to distinguish its place in the world from that held by former European imperial powers. Acutely aware of this situation, according to Mandler, Mead believed that the ethos of cultural pluralism and related principles of "Boasian internationalism" would play a central role in the making of a new, more democratic international order in the post-WWII world.

Frazer felt free to collect cultural facts from different places and to contemplate their meanings without necessarily taking an interest in what meanings these facts might have in their places and contexts of origin. These were the old days, whose legacies modern anthropology has since sought to put behind it. In the second half of the twentieth century, however, a philosophically pluralist world—such as that which Wittgenstein advocated and reproached Frazer for not understanding—remained a contested reality. Even in the heyday of decolonization, where political sovereignty and cultural integrity were becoming increasingly accepted, sanctified principles, the manifestation of these principles was heavily constricted within the global political order, then divided into what some historians call the empire of liberty and the empire of equality (Westad 2005). Cultural pluralism was a powerful instrument in the politics of the global Cold War and for both of this era's empires; it made the new imperial order appear different from the old, Europe-dominated one and thereby relatively more acceptable to the new nations in the postcolonial world. The era also saw forceful globalization of contrasting visions of modernity, in which the idea of a cultural pluralistic world was often a convenient instrument of power in the contest of influence over the postcolonial world (Kwon 2010).

A certain sense of "forms of life" advanced and flourished in anthropology during the era. Wittgenstein's second philosophy, and his critique of Frazer, became an important reference point for a number of anthropologists in the mid-twentieth century, starting with scholars interested in language and culture in the 1940s and leading to the interpretative turn and related rationality and relativism debates in the 1970s and 1980s (Hollis and Lukes 1982; Geertz 2000). Later, his influence was strongly felt in the advent of the so-called reflexive turn. However, this does not mean that Frazer had no place in the development of anthropology in recent times. His broad comparative historical interest in human customs contributed to efforts to make a historical turn in anthropological research (notably by scholars like Jack Goody [1977]). Some of Frazer's brilliant insights into the logical properties of magic, such as the idea of sympathetic or analogical magic, are cherished and revived by scholars interested in shamanism or spirit possessions; some scholars expand the meanings of these properties to address large historical questions such as the critique of colonialism (Taussig 1992). Moreover, *Golden Bough* continues to attract a literate audience in the urbanized world, well beyond the educated circles in Europe, which takes pleasure or finds consolation in getting to know the variety of magical thoughts and practices humans can devise. This attraction is in tune with what brought Frazer to write *Golden Bough* in the first place. I recently had opportunities to engage with groups of artists in East Asia, many of whom, to my surprise, were quite keen on some of the premises of *Golden Bough*. One artist said that she was interested in relearning what she called the wisdom and magical knowledge of the ancient world, and she believed that Frazer might serve as a guide in that quest.

Wittgenstein's second philosophy became a philosophical companion to anthropology's pluralistic ethos and contextualist practice in the second half of the

twentieth century. Sovereignty questions (whether cultural, political, or even religious) are still very much part of the human condition today. However, our age
is also one that seeks to go beyond the age of sovereignty in order to confront
larger questions of common human existence. Seen in this light, Wittgenstein's
truly valuable legacy today may not necessarily be what he advocated in his critique of Frazer. Rather, it may be his acute awareness of the emergent spirit of
the new era, which made him question, with such great confidence and in such
strong language, the senses and sensibility of the fading age.

***

Remark 23: I will begin with Remark 23 of *Wittgenstein's Remarks on Frazer's
Golden Bough*, which concerns certain distinctions between the concept of
"ghost" and that of "soul" or "spirit." In this remark, Wittgenstein expresses one
of his strongest objections to the way in which Frazer renders primitive beliefs
in *Golden Bough*. Wittgenstein says, "Nothing shows our kinship to those savages better than the fact that Frazer has at hand a word as familiar to us as
'ghost' or 'shade' to describe the views of these people. . . . Yes, the strangeness
of this relates not only to the expressions 'ghost' and 'shade,' and far too little
is made of the fact that we count the words 'soul' [*Seele*] and 'spirit' [*Geist*] into
our own civilized vocabulary.' The point he is making in this remark is one that
appears more or less consistently throughout *Remarks*—that is, the problem of
translation. In Wittgenstein's view, the descriptive strategy of *Golden Bough* is
problematic: On the one hand, it contents itself with a mere listing of forms of
magical beliefs rather than trying to situate a particular belief within a specific
cultural context that gives meaning to the belief. By assigning the idea of ghosts
to a belief in magical power, on the other hand, *Golden Bough* projects a distance
of presumed civilizational maturity between such magical beliefs and the ideas
of higher religions. It would have been different if the book introduced the
concept of spirit or soul—concepts that are familiar to modern Western cultures—instead of that of ghost or shade. That might have highlighted an affinity between primitive and modern civilizations, rather than a sense of distance
between them and us, between magic and religion.

The issue is not so simple, however. The attribution of the concept of soul
to the description of magical beliefs is not separate from *Golden Bough* but very
much part of its making. In E. B. Tylor's *Primitive Culture* ([1871] 1903), which
influenced Frazer as well as many other scholars of the late Victorian age, the

whole argument revolves around the concept of soul and its centrality in the constitution of what Tylor called "natural religion" or "animism." In animism, according to Tylor, all natural objects are potentially human-like entities endowed with a soul—a system of beliefs that should be distinguished from belief systems familiar to advanced societies that he called "moral religions," religious beliefs whose central role is to maintain a normative social order by distinguishing what is moral from what is not, and sanctifying the distinctions. As we know, Émile Durkheim ([1912] 1991) later turned Tylor's argument on its head with his sociological approach to religious practice, which presents primitive religions (and all religions) as fundamentally moral institutions.

The concept of the spirit is not an easy one, either. Tylor did not distinguish soul from spirit and used both concepts liberally and interchangeably in *Primitive Culture*. For Durkheim, however, spirit needs to be clearly differentiated from soul, on the one hand, and from ghost, on the other. Briefly put, the soul is a presocial, individual entity (imprisoned in the body), in contrast to the spirit, which is a thoroughly sociological concept constitutive of the moral integrity of collective life. The ghost is, for Durkheim, something in between the soul and the spirit, a vitality that is freed from the prison of the body (with death, for instance) but is not transformed into a spirit (due to the absence or failure of a collective rite to make this transformation) (Kwon 2008: 19–24).

Therefore, the substitution of "spirit" for "ghost," as Wittgenstein suggests, is much more than a question of translation. It involves a great shift of perspective in the rebirth of anthropology as a modern social science between the late Victorian era and the early twentieth century. Seen from this angle, it is not sufficient to argue, as Wittgenstein does, that the concept of spirit is more appropriate than that of ghost. The question is not which concept still exists meaningfully in the secularized West. The real question is how to thoroughly secularize the understanding of the concept of the spirit so that the distance between secularized modern society and the world of natural religions is finally put behind us.

Remark 12: This leads us to Wittgenstein's Remark 12: "What narrowness of spiritual life we find in Frazer! Hence the impossibility of grasping a life different from the English one of his time! Frazer cannot imagine a priest who is not basically an English person of our times, with all his stupidity and shallowness." There is no question that Frazer was heavily conditioned, while writing *Golden Bough*, by the atmosphere of the late Victorian era. This is particularly evident in changes made in the book's later editions. The first edition included a discussion of foundational Christian symbols alongside issues of European cultural and religious history that were associated, at the time of his writing and in later eras, with pagan traditions as well religious practices in other parts of the world. *Golden Bough* earned fame in the literary world of Britain and elsewhere in Europe (among avid readers of this book were such towering figures as James Joyce, Ezra Pound, William Yates, and T. S. Eliot) partly because of its approach to iconic symbols of the Christian doctrine in parallel with those of Europe's spiritual tradition that were rejected by the church. This audacious move drew considerable disapproval from members of the learned circles at the end of the nineteenth century. Frazer was apparently conscious of this disapproval; in later editions of the book, allusions to Christian symbols were taken out of the text and relegated instead to an index. Frazer's oeuvre had considerable influence in the advance of literary and intellectual interest in neopaganism, first after the mass destruction of the First World War and then in the 1950s, after the Second World War

Considering this background, it is difficult to believe that *Golden Bough* was primarily an expression of English ethnocentrism or an English superiority complex (Frazer was not even an Englishman but a Scot!). Quite the contrary, we may understand the book as an attempt to demonstrate that the multitude of strange magical beliefs and customs introduced would appear less strange once Victorian-era readers came to terms with a tradition in European cultural history that was lost and forgotten. *Golden Bough*'s original strategy of exposition goes beyond Tylor's idea of natural religion giving way to moral religion by showing how ideas of natural religion and those of moral religion are both present in the history of religious ideas and doctrines. Seen from this angle, Frazer's choice of the term "ghost" over that of "spirit" in discussing beliefs in spirits, which Wittgenstein criticizes in his Remark 23, may be understood as a natural choice for someone who was aware of the history of religious ideas in modern Europe since the sixteenth century, in which the struggle against the popular ideas of "ghost" or "specter" was a vital part of church politics.

Remark 19: Wittgenstein's objection that he expressed in the above remark closely relates to Frazer's idea of primitive science. He says, "Frazer seems capable of believing that a savage dies out of error. In the elementary school primers it says that Attila undertook his great campaigns because he believed he possessed the sword of the god of thunder." For Frazer, magical practices are grounded in a form of rationality, primarily instrumental. They are, however, according to him, prescientific and basically erroneous in that these practices are not compatible with the system of verification and falsification, which is the hallmark of modern scientific rationality. For Wittgenstein, Frazer's rendering of the error of the primitive philosopher is none but Frazer's own error, faulty intellectualizing of expressive actions that all humans, primitive or modern, perform as part of their common, ordinary language life.

Remark 26: Wittgenstein says, "What we have in the ancient rites is the use of a highly cultivated gestural language. And when I read Frazer, I keep wanting to say at every step: All these processes, these changes of meaning are still present to us in our word language. If what is called the 'corn-wolf' is what is hidden in the last sheaf, but [if this name applies] also to the last sheaf itself and the man who binds it, then we recognize in this a linguistic process with which we are perfectly familiar." For Tylor, a sacred stone or tree is a sacred object not because of the object's materiality but because of what is believed to be hidden in it (that is, some kind of soul). He was not interested in the move from a reference to what is hidden in the stone to the stone itself, but in explaining why a stone comes to have a magical property in the first place. For Wittgenstein, the transformation—or transubstantiation—from a concept (of the soul or of the hidden force) to the thing itself is a natural property of the human linguistic process, which is fundamentally symbolic. The corn-wolf was an imaginary wolf roaming around a corn field; the wolf gave way to a sheaf, and then to the man who handled it. So, following his rendition, there is nothing strange in the idea of a stone with magical power; what is strange, instead, is an orientation such as that found in *Golden Bough* that, in his view, magnifies the strangeness of this idea. In *Golden Bough*, Frazer introduces old French and German peasant beliefs in corn-wolves together with similar cases drawn from ethnological sources, including the idea of a sacred stone. He does this to generate an awareness of likeness between the phenomenon of corn-wolves (existing in European tradition) and that of sacred stones (drawn from magical beliefs elsewhere)—that is, to make the belief in the power of a stone appear less strange to the educated public of the late Victorian era. We might even call this expository strategy an extension of the work of sympathetic magic, one of the key analytical concepts Frazer introduced in *Golden Bough*, to the task of translation. This approach might be called, in contemporary language, cross-cultural understanding.

Remark 24: Wittgenstein says, "A whole mythology is deposited in our language." This follows his proposition in Remark 23 that the concept of "spirit" (instead of that of "ghost") might have helped narrow the gap between primitive magical beliefs and beliefs familiar to modern Europe. In doing so, however, he seems oblivious, unlike Frazer, to the fact that "spirit" is a problematic concept, and that hidden in the modern concept of "spirit" is a history of the purge of the concept of "ghost" from civilized society.

When he wrote this remark, moreover, Wittgenstein probably was thinking of both language as such and the philosophical language more specifically. The latter relates to his radical idea of metaphysics as a kind of magic (see Rhees 1979: 22). Here, Wittgenstein's frustration regarding Frazer may actually be his growing frustration and radical thought about the philosophy of his time. The real object of his frustration may have been someone like Bertrand Russell rather than Frazer. Wittgenstein knew both Frazer and Russell. The three were all members of a close community in their formative years as fellows of Trinity College, Cambridge.

Remark 17. If "a whole mythology is deposited in our language" (#24), the philosopher's work is then to discover the great treasure deposited deep down the tree of language, the richness and diversity of language and life. He says, "We must plow over language in its entirety." Wittgenstein briefly worked as a gardener and often compared philosophy to gardening, especially in his *Culture and Value*.

REFERENCES

Beard, Mary. 1992. "Frazer, Leach, and Virgil: The Popularity (and Unpopularity) of the Golden Bough." *Comparative Studies in Society and History* 34 (2): 203–24.

Durkheim, Emile. (1912) 1991. *The Elementary Forms of Religious Life*. New York: Free Press.

Geertz, Clifford. 2000. *Available Light*. Princeton, NJ: Princeton University Press.

Goody, Jack. 1977. *The Domestication of the Savage Mind*. Cambridge: Cambridge University Press.

Hollis, Martin, and Steven Lukes, eds. 1982. *Rationality and Relativism.* Cambridge, MA: MIT Press.

Kwon, Heonik. 2008. *Ghosts of War in Vietnam.* Cambridge: Cambridge University Press.

————. 2010. *The Other Cold War.* New York: Columbia University Press.

Mandler, Peter. 2013. *Return from the Natives: How Margaret Mead Won the Second World War and Lost the Cold War.* New Haven, CT: Yale University Press.

Rhees, Rush. 1979. "Afterword." In *Remarks on Frazer's Golden Bough*, by Ludwig Wittgenstein, 21–34. Edited by R. Rhees. Atlantic Highlands, NJ: Humanities Press.

Taussig, Michael. 1992. *Mimesis and Alterity: A Popular History of the Senses.* New York: Routledge.

Tylor, Edward B. (1871) 1903. *Primitive Culture: Researches into the Development of Mythology, Philosophy, Religion, Language, Art and Custom.* London: Murray.

Westad, Odd Arne. 2005. *The Global Cold War: Third World Interventions and the Making of Our Times.* Cambridge: Cambridge University Press.

CHAPTER 5

Deep Pragmatism

KNUT CHRISTIAN MYHRE

Ludwig Wittgenstein's work is commonly divided between an early and a later philosophy, which are considered to be in stark distinction even though both concern the nature of language and meaning. Moreover, both adopt a similar literary style, which consists of numbered clauses or paragraphs that eschew argumentation in favor of other rhetorical forms. In a broad sense, his early philosophy regards language as a system of representation, where words combine in propositions that "picture" or model possible states of affairs in the world, while his later philosophy approaches language as part of human practice or a form of life (Glock 2001). Accordingly, the former presents a formal system of propositions and statements, while the latter provides paragraph-long descriptive remarks. His early work influenced the development of logical positivism, while his later thinking was important for the development of ordinary language philosophy. In multiple ways, his work was crucial for the "linguistic turn" that first occurred in philosophy, and later took place in the human and social sciences, including anthropology.

However, Wittgenstein has not only influenced anthropology—his later philosophy in fact emerged from an encounter with anthropology. This encounter occasioned a conception of language and meaning that speaks to concerns for pragmatics and performativity, and a shift from representation to practice or action that increasingly interest and influence anthropology and related disciplines (see, for instance, Whyte 1997; Barad 2003; Latour 2005; Law 2009). Wittgenstein also invoked and engaged a notion of "life," and developed a descriptive mode and means that relate to and open up possibilities for ethnographic enquiry. He even hinted at an "ethnological approach" (CV: 45), and conjured anthropological fieldwork situations to shed light on philosophical questions.[1]

In this text, I draw and expand on my efforts to engage with Wittgenstein's thought (Myhre 2006, 2007, 2018) to sketch how his encounter with anthropology afforded a deep and deepening pragmatist approach to language and meaning. I demonstrate how his conception is of relevance to ethnography, and indicate ways in which his ideas are of significance to longstanding anthropological concerns, including translation and comparison. I emphasize that my remarks are neither exhaustive of Wittgenstein's thought nor its potential relationship and relevance to ethnography and anthropology. Instead, they furnish one entry for anthropologists into his work, which may spur further engagements.

ENCOUNTERING ANTHROPOLOGY

Wittgenstein's encounter with anthropology occurred in 1931, when he read James George Frazer's *The Golden Bough* with his student Maurice O'Connor Drury ([1984] 1996: 134). The experience resulted in a set of remarks, where Wittgenstein took exception with Frazer's view that magic and religion are erroneous attempts to explain and influence the world: "Frazer's representation of human magical and religious notions is unsatisfactory: it makes these notions appear as *mistakes*" (#1). Wittgenstein's objection was that explanation presupposes that the phenomena in question involve and rest on a hypothesis, which misconstrues the role they play in people's lives: "Every explanation is a hypothesis. But someone who, for example, is unsettled by love will be ill-assisted by a hypothetical explanation. It won't calm him or her" (#3). Explanations and hypotheses moreover postulate underlying phenomena that account for the

---

1.   I follow the convention in the commentary literature and cite Wittgenstein's works by using an abbreviation of the title in question, followed by a paragraph number or page reference. The only exception are citations to *Remarks on Frazer's Golden Bough*, which are prefixed with the number sign (#). The abbreviations of Wittgenstein's work are PI = *Philosophical Investigations*, CV = *Culture and Value*, BB = *The Blue and the Brown Books*, OC = *On Certainty*, and Z = *Zettel*.

notions and practices in question. However, these cannot resolve the meaning the latter have for those who use and engage in them. In Wittgenstein's view, "It could have been no insignificant reason—that is, no *reason* at all—for which certain races of man came to venerate the oak tree other than that they and the oak were united in a community of life, so that they came into being not by choice, but jointly, like the dog and the flea (were fleas to develop a ritual, it would relate to the dog)" (#32). Wittgenstein accordingly held: "I believe that the enterprise of explanation is already wrong because we only have to correctly put together what one already *knows*, without adding anything, and the kind of satisfaction that one attempts to attain through explanation comes of itself" (#2). To consider a particular practice, one must instead pay careful attention to what takes place in the given context: "One can only resort to *description* here, and say: such is human life" (#3).

Wittgenstein hence hinted at a descriptive approach, where life served as the ground for the phenomena in question and the object of their description. To grapple with this, Wittgenstein later adopted the notion of "form of life" (*Lebensform*), which had a long history in German philosophical and scientific enquiry (Helmreich and Roosth 2010). It appears only a handful of times in *Philosophical Investigations* (1953), in both the singular and the plural, and in indeterminate and determinate forms. Its scarce and seemingly careless usage may obscure how *Lebensform* conjoins with other ideas in Wittgenstein's effort to consider language as a human practice that grants privilege to description at the expense of explanation and theory (Allen and Turvey 2001; Glock 2001: Hacker 2001a; Bouveresse 2007).

COINING LANGUAGE-GAMES

Central in this regard is the concept of "language-game" (*Sprachspiel*), which Wittgenstein introduced in 1933–34, after his encounter with Frazer. Initially coined to mean simple forms of language-use (BB: 17), the notion was later employed to highlight how language embeds in nonlinguistic practices: "Here the term language-*game* is meant to bring into prominence the fact that the *speaking* of a language is part of an activity, or a form of life" (PI: §23). If *Lebensform* is borrowed from elsewhere, *Sprachspiel* is Wittgenstein's invention for grasping how language is a practice, where the meaning of a word is its use, and not the object to which it refers: "For a *large* class of cases—though not for all—in which we employ the word 'meaning' it can be defined thus: the meaning of a word is its use in language" (PI: §43). Accordingly, Wittgenstein argues that, "The grammar of the word 'knows' is evidently closely related to that of 'can,' 'is able to.' But also closely related to that of 'understands.' ('Mastery' of a technique)" (PI: §150). Enhancing his pragmatist approach, Wittgenstein stresses how such concepts concern capacities or dispositions to act in certain ways, and not mental states that are only accessible to the person concerned, as philosophers often tend to think.[2]

However, the notion of language-game also attends to the diversity of uses that words have. To illustrate this, Wittgenstein considers the concept of "game" itself:

> Consider for example the proceedings that we call "games." I mean board-games, card-games, ball-games, Olympic games, and so on. What is common to them all? —Don't say: "There *must* be something common, or they would not be called 'games'" —but *look and see* whether there is anything common to all. —For if you look at them you will not see something that is common to *all*, but similarities, relationships, and a whole series of them at that. To repeat: don't think, but look! —Look for example at board-games, with their multifarious relationships. Now pass to card-games; here you may find many correspondences with the first group, but many common features drop out, and others appear. When we pass next to ball-games, much that is common is retained, but much is lost. —Are they all "amusing"? Compare chess with noughts and crosses. Or is there always winning and losing, or competition between players? Think of patience. In ball games there is winning and losing; but when a child throws his ball at the wall and catches it again, this feature has disappeared. Look at the parts played by skill and luck; and at the differences between skill in chess and skill in tennis. Think now of games like ring-a-ring-a-roses; here is the element of amusement, but how many other characteristic features have disappeared! And we can go through the many, many other groups of games in the same way; can see how similarities crop up and disappear. And the result of this examination is: we see a complicated network of similarities overlapping and criss-crossing: sometimes overall similarities, sometimes similarities of detail. (PI: §66)

---

2.   The ordinary language philosopher Gilbert Ryle (1949) made a similar point.

It is Wittgenstein's point that the multiple uses and meanings of a single word need not have any feature in common, even if our "craving for generality" (BB: 17) compels the search for one. Instead, there are overlapping and crisscrossing similarities between their multiple meanings, which Wittgenstein terms "family resemblances": 'I can think of no better expression to characterize these similarities than 'family resemblances'; for the various resemblances between members of a family: build, features, colour of eyes, gait, temperament, etc. etc. overlap and criss-cross in the same way. —And I shall say: 'games' form a family" (PI: §67). Family resemblances entail that the multiple uses and meanings of the singular term lack an essence or a shared feature, and instead exist through a range of relationships. In fact, these extend to encompass language itself: "Instead of producing something common to all that we call language, I am saying that these phenomena have no one thing in common which makes us use the same word for all, —but that they are *related* to one another in many different ways. And it is because of this relationship, or these relationships, that we call them all 'language'" (PI: §65). It is because language consists of a multitude of relationships of different kinds that words and meanings must be considered and described in their concrete use: "In order to see more clearly, here as in countless similar cases, we must focus on the details of what goes on; must look at them from close to" (PI: §51).

However, the notion of language-game not only serves to embed language in other activities, it conversely captures how language-use enables, entwines, and entails nonlinguistic actions. Thus, Wittgenstein says: "I shall also call the whole, consisting of language and the actions into which it is woven, the 'language-game'" (PI: §7). Indeed, linguistic practice not only has bodily concomitants, but in a sense extends out of such activities: "Language—I want to say—is a refinement, 'in the beginning was the deed'" (CV: 31).[3] Or, as Wittgenstein states in a remark on Frazer, language forms part of "the *environment* of a way of acting" (#44). In turn, these pragmatic imbrications curtail the role that explanation, justification, and even interpretation, play in the use of language: "Giving grounds, however, justifying the evidence, comes to an end; —but the end is not certain propositions' striking us immediately as true, i.e., it is not a kind of *seeing* on our part; it is our *acting*, which lies at the bottom of the language-game" (OC: §204). These comments aim to grasp the multiple and variegated

---

3.   Wittgenstein borrows the dictum from Goethe's Faust, in opposition to the Biblical "in the beginning was the word."

relationships that obtain between language and action and by extension the objects that these involve in concrete language-games. Along with Wittgenstein's equation between meaning and use, the result is that words and notions neither refer to nor index objects and practices, but surround, contain, and entail activities that entangle and engage things in specific language-games. Phrased differently, language-games gather up objects in multiple ways (Myhre 2012) and hence involve a plethora of world-relations.

CREATING PERSPICUOUS PRESENTATIONS

The relational character of Wittgenstein's notions entail that the language-game constitutes the semantic unit: "Look on the language-games as the *primary* thing" (PI: §656). Its relations require description to lay out the uses of words, along with the activities they entail and the objects these involve. In this way, the description affords a "surview" or "overview" (*Übersicht*) of a portion of language of which it aims to provide a "perspicuous presentation" (*übersichtliche Darstellung*): "For us the concept of perspicuous presentation is of fundamental importance. It designates our form of presentation, the way we see things. . . . This perspicuous presentation transmits an understanding of the kind that what we see are 'just the connections.' Hence the importance of finding *intermediate links*. However, in this case, a hypothetical link is not meant to do anything other than draw attention to the similarity, the connection between the *facts*" (#22). The idea of perspicuous presentation or representation is the only element of the *Remarks on Frazer* that Wittgenstein retained for his *Philosophical Investigations*. It became central for his effort to describe the "conceptual topology" of language that replaced the "conceptual geology" of his earlier philosophy (Hacker 2001b) once "nothing is hidden" (PI: §435). Along with the idea of family resemblance, the emphasis on "seeing connections" and "finding intermediate links" could suggest that Wittgenstein conceives of language and meaning in terms of identity or commonality, but he is in fact as concerned with difference and dissimilarity: "The language-games are rather set up as *objects of comparison* which are meant to throw light on the facts of our language by way not only of similarities, but also of dissimilarities" (PI: §130). O'Connor Drury (1996: 157) accordingly recalled Wittgenstein arguing that, "Hegel seems to me to be always wanting to say that things which look different are really the same. Whereas my interest is in showing that things which look the same are really different. I was thinking of using as a motto for my book a quotation from *King Lear*: 'I'll teach you differences.'" The emphasis on difference entails that Wittgenstein provides an otherness-oriented conception of language and meaning. Such conceptions go back at least to Ferdinand de Saussure's ([1916] 1983) approach to linguistics, but Wittgenstein's differ in that he does not conceive of and trace systematic contrasts or structural oppositions between signifiers and the signified. He rejects the relationship of reference that underpins this conception and instead pursues the multifarious uses of language that its uniform appearance belies: "It is like looking into the cabin of a locomotive. We see handles all looking more or less alike. (Naturally since they are all supposed to be handled.) But one is the handle of a crank which can be moved continuously (it regulates the opening of a valve); another is the handle of a switch, which has only two effective positions, it is either on or off; a third is the handle of a brake-lever, the harder one pulls on it, the harder it brakes; a fourth, the handle of a pump: it has an effect only so long as it is moved to and fro" (PI: §12). The example highlights Wittgenstein's pragmatist approach to bring out how language involves a diversity of uses and effects, which create a braid of similarities and differences, where many relationships are of an analog rather than digital kind presumed by structural linguistics (Myhre 2012).

A perspicuous presentation charts what Wittgenstein calls the "grammar" that determines the uses and meanings of particular words. For Wittgenstein, the purpose of such a representation is to resolve or dissolve philosophical problems, which arise from conceptual confusion and misuse of words that are due to our entanglement in the variety of linguistic expressions. Wittgenstein underscores the pragmatics of language when he claims: "The confusions which occupy us arise when language is like an engine idling, not when it is doing work" (PI: §132). His pragmatist approach is emphasized when O'Connor Drury (1996: 110) recounts Wittgenstein saying, "My father was a businessman and I am a businessman: I want to get something settled." However, Wittgenstein has no intention to reform the use of language, but instead argues, "Philosophy may in no way interfere with the actual use of language; it can in the end only describe it. For it cannot give it any foundation either. It leaves everything as it is" (PI: §124). This departs from his early work, where analysis aimed to burrow beneath language and uncover the essential form of reality. His early work thus aimed for a critique of language, while his later philosophy seeks to find value in and leave language as it is.

The resolution or dissolution of philosophical problems occurs through a conceptual clarification that disentangles and lays out the use of particular words and the workings of language. The account does not refer to anything hidden or underlying, since the use and meaning of words cannot depend on something concealed to those who speak the language. The solution to philosophical problems therefore cannot involve explanation of any kind, but can only consist of description: "Philosophy simply puts everything before us, and neither explains nor deduces anything. —Since everything lies open to view there is nothing to explain. For what is hidden, for example, is of no interest to us" (PI: §126). A perspicuous presentation therefore does not discover anything new, but arranges or rearranges what competent speakers already know and do: "The problems are solved, not by giving new information, but by arranging what we have always known" (PI: §109). The task is therefore to recall how specific words are used: "The work of the philosopher consists in assembling reminders for a particular purpose" (PI: §127). The purpose varies with the problem involved, so the arrangement required and achieved varies accordingly. The perspicuous presentation thus affords *Übersicht* of a particular segment of language, which depends on the purpose and problem concerned. The description involved is not a uniform concept but a family resemblance phenomenon whose form depends on the words and issues involved (Hacker 2001b: 24). The perspicuous presentation therefore provides *a* conceptual order of a portion of language through a description that is partial in the sense that it is incomplete and infused by a specific interest: "We want to establish an order in our knowledge of the use of language: an order with a particular end in view; one out of many possible orders; not *the* order" (PI: §132). To paraphrase Martin Holbraad and Morten Pedersen (2009: 381), the effect "is to provide, not a point of more general vantage, but rather one of further departure." In a related way, Avrum Stroll (2002: 93) points out with regard to Wittgenstein's literary form, "One is moved conceptually and presumably will eventually come to possess a point of view one did not hold before."

The task then is to describe the uses and meanings of particular words together with the activities they entail and the objects they involve. The relations that language-games involve mean that such description does not consist simply in the portrayal of a state of affairs. Instead, it involves the act of *unfolding* a language-game to lay out the uses of words, along with their attendant practices and things. The description must also chart the family resemblances between the different uses of the singular notions across the language-games in which they occur, and sketch the additional words and concepts with which they combine. It is in this sense that Wittgenstein states: "We must plow over language in its entirety" (#17). In methodological terms, it means that the description can trace relationships from anywhere, as the language-game can be unfurled from the words, practices, or objects it contains or entails, or folded out of any of the other language-games with which it interlinks. Since neither things nor practices or words ground or anchor each other, the description can and must proceed pragmatically from one to the other, depending on the problem and the language-game involved.

To provide a perspicuous presentation one must describe the multifarious uses of particular words or expressions, along with activities they involve and the objects they engage. Elsewhere, I adopt this approach to explore a cluster of evasive notions among the Chagga-speaking people of Rombo District on the eastern slopes of Mount Kilimanjaro in northern Tanzania (Myhre 2018). The notions include that of *horu* or "life-force," which is transformed by and transferred between humans, houses, livestock, and crops through various yet interrelated activities, and that enables and constitutes their existence, capacity, health, and well-being. In combination, these activities constitute the notion of "dwelling" (*ikaa*), which takes place in and around the homestead (*kaa*), where the transfers and transformations of *horu* engage or occur by means of places, processes, substances, conducts, and beings that derive their terms from the notion of *moo* or "life." As I argue, Wittgenstein's ideas are especially pertinent in this regard since *horu* has a multiplicity of uses and imbricates with an array of activities that constitute a diversity of language-games. *Horu* is hence a family resemblance concept that both entails and forms part of a multiplicity of relationships that I describe in detail. Moreover, *horu* is not some*thing*, but concerns movements or interactions that manifest as beings of different kinds, which become, exist, and pass away as transformations of each other. Since *horu* does not designate an object, the various language-games played with this notion can only be approached through its pragmatics, which reveal how the notion concerns the capacity of different beings to affect each other through the activities that constitute *ikaa*.

BEYOND TRANSLATION

Combined with Wittgenstein's point that the language-game is the semantic unit, these ideas contravene the common idea that translation consists in matching words, sentences, or meanings from one language in that of another (see Hanks and Severi 2014). As Talal Asad (1986: 151) points out, "We are dealing not with an abstract matching of two sets of sentences, but with a social practice rooted in modes of life." In fact, the language-games played with the notions that derive from *moo* surpass this claim, as they concern the beings, places, conduits, substances, and processes whereby *horu* converts and conveys to afford the becoming and constitute the being of persons, houses, livestock, and crops. Paraphrasing Wittgenstein, the language-games show how *moo*, along with its derivate terms, is "a widely ramified concept. A concept that comprises many manifestations of life" (Z: §110). In combination, they provide for an anthropological concept of life, which enunciates how life and the world in which it occurs are effects of the transfers and transformations of *horu* that project through beings of different kinds and take place in the activity of dwelling.

These ideas may moreover nuance Eduardo Viveiros de Castro's (2004) conception of translation and comparison as forms of "controlled equivocation." In his view, the task is not to discover or create common concepts that can unify a multitude of different representations of the same underlying reality, but to heed and respect how different beings refer to different things by means of shared terms and concepts. While I do not dispute the importance and potential of Viveiros de Castro's project, it remains the fact that it and the Amerindian perspectivism from which it departs presuppose that meaning resides in a relation of reference between words and objects. Thus, Viveiros de Castro (1998: 477) argues, "Animals impose the same categories and values on reality as humans do; their worlds, like ours, revolve around hunting and fishing, cooking and fermented drinks, cross-cousins and war, initiation rituals, shamans, chiefs, spirits." By contrast, Wittgenstein's approach can provide a view of how humans and animals of different kinds use the same concepts ("beer," "marriage," "house," and "prey"), yet engage with different elements of the world (beer/blood, house/salt-lick, animals/humans) in a diversity of similar yet different and therefore overlapping language-games. The effort speaks to Wittgenstein's remark: "(The Malays conceive the human soul as a little man . . . who corresponds exactly in shape, proportion, and even in complexion to the man in whose body he resides . . .) How much more truth in granting the soul the same multiplicity as the body than in a watered-down modern theory" (#38). By contrast to the Amerindian version, Wittgenstein urges a regard of the soul as not involving a singular capacity to impose categories but as multifarious dispositions to engage the world in manifold ways, as bodies do. It recalls how the Chagga *moo* is the root form of multiple terms that concern transfers and transformations of *horu* that occur by means of different parts of the body (Myhre 2017, 2018, 2019), which contrast with Günter Wagner's (1949: 160) translation of the Kavirondo cognate *omwoyo* as "soul." Like Viveiros de Castro's approach, this position departs from epistemological perspectives, where persons confront a singular world that is distinct from them and their description of it. Yet it also averts the ontological position, where uniform representations constitute different worlds for different beings through different relations of reference. By contrast, Wittgenstein deals with matters neither epistemological nor ontological, but the logic—in a loose sense—on which both turn. Paradoxically perhaps, the result is a move beyond translation that instead concerns the unfolding of language-games and the multiple world-relations they entail.

FORM OF LIFE

A reconception of Amerindian perspectivism in terms of Wittgenstein's later philosophy can reveal how human and nonhuman beings share a common form of life, yet play different and interlocking language-games where they engage the world in different ways. It recalls his remark regarding humans and the oak conjoined in a community of life, and fleas developing a ritual relating to the dog. It allows for the notion that different beings use and imbricate the same words with different practices and objects, and thus provides for Viveiros de Castro's point that subjects share conceptual and perceptual capacities, but differ in terms of bodies and affects. It moreover affords an understanding of how Wittgenstein's notion of language-game relates to that of form of life. Wittgenstein propounds a lateral conception of language and meaning, where words, practices, and things combine in language-games that extend into and out of each other. This forms the basis for the common interpretations of "form of life," like in Oswald Hanfling's (1989: 162) view: "The expression 'forms of life' is meant to convey the wholeness of the system, and also the fact that it includes action ('life') as well as passive observation or experience." Similarly, Jerry Gill (1991: xii) claims that Wittgenstein 'saw this form of life as constituting a vast and ever-developing network of overlapping and criss-crossing 'language-games,' each tied in its own way to specific physical and social activity." The idea of an interlocking web of games that enfold words, practices, and objects conceptualizes language as an extensive phenomenon that exists and unfolds through time and space.

Accordingly, Wittgenstein uses a temporal and spatial image for the character of language: "Our language can be seen as an ancient city: a maze of little streets and squares, of old and new houses with additions from various periods; and this surrounded by a multitude of new boroughs with straight regular streets and uniform houses" (PI: §18). Elsewhere, however, he argues that, "What has to be accepted, the given, is—so one could say—*forms of life*" (PI: ¶226). Its given character means that form of life is not the result of language-games combining as parts of a whole; instead, the latter arise from the former as elaborations that determine particular aspects of it. It accords with the idea that language-games are descriptive means that elicit similarities and differences between situations of use, and unfold the activities and objects they involve and engage. Language-games thus unfold from the form of life to emerge and exit as multiples of "one" that eventually fold back into the form of life. Charles Taylor (1995: 96) grapples with this when he points out that for Wittgenstein, "language is rather something in the nature of a web, which, to complicate the image, is present as a whole in any one of its parts." As singular relational composites, language-games are self-similar iterations, where each "one" contains and retains connections to other "ones," which constitute the form of life from which they emerge and to which they return. The idea gains support from Wittgenstein's notion of "back-ground," against which one distinguishes between true and false, and something appears as significant and meaningful (OC: §94, §461). It moreover gives sense to his remark: "The crowding of thoughts that will not come out because they all try to push ahead and are wedged at the door" (#4). It concerns how Frazer's concept of and attempt at explanation presupposes and occurs against a back-ground or a form of life, which entails a plethora of notions and practices that can neither be released nor grasped at once, but must be separated and described as elements of separate language-games. It recalls Gregory Bateson's (1958: 3) point that it is "impossible to present the whole of a culture simultaneously in a single flash" (see Palmié, this volume), yet tempers the remark that "We must plow over language in its entirety" (#17), as description must consider specific uses and games that concern particular issues.

PROPORTIONING RELATIONS

The world-relations that the language-games entail provide a view of how language and meaning involve and emerge from engagements and relations between persons and the world. Conversely, to know and to describe a language amounts to moving in and engaging with a world. Thus, Wittgenstein uses the temporal and spatial simile of the city to grasp the character of language. He moreover writes in the Preface to *Philosophical Investigations* regarding its form, "The best that I could write would never be more than philosophical remarks; my thoughts were soon crippled if I tried to force them on in any single direction against their natural inclination. —And this was, of course, connected with the very nature of the investigation. For this compels us to travel over a wide field of thought criss-cross in every direction. —The philosophical remarks in this book are, as it were, a number of sketches of landscapes, which were made in the course of these long and involved journeyings." His statement suggests that the remarks emerged and took their form from a simultaneous engagement with and movement in language and the world. Moreover, it gives sense to Wittgenstein's claim that "Frazer is more savage than most of his savages, for these savages will not be as far removed from an understanding of spiritual matters as an Englishman of the twentieth century. His explanations of primitive practices are much cruder than the meaning of these practices themselves" (#19). The remark can be read as an admonition and accusation of a failure to approach and engage that which takes one's interest. It echoes Asad's (1986: 155) critique that the concept of cultural translation involves "the privileged position of someone who does not, and can afford not to, engage in a genuine dialogue with those he or she once lived with and now *writes* about." The call for engagement and dialogue resonates with Wittgenstein's point that one "must focus on the details" and "look at them from close to." Elsewhere, however, he argues: "If we look at things from an ethnological point of view, does that mean we are saying that philosophy is ethnology? No, it only means that we are taking up a position right outside so as to be able to see things more *objectively*" (CV: 37). In combination, the remarks concern how the description is required to proportion a relation in order to provide a perspective on a particular phenomenon. On this basis, one can nuance the point to say that Frazer does not fail to engage, but his idea of explanation fails to proportion an adequate relationship, and thereby misrepresents the phenomena in question.

These points link to Marilyn Strathern's (1999: 6) idea that anthropological knowledge and insight is an effect of the ethnographic moment, which involves a relation between immersion and movement that in turn contains and combines observation and analysis. In anthropology, observation entails a relation to participation, which in combination constitutes the bedrock of fieldwork.

In fact, participant observation itself requires proportioning a relation, but this must be commensurate with that which one studies. In other words, it is the world-relations involved that determine the form and character that fieldwork must assume. The point then is not that Frazer failed because he never did field-work—it is rather that anthropologists are required to constantly retool partici-pant observation and ethnographic description as they approach new fields and phenomena.

One can, in fact, trace further affinities between the anthropological work of Strathern and Wittgenstein's later philosophy. For instance, perspicuous presen-tation affords what Peter Hacker (2001b: 23) calls connective analysis, "that is, a description of the conceptual connections and exclusions in the web of words." Description affords ethnographic openness, while the idea of taking something apart by joining it to something else, and combining something through tak-ing it apart, recalls Strathern's (1988, 1995, 2005) account of anthropology's relation, and of elicitation, detachment, and decomposition as social processes. In fact, Wittgenstein's descriptive tools are means of connection and distinc-tion, which constitute philosophical versions of the relation. Strathern (1988) endeavors to displace certain analytics in order to describe social life without their attendant problems and effects (Lebner 2016; Myhre 2019). Similarly, Wittgenstein removes the idea that meaning resides in a relation of reference to favor description of the use words, and his method and mode of writing is meant to break the grip of certain conceptual models (Stroll 2002: 93–94). Strathern's account involves a redescription of Melanesian ethnography, and hence a rearrangement of what one already knows. Like Wittgenstein's dis-solution of philosophical problems, her description also involves "assembling reminders for a particular purpose" (PI: §127). Indeed, as Rush Rees points out in the introductory note to *Remarks on Frazer's Golden Bough*, Wittgenstein endlessly endeavored to rearrange his remarks, and hence adopted a mode of work that resonates with redescription. Aiming for a perspicuous presentation, he offers up language-games that on my reading emerge from and revert to life as multiples of "one," or fractals of the kind Strathern ([1991] 2004) explores to address questions of scale and proportion in representation and comparison. Fi-nally, Wittgenstein states: "If I have exhausted the justifications I have reached bedrock, and my spade is turned. Then I am inclined to say: 'This is simply what I do'" (PI: §217). As such, his philosophy trains on the moments and activities that curtail and contain the uses of words, and thus recalls Strathern's (1996) concern for limits and end-points.

CONCLUSION

Perspicuous presentations consist of descriptions that use language to chart the grammar or use of words. It follows that there is an internal relationship or self-similarity between their means and ends (cf. Myhre 1998), and that they do not involve conventional analysis, where concepts are applied to a material that is different in scope or character. Instead, it consists in a moment and movement of unfolding and enfolding, where descriptions effectuate and multiply concepts as their result (Corsín Jímenez and Willerslev 2007; Myhre 2014, 2015). Despite the connotations of "surview" and "overview," the perspicuous presentation locks into ordinary language, on which it provides a peripheral perspective that traces relationships within and between language-games to describe conceptual structures from within. The description hence affords and involves a reverse or inverse move that confounds the distinction between the analytical and the empirical, and destabilizes the separation between anthropological and vernacular concepts (cf. Myhre 2013). Vernacular concepts consequently become the subject of ethnography, which generates anthropological notions that it places on the same footing (cf. Viveiros de Castro 2003, 2013). The approach allows the ethnographic to shape the anthropological, as vernacular and analytical concepts emerge together as transformed instances of each other. The challenge is not to provide a translation of a vernacular term but to afford space where language-games may unfold so the concepts they involve can emerge to explore "the further potentialities of our thought and language" (Lienhardt 1954, in Asad 1986: 159). Wittgenstein's ideas provide what Bruno Latour (2005: 30) calls an "infra-language," where unfamiliar concepts can appear and "be given a chance" they otherwise may not get (Latour 2000: 368). As descriptive devices, Wittgenstein's notions posit empty relations of similarity and difference, and are thus "thin" concepts that allow for "thick" descriptions from which vernacular notions may emerge as concepts in their own right. His later philosophy of language and meaning therefore complement virtue ethics as "a philosophy with an ethnographic stance" (Laidlaw 2014), as well as an anthropological import.[4]

---

4. As James Laidlaw (2014: 49) points out, modern virtue ethics grew out of a Wittgensteinian tradition, and perhaps most strongly from the work of his student Elizabeth Anscombe.

ACKNOWLEDGEMENTS

I thank Stephan Palmié for the invitation to contribute to this book and for his suggestions for improving my text. I am also grateful to Douglas Holmes for regular conversations regarding resonant ideas. The text is part of the research project *Forms of Ethics, Shapes of Finance: Ethnographic Explorations of the Limits of Contemporary Capital*, financed by the Research Council of Norway (grant number 259495).

REFERENCES

Allen, Richard, and Michael Turvey. 2001. "Wittgenstein's Later Philosophy: A Prophylaxis against Theory." In *Wittgenstein, Theory and the Arts*, edited by Richard Allen and Michael Turvey, 1–35. London: Routledge.

Asad, Talal. 1986. "The Concept of Cultural Translation." In *Writing Culture: The Poetics and Politics of Ethnography*, edited by James Clifford and George E. Marcus, 141–64. Berkeley: University of California Press.

Barad, Karen. 2003. "Posthumanist Performativity: Toward an Understanding of How Matter Comes to Matter." *Signs: Journal of Women in Culture and Society* 28 (3): 801–31.

Bateson, Gregory. 1958. *Naven: A Survey of the Problems Suggested by a Composite Picture of the Culture of a New Guinea Tribe Drawn from Three Points of View.* Stanford, CA: Stanford University Press.

Bouveresse, Jacques. 2007. "Wittgenstein's Critique of Frazer." *Ratio*, n.s., 20 (4): 357–76.

Corsín Jiménez, Alberto, and Rane Willerslev. 2007. "'An Anthropological Concept of the Concept': Reversibility among the Siberian Yukaghirs." *Journal of the Royal Anthropological Institute*, n.s., 13 (4): 527–44.

Gill, Jerry H. 1991 *Merleau-Ponty and Metaphor.* Atlantic Highlands, NJ: Humanities Press.

Glock, Hans-Johann. 2001. "The Development of Wittgenstein's Philosophy." In *Wittgenstein: A Critical Reader*, edited by Hans-Johann Glock, 1–25. Oxford: Blackwell.

Hacker, Peter M. S. 2001a. "Developmental Hypotheses and Perspicuous Representations: Wittgenstein on Frazer's *Golden Bough*." In *Wittgenstein:*

Connections and Controversies, edited by Peter M. S. Hacker, 74–97. Oxford: Clarendon Press.

———. 2001b. "Wittgenstein: An Overview." In *Wittgenstein: Connections and Controversies*, edited by Peter M. S. Hacker, 1–33. Oxford: Clarendon Press.

Hanfling, Oswald. 1989. *Wittgenstein's Later Philosophy*. Basingstoke, UK: Macmillan.

Hanks, William F., and Carlo Severi. 2014. "Translating Worlds: The Epistemological Space of Translation." *HAU: Journal of Ethnographic Theory* 4 (2):1–16.

Helmreich, Stefan, and Sophia Roosth. 2010. "Life Forms: A Keyword Entry." *Representations* 112 (1): 27–53.

Holbraad, Martin, and Morten Axel Pedersen. 2009. "Planet M: The Intense Abstraction of Marilyn Strathern." *Anthropological Theory* 9 (4): 371–94.

Laidlaw, James. 2014. *The Subject of Virtue: An Anthropology of Ethics and Freedom*. Cambridge: Cambridge University Press.

Latour, Bruno. 2000. "A Well-Articulated Primatology: Reflections of a Fellow-Traveller." In *Primate Encounters: Models of Science, Gender, and Society*, edited by Shirley C. Strum and Linda Marie Fedigan, 358–81. Chicago: University of Chicago Press.

———. 2005. *Reassembling the Social: An Introduction to Actor-Network Theory*. Oxford: Oxford University Press.

Law, John. 2009. "Actor Network Theory and Material Semiotics." In *The New Blackwell Companion to Social Theory*, edited by Bryan S. Turner, 141–58. Oxford: Wiley-Blackwell.

Lebner, Ashley. 2016. "La redescription de l'anthropologie selon Marilyn Strathern." *L'Homme* 2 (218): 117–50.

Myhre, Knut Christian. 1998. "The Anthropological Concept of Action and Its Problems: A 'New' Approach Based on Marcel Mauss and Aristotle." *Journal of the Anthropological Society Oxford* 29 (2): 121–34.

———. 2006. "The Truth of Anthropology: Epistemology, Meaning and Residual Positivism." *Anthropology Today* 22 (6): 16–19.

———. 2007. "Family Resemblances, Practical Interrelations and Material Extensions: Understanding Sexual Prohibitions, Production and Consumption in Kilimanjaro." *Africa* 77 (3): 307–30.

———. 2012. "The Pitch of Ethnography: Language, Relations and the Significance of Listening." *Anthropological Theory* 12 (2): 185–208.

———. 2013. "Cutting and Connecting: 'Afrinesian' Perspectives on Networks, Exchange, and Relationality." *Social Analysis* 57 (3): 1–24.

———. 2014. "The Multiple Meanings of *Moongo*: On the Conceptual Character of Doorways and Backbones in Kilimanjaro." *Journal of the Royal Anthropological Institute* 20 (3): 505–25.

———. 2015. "What the Beer Shows: Exploring Ritual and Ontology in Kilimanjaro." *American Ethnologist* 42 (1): 97–115.

———. 2017. "The Power of a Severed Arm: Life, Witchcraft, and Christianity in Kilimanjaro." In *Pentecostalism and Witchcraft in Melanesia and Africa*, edited by Knut Rio, Michelle MacCarthy, and Ruy Blanes, 163–87. London: Palgrave.

———. 2018. *Returning Life: Language, Life Force and History in Kilimanjaro*. Oxford: Berghahn.

———. 2019. "Tales of a Stitched Anus: Fictions, Analytics, and Personhood in Kilimanjaro." *Journal of the Royal Anthropological Institute* 25 (1).

O'Connor Drury, Maurice. (1984) 1996. *The Danger of Words and Writings on Wittgenstein*. Bristol, UK: Thoemmes Press.

Ryle, Gilbert. 1949. *The Concept of Mind*. London: Hutchinson.

Taylor, Charles. 1995. *Philosophical Arguments*. Cambridge, MA: Harvard University Press.

Saussure, Ferdinand de. (1916) 1983. *Course in General Linguistics*. London: Duckworth.

Strathern, Marilyn. 1988. *The Gender of the Gift: Problems with Women and Problems with Society in Melanesia*. Berkeley: University of California Press.

———. (1991) 2004. *Partial Connections*. Walnut Creek, CA: Altamira Press.

———. 1995. *The Relation: Issues in Complexity and Scale*. Cambridge: Prickly Pear.

———. 1999. *Property, Substance, and Effect: Anthropological Essays on Persons and Things*. London: Athlone Press.

———. 2005. *Kinship, Law and the Unexpected: Relatives Are Always a Surprise*. Cambridge: Cambridge University Press.

Stroll, Avrum. 2002. *Wittgenstein*. Oxford: One World Thinkers.

Viveiros de Castro, Eduardo. 1998. "Cosmological Deixis and Amerindian Perspectivism." *Journal of the Royal Anthropological Institute* 4 (3): 469–88.

———. 2003. *And*. Manchester: Manchester Papers in Social Anthropology.

———. 2004. "Perspectival Anthropology and the Method of Controlled Equivocation." *Tipití: Journal of the Society for the Anthropology of Lowland South America* 2 (1): 1–22.

———. 2013. "The Relative Native." *HAU: Journal of Ethnographic Theory* 3 (3): 473–502.

Wagner, Günter. 1949. *The Bantu of North Kavirondo*. Vol. 1. Oxford: Oxford University Press.

Whyte, Susan Reynolds. 1997. *Questioning Misfortune: The Pragmatics of Uncertainty in Eastern Uganda*. Cambridge: Cambridge University Press.

Wittgenstein, Ludwig. 1953. *Philosophical Investigations*. Oxford: Blackwell.

———. 1958. *The Blue and the Brown Books*. Oxford: Blackwell.

———. 1967. *Zettel*. Oxford: Basil Blackwell.

———. 1969. *On Certainty*. Oxford: Blackwell.

———. 1980. *Culture and Value*. Oxford: Blackwell.

CHAPTER 6

Wittgenstein Exercise

WENDY JAMES

PART I: INTRODUCTION

The anthropologist today can draw inspiration from both James Frazer and Ludwig Wittgenstein. Both seek to grasp in some way a common human sensibility by moving from ethnographic or historical texts about strange practices to "myself," a feeling, thinking person of today responding to the world: what I feel, how I reason, how I react to danger, to anger, and so forth. However, no one lives, feels, or speaks alone. Of course our discipline would be the poorer without the work of these iconic writers. But as anthropologists, we need to transpose what they have offered us into the inescapably social context of human life—that is, of social *interaction*, of the processes of shared experience and the mutual creation of "meanings" through participatory action.

The mass of cases presented by Frazer concerning the world's "magical" practices relating to kingship, fire, food, sacrifice, birth, illness, blood, death, and so on provides an invaluable resource, despite his own somewhat blinkered search for a clear evolutionary process from magic, through religion, to science. Frazer's massive demonstration of similarity between reports of beliefs and practices from around the world is indeed sufficient to impinge upon ourselves and our imaginations as much as their "magic" might be supposed to have impinged on supposedly "prerational" peoples. Perhaps it was the very scale of his ethnographic comparisons that helped stimulate Wittgenstein's own reflections on the significance of the material—for its ability to provoke us all into recognizing "ourselves" in it.

MY OWN PERSPECTIVE

As an anthropologist who once undervalued, even scorned, Frazer and his works, I have come around to appreciating him more positively. I was interested to find among my father's books the 1922 abridged edition of the *Golden Bough*, reprinted in 1932 by the Rationalist Press Association and signed by his own father. Once taught in part by Rodney Needham, though feeling it was all rather beyond me, I did read Wittgenstein's *Philosophical Investigations* and later the *Remarks on Frazer's Golden Bough*. I then took Frazer more seriously—partly because I went to the Sudan for my fieldwork, not far from Shillukland—and needed to know what all the fuss was about divine kingship (I was also taught by E. E. Evans-Pritchard, who later supervised my doctoral thesis). I remember attending the 1965 London conference organized by Julian Huxley on ritualization in animals and in humans, where contributions were made by key scientific figures such as Konrad Lorenz and Nikolaas Tinbergen alongside social anthropologists such as Edmund Leach and Victor Turner (see Huxley 1966). I began to realize there were major problems in the way academic language was being stretched in different directions on this issue.

In due course, I decided to leave aside the complications that came with the term "ritual" in favor of the phrase "The Ceremonial Animal," which I believe was first suggested by Wittgenstein in #15 of the *Remarks* under discussion here, and adopt it as the title of my own general book on anthropology (2003).[1] There, I tried to escape the old dualisms (e.g., of the individual vs. the social whole, the sacred vs. the profane, etc.), and to draw rather on the imagery of games, dancing, and drama, all with their own rules of shaping and interaction within the wider processes of economic and political history. I deliberately avoided adopting the language of "ritual" and "rite" because they seem to imply such a sharp distinction between what is and is not "ritual." I was also very aware of Talal Asad's important point, clearly explaining to anthropologists that the

---

1.   I have to confess I was not aware of the 1977 paper by Jacques Bouveresse that used the same phrase as a title (in French).

very word "ritual" actually once meant a book, specifically the book of instructions as to how to perform the church liturgy and sacraments (Asad 1993). The word then escaped into general usage, but still carries with it an aura, almost the religiosity of the sacraments. Much the same applies to "sacred"; the general use of these terms in comparative anthropology seems to beg too many questions. The same issues do not complicate our use of the term "ceremony"; it has not so obviously escaped from the church, or any established world religion, and there is no necessary sharp distinction between what is "ceremonial" and what is not. As I argue in an early chapter of the book mentioned above, it is not possible to separate spoken language from meaningful rhythm and gesture; ceremoniality is a matter of degree, and of the mixing and matching of sometimes very different modes of communication (James 2003: 74–99; "Life in Motion: Daughters of the Dance).

In the translator's introduction to the present collection, Stephan Palmié draws on Gregory Bateson's analysis of the seemingly marginal but ubiquitous ceremonial of *naven* among the Iatmul; recognizing achievement among maturing individuals in a fairly structured kinship system, this is far from religion as commonly understood. We should recall also a number of classics in the field of "ritual" that explore the foundations of socio-symbolic distinction and process, rather than what may well be in some cases their "religious" expression: for example, Robert Hertz's essays in *Death and the Right Hand* (1960); Arnold van Gennep, *The Rites of Passage* (1960); Franz Steiner, *Taboo* (1956); Audrey Richards, *Chisungu* (1956); Mary Douglas, *Purity & Danger* (1966); Victor Turner, *The Ritual Process, Structure and Anti-Structure* (1969). Linguistic and social imagery running through the works of many of these authors—in these well-known books and elsewhere—moves away from a recognizably religious perspective to fields such as those stemming from our universal appetite for the making, and marking, of difference in the human world; the regular celebration of changing times and spaces; and the idealized expression of social relations through the arts, especially the theater.

From Van Gennep onward, it has been clear that "rituals" have little to do with individual belief, or individual spontaneous feeling (although compare Wittgenstein's vignette of banging his stick on the ground in anger, labeling this a "rite," and his references to a "ritual instinct" that seems to be present in individuals). However, actual "rituals" are almost in essence participatory, and while not necessarily prescribed in form, they do embrace generally recognizable elements of design in their choreography and action (James 2007). They are very rarely the direct outcome of emotions, even shared emotions, though certainly often productive of them. It is difficult, moreover, to think of any "rituals" (or important ceremonies) that do not involve *passage* in some sense, a transformation of persons, places, or the redefinition of social relations. Whatever "behavior" is involved, the overall effect is to mark a threshold of arriving at a time or place; or changes in the condition of the body; or a transition from one phase of political order to another; or shifting relations between living humanity and the imagined beings of a world beyond them—the dead, or the divinities, or the wider cosmic forces within which we all see ourselves to be placed one way or another—including the evolutionary scientists.

"LANGUAGE" BETWEEN WRITING AND SPEECH

Frazer's monumental work of comparative ethnography, while dealing in large part with tribal or at least rural communities wholly or predominantly innocent of writing, is derived almost entirely from written sources. And while it is true that some of his written sources were firsthand letters from missionaries or travelers (along with occasional live conversations with them on their return), he almost never referred to the live communications of the tribes in question as being part of what he was investigating—let alone those of his own social world.

Neither Frazer nor Wittgenstein deal with this basic issue about language that faces the fieldworking anthropologist. In the field, the anthropologist is immersed in the to-and-fro life of the oral, gestural, and art-like languages of social communication. This is so not only in nonliterate communities but also in highly literate ones, too. This "oral culture" is the past world in which Frazer locates "magic," and through the clear explanatory possibilities of written historical analysis it finds its legacy even today. It is true that Wittgenstein draws attention to its presence around us still, though mainly through writing down fragments from his own inner voice—full of hints and unfinished arguments, mentions of personal experience, and feelings of dread, happiness, and so on. At the same time, there are very few references to extended conversations or situated contacts with others.

As far as I am aware, Frazer does not examine *language* as a phenomenon in itself, as of course the professional philosophers typically do. But for an anthropologist in the fieldworking tradition, a scholar who has to penetrate somehow *through* the language being spoken all around him or her in order to describe social life at any level, the importance of words, gestures, rhetoric, poetry, memories of life experience, and so on surely shape the options for entering into ongoing relations with local people. The quality of such live interconnections as a crucible of language are not always transparent in a written text, or in the process of translating such texts from one language to another. Not only "science" but also academic philosophy and history depend upon the phenomenon of writing, which itself (despite the advance of the digital age) underpins modern forms of social and political order. At the same time, spoken language—along with its analogues and accompaniments—pervades all communication, morphing over time and space into the creation of changing speech communities, along with shifts in their relation to each other and to surviving written texts.

Of course, like other academic disciplines, anthropology requires a degree of sustained rational argument, or "explanation," in the context of written language, whether presented in a book or in the form of the internally contained logic of an academic lecture, a monologue. However, the kind of language it needs to understand even better is the living form of discourse between people, which is rarely that of a formal conversation but commonly a part of the whole milieu of communicative exchange arising from personal experience of the actions, sounds, sights, and bodily movements of social life. This, however, is indeed the kind of language on which Wittgenstein himself does focus, almost as a fieldworker among his own people—though still confined to the armchair.

Language in this wider sense goes beyond the two parties to a conversation: it can morph and enter into the collective repatterning of hunting, harvesting, dancing, protests, and so on. As Theodore Schatzki (1996) has pointed out, as overlapping active "games," such practices of social life are perhaps beyond the language games as such to which Wittgenstein introduced us. Consider Shakespeare's plays. Though defined in the narrow sense by the written texts that have come down to us, these plays have been performed live for several centuries in front of changing audiences. They can be set in quite different geographical and historical settings from the original, offering new perspectives on the love, politics, tragedy, and comedy at their core. A recent popular production of *Romeo and Juliet* was set in Canada: the Montagues speak French and the Capulets speak English.[2]

The written forms of language, in addition to giving primacy to the single voice, tend to embrace logical opposites, such as true/false. But in the spoken

---

2. Details of a Kindle version of the play in English and French can be found online.

exchanges of social life, in the context of action and response, we do not find the sharp oppositions of reason versus emotion, of logical explanation as against gestures and exclamations. Nor do we find a sharp opposition between language and ritual. Social interaction can have multiple forms and components; it cannot easily be classified as either rational or ritual. One might do better adopting Wittgenstein's image of a sliding scale of ceremonial significance from hot to cold, with the unmarked lukewarm category of the everyday in the middle, and seeing everything else circling around it (#13). Stephan Palmié has suggested in our exchanges that anthropologists might regard even limited examples of human communication as a "total social fact," a perspective that I find very helpful.

The French philosopher Philippe de Lara has argued for an affinity between the insights of Evans-Pritchard into the "rational" understandings of the Azande in relation to magical practice and the earlier ideas of Lucien Lévy-Bruhl he criticized. The Azande were more than simply logic-choppers; their world was rich also in imagery, alternative theories, poetic insights, and so on. De Lara argued for the "anthropological" character of Wittgenstein's philosophy when considered in relation to such rich ethnographic work—for example, in his broad survey *Le rite et la raison: Wittgenstein anthropologue* (2005).

CONCLUDING NOTE ON LONG-TERM HUMAN HISTORY

More than a decade ago, Bruce Kapferer edited a short book under the title *Retreat of the Social* (2005). I feel the time is ripe for us to endorse his plea to return boldly to "the social" right across the various subfields of anthropology, a perspective without which human nature can scarcely be understood.

In arguing for the primacy of "sociality" in any understanding of "human nature," we must draw not only on ethnography but also "history" in the broadest sense—including material evidences from archaeology. Today's approaches to human evolution and early human history go far beyond a study of skeletons and genes and stone axes. Collaborative research now seeks evidence for patterning in early human social life; for example, of the development of home bases and a division of labor among hunter-gatherers, long-distance exchange, and an increased focus on collective care in child-rearing. One of the most exciting areas linked with these developments in archaeology concerns the beginnings of fire, and human control and uses of fire. The commentaries I offer below are largely linked with this theme of fire, which first fascinated Frazer and then Wittgenstein in his *Remarks on Frazer*.

***

PART II: NOTES AND COMMENTS ON SPECIFIC REMARKS

Remark 13, last para.

Toward the end of Remark 13, Wittgenstein poses a very interesting question: "How could the fire or the fire's resemblance to the sun have failed to make an impression on the awakening mind of man?" This thought, found among some of his brief notes on Frazer of the early 1930s, prefigures a theme that would recur in the early fragments and then gather real focus in the second set of notes dated from post-1936 and possibly even later than 1948 (from #39 onward; see below).

   What did Wittgenstein mean by an impression made on the "awakening mind"? This could be applied to the experience of any child (or indeed of any living creature, from fox cubs to flamingoes); but it surely evokes for us afresh today, though in a much-revised context of evolutionary theory from that of Frazer, the very early evidences for human control of fire in the archaeological record. Our experience of "fire" is far more than simply the impression it makes on an individual mind; it has a direct effect on the body too, producing fear, and retreat—and beyond this, it calls out for coordinated action and cooperation, especially in its potential for enhancing life as well as the need to control its potential for death. The impact of fire often leaves material traces, and here we can turn to a few of the new findings by archaeologists. John Gowlett has led much of this research from the United Kingdom (see for example 2010), while the work of Richard Wrangham, based in the United States, has become well known for his arguments that the early controlled use of fire for cooking food led to enormous improvements in the early human diet, with particular nutritional benefits to young children and to brain development (see, for example, 2009). These two authors recently provided a summing up of our state of knowledge in this area from which I shall select a few general points (Gowlett and Wrangham 2013).

While it used to be assumed that fire use was either present or absent in the record, researchers have recently begun to focus on the way that in early human history there was significant interaction with wild fires, mainly caused by lightning. Landscapes can be studied and experimented on to understand better how this might have happened. A lightning strike, very often on higher ground, would cause a fire in the first place. As it spread downslope and faded out in the grass and bushland below, it could sometimes be approached and elements of still-burning material (including animal dung) could be collected. These could be transported from the open spaces to local home settlements, necessarily near water. The wild fire could thus be "stretched" beyond the natural limits of its area. To keep a fire going, of course, firewood had to be collected and a hearth maintained. Here, even from very early times, females were likely to gather as a home community to which males would return periodically from hunting and foraging, and where cooked food could be deliberately produced. Such a hearth made it possible to extend the daily cycle of work and sleep, with evening socializing around the fire. Light, warmth, and regular company could facilitate exchanges of all kinds, from chorusing and gestural communication to song, dance, and language, to a formalization of patterns (even local "rules of the game"?) regulating sexual relations, responsibility for childcare, and the negotiation of exchange dealings with like communities elsewhere, whether economic or cultural. The controlled fire has ever since represented a focus for sociality in all its forms; as John Gowlett remarked after a lecture, "In a sense, fire is its own ceremony"; "it structures things."[3]

The implications are vast, and arguably connected with increasingly complex forms of social practice, and of communication. The warmth of the fire is even relevant to the emergence of language as such, along with the collective celebration of gatherings heightened through shared emotion. Here, the biologists would point to a rise of endorphins to the brain (Dunbar et al. 2010); surely making for something of the kind that Émile Durkheim (1995) famously identified as "effervescence" or the heightened emotional intensity in social contact, as in excited crowds. The convergence emerging from several different such lines of research enhances the edge of Wittgenstein's insights. For me, one of the prime contrasts between the social life of animals and that of any "human" group is the capacity to imagine how things might be

---

3.   John Gowlett, in a research seminar presented at the RAI in London, October 8, 2014.

otherwise than they are, and to innovate in helping create such a new world, as happens all the time through the endless imagination of fresh "drama," new styles in fashion, or even in politics, to the point of revolution (cf. James 2014). As Palmié has emphasized to me, "While there is research on animal tool use in problem solving (which would imply 'imagining otherwise'), humans *socially* create such new worlds, *and pass them on* to their successors (for better or worse). No other animal seems to be capable of doing so, and we are, because we rely on symbolic media capable of transcending our lifespans" (Stephan Palmié, pers. comm.).

What was the threshold for the passing on of such socially created worlds? Was it the community fire, or the domestic hearth, plus the way performers and even strangers might be attracted there for games of gesture, chorusing and other basic musical expressions, enactments, and dance? Well, by such a definition it would have to have been very early indeed, preceding the emergence of *Homo sapiens*. The earliest date at which evidence has been found of the controlled use of fire in hearths was possibly a little more than two million years ago, while evidence of cooking may indicate its emergence around 1.7 million years ago, followed by significant enlargement of the brain, making plausible the beginnings of "language," myth, song, and what we might think of as ceremonial enactments probably at around 0.5 million years ago (see contributions in Dunbar et al. 2010).

Remark 15. In another of the early notes, Wittgenstein here seems to retreat from his suggestion above that fire has a special significance for human beings. "For no phenomenon is particularly mysterious in itself, but any of them can become so to us," being, he suggests, a characteristic of the "awakening" human mind to see significance in any phenomenon.

However, we should ourselves recognize that it is not so much what fire *is* but what fire *does* that makes its impression on us. Here it stands out as something extremely distinctive. You can't avoid its felt quality, along with its visual impact. It can injure and kill. You have to do something about it, even just getting the children out of the way—or putting it out. All such active response is likely to involve others—fire provokes social collaboration, even in a purely defensive situation of this kind. And collaboration becomes more complex as we begin to "tame" its fearful powers of destruction, using it as a focus for the home community (whether ancient or modern), for cooking, and for transforming raw materials. And it can be used in hostile ways—such as burning the huts of enemies—long before its incorporation into modern weapons of war.

It is in this same Remark that Wittgenstein makes his memorable suggestion: "One could almost say that man is a ceremonial animal." He adds that besides "animal" behavior, humans also carry out peculiar actions that might be called "ritual" actions. Anthropologists would demur over "taking food" as merely animal behavior, but be very interested in the width of this conception of "ritual action." But if there are so many of these actions, why should we use a descriptive term that carries so much religious import? Is there nothing in between the animal and the religious side of human action? And Wittgenstein seems to be thinking in terms of the individual human person rather than the socially interactive context in which persons usually act upon the basis of understandings they have in common with other persons. It need not be a Christmas dinner for ceremoniality to be enacted; even the plain "taking of food" as a private snack on a crowded train has its own decencies.

Remark 39. Wittgenstein's discussions of the similarities—but also differences—between fire festivals through time have highlighted some of the most memorable scenes from the *Golden Bough*. Here, I think we should defend Frazer's anthropology against the first generation of his modern academic critics who rubbished his theory of a linear development of ideas about magic, through religion, to the white light of science. We should recognize Wittgenstein's success in rescuing something of the value of what Frazer put before us. One does read through the long accounts of fire festivals, especially the old Celtic Beltane Fire Festival, with growing wonderment—even in the abridged edition (1922: 609–58); and there is more in the set of volumes as a whole.

However, in discussions by philosophers and historians of the significance of Frazer's fire festivals, I have not often found any recognition of the fact that closely similar festivals still take place regularly, including in the relatively "modern" countries of the United Kingdom and the United States. My own earlier brief discussion of Wittgenstein's *Remarks on Frazer* does, however, include two photographs of a related event in Northumberland in 1910 (James 2003: 110–14; illustrations on p. 113). As yet, I have not found any reference in the volumes of *Golden Bough* to Guy Fawkes and the Gunpowder Plot of 1605, though today's British festival of Bonfire Night on November 5th is over four hundred years old—considerably older than the classic Beltane festivals in eighteenth-century Scotland. It celebrates the failure of Guido Fawkes and his fellow Catholic plotters to blow up the House of Commons and unseat King James I. Effigies burned in today's neighborhood bonfires are usually put together a couple of days beforehand, just for fun. But in the past, the effigies were sometimes figures of hate, including the Pope. The customary practices involved in Bonfire Night have gone through various changes and "explanations" over the years, but there is no sign of decline in ceremoniality or public interest in the event. The Sussex town of Lewes is sometimes known as the Bonfire capital of the world, regularly hosting an astonishing—and increasing—array of torch-carrying processions, bonfires, and firework displays on Guy Fawkes Day. Plenty of information can be found online.[4] Reflecting on this example of a modern fire festival, despite its nasty political beginnings, we have to endorse Wittgenstein's skepticism about the relevance of "historical explanations" behind the impulse to mount these special occasions. Almost no one, we suspect, would really want Bonfire Night to reignite Protestant/ Catholic hatreds. And the actual attempt to blow up Parliament was so long ago that it scarcely seems real—or in any way plausibly connected with current terrorist activity.

There are, moreover, several examples over the last few decades of newly coined, or newly reinvented "fire festivals" in "modern" conditions. In 1712, Spanish colonists had established a religious Fiesta in the city of Santa Fe, with Mass and Catholic rituals, following their "peaceful" reconquest of the Pueblo settlements in 1692. By 1848, the United States had formally annexed the region, making Santa Fe the capital of New Mexico. It soon acquired a romantic aura and many English-speaking artists and writers were drawn there; the Museum of New Mexico was founded in 1909, and it was not long before the art colony and the museum crowd had set up a "counter Fiesta" for the people at large. Since 1926, this has included the fabrication of a truly giant figure of Zozobra ("Old Man Gloom"), burned in an enormous bonfire every September ("to chase away the glooms"). Although there are records of enormous wicker figures in some of the early European festivals, as an invented tradition, Santa Fe's big bonfire is by any standards an astonishing spectacle and watched by thousands (see James 2003: 252–56; photo from the 1940s on p. 255). The detail and the scale of the event has persisted to the present (see Figs. 1 and 2, taken on September 10, 2011).

Frazer and Wittgenstein obviously could not have known that the city of Edinburgh would reinvent the Beltane Fire Festival in 1988: but the latter might have been able to guess at something of the kind happening, and would not have been surprised. It was started as a Celtic revival by a number of musical

4.   See, for example, en.wikipedia.org/wiki/Guy_Fawkes and http://en.wikipedia.org/wiki/Lewes_Bonfire.

Figure 1. Zozobra limbering 2011, Douglas H. Johnson

Figure 2. Zozobra burns 2011, Douglas H. Johnson

enthusiasts along with academics from the School of Scottish Studies at the University of Edinburgh, and is now run by the Beltane Fire Society. Taking explicit cues from the older European sources, what Wittgenstein called the "Neid" fire is started from scratch, by friction against wood;[5] but Scotland's version also includes multiple other elements—such as the Trinidadian carnival. The event was originally a community festival, but it has grown so large that the city council requires it to be ticketed. Further information is plentiful on the internet. See, for example, a site where it is stated that "The event was intended as a celebration of traditional rituals as a local manifestation of an international spirit."[6] Are there still echoes of "ritual sacrifice" that would have specially interested both Frazer and Wittgenstein? Well, I have not seen the festival, but there are plenty of suggestive pictures—for example, the burning phoenix; the new-lit Beltane Fire with a ritual dancer; or the procession passing under the Fire Arch.[7] The City Council naturally has particular concerns over health and safety on the night of Beltane, and no doubt the fire engines are never far away. Indeed, just over the English border in Carlisle, in November 2014, the City Council became nervous about a similar festival, which had a Tudor theme. In the context of growing Scottish support for the idea of independence from the United Kingdom, local councilors and security officials decided at the last moment that the Carlisle Fireshow should not include the burning of an effigy of Mary, Queen of Scots (once a longtime captive held in Carlisle Castle).[8]

Remark 40. Wittgenstein's point here is absolutely clear and helpful for the anthropologist. It is true that Frazer, too, was seeking evidence for ideas partly through the ethnographic record of practices. But it is indeed more fruitful to take account of the overlap of ideas within any practice, as illustrated by the variable "explanations" and ideas there have been within the history of Guy Fawkes events, as well as the multiple ideas deliberately brought together in the practices of Edinburgh's modern reinvention of the Beltane Fire Festival. Certainly, anthropologists rarely focus exclusively on "ideas," and almost never on "practices" in isolation (as an animal behaviorist inevitably has to do). Social

---

5. Frazer Anglicized the term as the "Need-fire" practiced in times of distress or calamity (1922: 638–41).

6. http://en.wikipedia.org/wiki/Beltane_Fire_Festival.

7. http://en.wikipedia.org/wiki/Beltane_Fire_Festival.

8. www.itv.com/news/border/.../carlisle-fireshow-controversy.

and cultural anthropology always seeks the relation, not only between one idea and one practice but also between multiple and overlapping ideas both within "a practice" and across associated practices. An association of practices, which cannot be assumed to form a coherent "whole" from an explanatory perspective, may be somewhat miscellaneous but nevertheless acceptable in the main to wide swathes of a population (recall the very miscellaneous nature of what goes on around Christmas these days).

Frazer picks up a point here about the production of new fire from friction. He further explains that in some of the western Scottish islands, this would be done with a wooden drill rolled between the hands in a plank of oak—a method similar to what I have seen many times in my own fieldwork among peoples of the Sudan-Ethiopian border, when "new fire" is required for particular rituals (James 1979: 144–45, fig. 5b). On the Scottish mainland, according to Frazer's continuing account, the old system was more cumbersome, requiring a large number of people to wind an axle-tree; however, if any of them had been guilty of an atrocious crime, the fire would not kindle, or might be without its usual virtue. When sparks were produced, a combustible variety of tree fungus—or gilled mushroom—that grows on old birches, was applied. Wittgenstein, ever the armchair anthropologist, does not recognize why this spurt of new fire should have the appearance of coming from heaven. The obvious association seems to be the way that lightning always strikes from the sky, and as the archaeologists have recently been explaining, it is very likely that the earliest human actions in responding to or controlling fire would have been direct efforts to escape, limit, or harness the phenomenon of wildfire caused by lightning.

Remark 41. The discussion here leads on from the previous notes. Anyone who has been camping overnight can surely understand why fire should be surrounded by a "nimbus" (a sort of cloud or halo)—but most especially if it appears to come from "heaven," perhaps as part of a thunderstorm. But of course the sky does not necessarily carry such religious significance, and ethnographers should perhaps take care in translating what people might mean by gesturing to the sky.

The accounts of dividing up and sharing the Beltane cake, with one unlucky recipient getting the inauspicious slice, is closely parallel with many other means of "casting lots," as noted in the Bible, and a very effective public dramatization of the consequences of good and bad luck. The company make a show of putting the unlucky person in the fire. The whole thing is rather more like a form of ceremonial play upon a theme (maybe like children playing cops and robbers).

Remark 42. And as Wittgenstein observes in his continuing discussion of the Beltane fire, the practice itself, today, is "harmless." It is only a "hypothesis" that might give the matter "depth." We understand from this that whether or not there was historical continuity from a time when human sacrifice was actually played out, in old Celtic society or from a more remote source, the idea suggests itself from the practice. He then evokes the opera, where evidence for historical continuity in every case more or less disappears into myth. The theme of fire runs right through the operatic cycle of Richard Wagner's *Nibelungenlied,* based on the early epic stories of Siegfried and Brunhild. Angry with the gods, she eventually lights a funeral pyre and leaps into the flames, as Valhalla burns in the distance.

Opera brings together music, song, dance, extraordinary out-of-this world adventures, human characters, fate, and sacrifice on a cosmic scale. Does it not share much with the "ritual" dramas of religion, which we do not need to remind ourselves, not least in the case of Judaism and Christianity, which take their bearings from various images of sacrifice? And as Wittgenstein noted for the Beltane fire, if we observe the people that take part, their usual way of behaving, the kinds of games they play on other occasions (we can include the opera audience here, perhaps)—then we can describe the "spirit of the festival." We can see that "what is sinister lies in the character of these people themselves"; we should also remember that the Beltane fire used to mark the opening up of the summer pastures, where the cattle could be taken and a warm, fruitful summer would follow. This was celebration in the nicest sense (as some of us may recall from childhood the ongoing fun of English Mayday), with dancing round the maypole. And the spring fires of Beltane would be followed in the autumn by a closing of the cycle through another festival that marked the return of the cattle to their local winter quarters.

Wittgenstein then returns to the evidence of casting lots through the knobs baked on cakes; this is followed in much greater detail in the next note.

Remark 43. Wittgenstein continues his discussion of the way that the Celtic festivals may involve the use of a cake, baked perhaps with buttons on the top, as a method of casting lots—to identify the person who will become a victim, supposedly to be thrown on the fire. Although this is in practice only a show, he speculates on why we should feel there is something sinister about this. Clearly, we have some sense of apprehension, as of course the people present would obviously have, that something awful might actually happen. Although they are "only acting," we ourselves recoil with apprehension when watching cruel violence "enacted" on the stage (think of *King Lear* and Gloucester's eyes). For those of us who have read about practices of the burning of witches or "human sacrifice" in the past, there will of course be a sense of possible direct links with the "play" of the Beltane performance. But as Wittgenstein's notes perhaps suggest—though do not spell this out—the more history you have read, the more likely you are to "see connections" of a plausibly historical kind in events of this sort (as Frazer did). If you have never read any history, or ethnography, your fears are likely to feed off the atmosphere of the day, and what people around you are talking and singing about, or mentioned quietly the night before. Wittgenstein suggests the use of a cake for choosing a victim is "especially horrible" because of the cake. This may ring true locally for a reason he does not, I think, mention—that is, the practice, certainly common in the north of England when I was young, of hiding a nice surprise in the Christmas pudding. We used to put a silver threepenny bit or sixpence in the pudding, for one lucky person to find it in their slice. So, taking the region of northern Britain for a start (and proceeding round the world!) there might well have been a long history to the widely understood perceptions of the ambiguity of the common method; being chosen through sharing out the portions of a cake or pudding could be presented as a way of casting either very bad, or very good, fortune.

Remark 44. The "environment" of a way of acting. Of course, this invokes not simply the natural environment but also the unfolding situations of the human environment. Ceremonial action is not simply a personal instinct, in relation to fire, trees, or whatever, but something like taking part in a game, a stage drama, of which the story line, the rules, or scenery provide the relevant "environment" for an actor. Such environments are not simply given. Nor are they just "fictional." We invent them all the time, and live by them, building on what we used to do in childhood, what we have learned from travel, and noticing the differences and similarities of the way that foreigners do these things. If you have already heard about torture by fire, or have directly experienced the actuality of killing in the field of battle, you will dread Guy Fawkes night more than if you have not.

Remark 45. The discussion is extended in the notes here. We are impressed not with the hypothesis of the historical origin of a custom like the Beltane festival but simply by being shown "the material." A pile of stones could be arranged to resemble ruins; as with the Beltane fire, the passerby will feel an "immense probability" that the form itself is derived from a collapsed house.

Wittgenstein's continuing arguments for our own sense of recognizing what is going on in such a performance as the Beltane festival help lay any simplistic sense of "cultural relativism." It is surely our deep-seated capacity for "recognition" that makes good fieldwork possible for the anthropologist; or, of course for the linguist, the general traveler, etcetera. Of the various forms of cultural communication, beyond food, it is probably music that "travels" best across frontiers. Japanese or African styles of music can be loved far from their local roots, and performed to delighted audiences, feeding into new forms (consider jazz) over time and space. "Recognition" here seems relatively straightforward, but cannot be too different from the recognition that we can experience in relation to ceremonial performances we may not have seen before.

The history of social phenomena is, of course, important: here, even if we have to rely on guesswork and imagination to some extent, we are not narrowly following Frazer in providing a rational explanation of how the early magic of lightning and bonfires led to religion and science but rather evoking Wittgenstein in appealing to something common to the imagination and feelings of humanity in whatever period or context of civilization. History necessarily depends, in any case, on such extendable human understanding. A mere time chart of events and practices is not in itself a historical record; as R. G. Collingwood pointed out so effectively, the understanding of history depends in some way upon our ability to *re-enact* the past, to use our imagination to the fullest in making the most of the evidence about how life would have been for ourselves (Collingwood 1946).

Wittgenstein admits that the Beltane festival has "come down to us" as a play, rather like children playing at robbers. "But then again, it is not like this . . ." and he adds that it possesses something more than a "mere theatrical performance" or a practical jest for entertainment. We might demur over the reference to mere theatrical performance, for as I have suggested above, Wagner's operas or Shakespeare's plays can be more than "entertainment"; they can potentially have tremendous impact on the feelings, moral understandings, and self-knowledge of people in the audience, not to mention the actors themselves. In the last paragraph of these notes, Wittgenstein suggests it is not just the *idea* of children's games such as burning a straw man that is frightening; this comes as much from what one has heard about such things—"through the thought of humans and their past" and through "all the strangeness of what I see in myself" as well as others.

Remark 46. Wittgenstein seems to be suggesting here that even when religious authorities differ in their prescriptions for rituals, through our own capacities we can grasp their differing significance—by extending the ritual "instinct" perhaps. Through a "commonality of spirit," we ourselves could invent all the ceremonies of human history. This capacity surely is essential for the practitioners and innovators of religion as such, as much as for the anthropologist and archaeologist, who ponder all the time how a ceremony ought to have looked if it hadn't been raining and the proper type of white ox couldn't be found, or how the material evidence of rock drawings and fires and bones suggests how a ceremony might have been conducted in the remote past.

Remark 47. Returning to the Celtic Beltane festivals, this Remark focuses on water, but water warmed by the rekindling of the freshly-created Neid fire. Recall how those kindling the fire itself were not to be murderers, adulterers, etcetera; it follows on clearly that the water now heated over the fire would have a cleansing effect when sprinkled on people infected with the plague or upon sick cattle. This practice confronts the disease, or the idea of the disease as "dirty," with washing, or the idea of water as cleansing. Wittgenstein makes it clear that this simple or "infantile" theory—that disease is like dirt and can be washed off—does not mean the practice has come from that theory, any more than "infantile" theories of sexuality can account for everything that children do. But in such cases, we should recognize that the practice might have come from such ideas.

Wittgenstein then defends the "solar" theory of cleansing, despite other theories of purification drawing mainly on water. He noted earlier that fire is needed to produce hot water for cleansing, and that fire itself can be used for cleaning up. We might emphasize its uses for clearing the land, burning the rubbish, and even modern medical uses such as cauterizing a wound; perhaps it would be going too far to add here the obvious relevance of doing away with evil persons in a big bonfire. He goes on to argue that the association of fire with the sun must also be very common, and that the two thoughts are more than likely to come together in any one person's mind. He seems to mock the scholars "who always want to have a theory"—that is, presumably, a single theory. Against this caricature, he places the ordinary populace, who might not actually *know* of a connection between cleansing and the sun, but among whom the link would be likely to have occurred somewhere. And people (presumably everywhere) must have noticed the way that fire can cause *total* destruction; the lingering image in our minds, on reading these words of Wittgenstein after the earlier discussion, is inevitably not only clearing up the garden rubbish with a domestic fire but also the threat of larger-scale destruction posed by the use of a ceremonial fire for ceremonial clearsing, and the disturbing memory, or part-imagined scene, of deliberate human destruction in this uniquely disturbing manner.

REFERENCES

Asad, Talal. 1993. *Genealogies of Religion: Discipline and Reasons of Power in Christianity and Islam*. Baltimore: Johns Hopkins University Press.

Bouveresse, Jacques. 1977. "L'animal cérémoniel: Wittgenstein et l'anthropologie.' *Actes de la recherche en sciences sociales* (16): 43–54.

Collingwood, R. G 1946. *The Idea of History*. Oxford: Clarendon Press.

De Lara, Philippe. 2005. *Le rite et la raison: Wittgenstein anthropologue*. Paris: Ellipses.

Douglas, Mary. 1966. *Purity and Danger: An Analysis of Concepts of Pollution and Taboo*. London: Routledge and Kegan Paul.

Dunbar, Robin, Clive Gamble, and John Gowlett, eds. 2010. *Social Brain: Distributed Mind*. Oxford: Oxford University Press for the British Academy.

Durkheim, Émile. (1912) 1995. *Elementary Forms of the Religious Life*. Translated by Karen E. Fields. New York: Free Press.

Frazer, Sir James. 1922. *The Golden Bough: A Study in Magic and Religion*. Abridged edition. London: Macmillan & Co. Reprinted in 1932 by the Rationalist Press Association.

Gowlett, John. 2010. "Firing up the Social Brain." In *Social Brain: Distributed Mind*, edited by Robin Dunbar, Clive Gamble, and John Gowlett, 341–66. Oxford: Oxford University Press for the British Academy.

Gowlett, John, and Richard Wrangham. 2013. "Earliest Fire in Africa: Towards the Convergence of Archaeological Evidence and the Cooking Hypothesis." *Azania: Archaeological Research in Africa* 48 (1): 5–30.

Hertz, Robert. 1960. *Death and the Right Hand*. Translated by Rodney Needham and Claudia Needham. London: Cohen and West.

Huxley, Julian, ed. 1966. "A Discussion on Ritualization of Behaviour in Animals and Man." *Philosophical Transactions of the Royal Society of London, Series B: Biological Sciences* 251: 249–71.

James, Wendy. 1979. *'Kwanim Pa: The Making of the Uduk People: An Ethnographic Study of Survival in the Sudan-Ethiopian Borderlands*. Oxford: Oxford University Press.

———. 2003. *The Ceremonial Animal: A New Portrait of Anthropology*. Oxford: Oxford University Press.

———. 2007. "Choreography and Ceremony: The Artful Side of Action." *Human Affairs: A Postdisciplinary Journal for Humanities & Social Sciences* 17 (2): 126–37.

———. 2014. "Human Life as Drama: A Maussian Insight." *Journal of Classical Sociology* 14 (1): 78–90.

Kapferer, Bruce, ed. 2005. *Retreat of the Social: The Rise and Rise of Reductionism*. New York: Berghahn.

Richards, Audrey I. 1956. *Chisungu: A Girls' Initiation Ceremony among the Bemba of Northern Rhodesia*. London: Faber and Faber.

Schatzki, Theodore R. 1996. *Social Practices: A Wittgensteinian Approach to Human Activity and the Social*. Cambridge: Cambridge University Press.

Steiner, Franz. 1956. *Taboo*. London: Cohen and West.

Turner, Victor. 1969. *The Ritual Process: Structure and Anti-Structure*. New York: Transaction Publishers.

Van Gennep, Arnold. (1909) 1960. *The Rites of Passage*. Translated by Monika B. Vizedom and Gabrielle L. Caffee. Chicago: University of Chicago Press.

Wrangham, Richard. 2009. *Catching Fire: How Cooking Made Us Human*. New York: Basic Books.

CHAPTER 7

Wittgenstein on Frazer

Michael Puett

PART I: INTRODUCTION

In his critique of James Frazer, Ludwig Wittgenstein consistently takes rituals that Frazer presented as based upon mistaken, prescientific understandings of the world and instead demonstrates that if the ritual actions are on the contrary understood *as* rituals, they can be understood in entirely different ways. But the ways in which Wittgenstein then discusses ritual are often quite counterintuitive and worth discussing in depth.

Let's begin by looking at Wittgenstein's critiques:

> How misleading Frazer's explanations are becomes clear, I think, from the fact that one could very well invent primitive practices oneself, and it would only be by chance if they were not actually found somewhere. That is, the principle according to which these practices are ordered is a much more general one than [it appears] in Frazer's explanation, and it exists in our own soul, so that we could think up all the possibilities ourselves. (#13)

The basis of ritual practice is to be found in the souls of all humans. The practices that emerge from humans are thus readily understandable and even predictable when understood as such:

We can thus readily imagine that, for instance, the king of a tribe becomes visible for no one, but also that every member of the tribe is obliged to see him. The latter will then certainly not occur in a manner more or less left to chance; instead, he will be *shown* to the people. Perhaps no one will be allowed to touch him, or perhaps they will be *compelled* to touch him. Think how after Schubert's death his brother cut Schubert's scores into small pieces and gave to his favorite pupils these pieces of a few bars. As a gesture of piety, this action is *just* as comprehensible as that of preserving the scores untouched and accessible to no one. And if Schubert's brother had burned the scores, this could still be understood as a gesture of piety. The ceremonial (hot or cold) as opposed to the haphazard (lukewarm) is what characterizes piety. (#13)

The content of the ritual is not what matters. The goal is to understand the sensibilities and dispositions that rituals express—sensibilities and dispositions embedded in the soul of any human. The comparative principle is then to find (or even imagine) possible ways that such dispositions have been or could be expressed.

The way such expression occurs is of less relevance than the fact of the expression. People being prevented from seeing a king, or being compelled to do so, are expressions of the same sense of extraordinary power; cutting up Schubert's scores and handing them out to disciples, or preserving them and making them inaccessible, are expressions of the same sense of piety. Unlike the world of chance and the haphazard, ritual is a world of required activity expressing a given sensibility. It is either hot or cold as opposed to the random lukewarm.

As Wittgenstein states elsewhere,

All these *various* practices show that we are not dealing with the descent of one from the other, but with a commonality of spirit. And one could invent (confabulate) all of these ceremonies on one's own. And the spirit in which one would invent them is their common one. (#46)

One is looking for the common spirit that underlies the various practices (whether real or invented).

What interests Wittgenstein is thus a framework in which we would connect ceremonies based upon their common rootedness in such a given, human sensibility:

If one sets the phrase "majesty of death" next to the story of the priest king of Nemi, one sees that they are one and the same. The life of the priest king represents what is meant by that phrase. Whoever is gripped by the [idea of] majesty of death can express this through just such a life. —Of course, this is also not an explanation, it just puts one symbol for another. Or one ceremony in place of another. (#5)

The interest in this work comes precisely from the fact that we are exploring inclinations that we ourselves have as well: "Frazer's explanations would not be explanations at all if they did not, in the end, appeal to an inclination in ourselves" (#13).

Wittgenstein elsewhere elaborates on the method:

There is a manifold of faces with common features that keep surfacing here and there. And what one would like to do is draw lines that connect the components in common. What would still be lacking then is a part of our contemplation, and it is the one that connects this picture with our own feelings and thoughts. This part gives such contemplation its depth. (#39)

The first step would be to connect the common features that appear among these rituals. And the next part is the contemplation, a contemplation that will connect the general picture that emerges with our own feelings and thoughts. This gives the contemplation its depth.

Such depth, it must be emphasized, can be a difficult thing to contemplate, as it opens up the darker aspects of human life. For Wittgenstein, these darker aspects are precisely one of the things we preclude ourselves from contemplating fully when we use the sort of framework employed by Frazer. Take, for example, the Beltane fire ritual. From Frazer's perspective, the darker aspect of the ritual comes from the fact that it *may* once have included human sacrifice. But for Wittgenstein this won't do. The depth only comes if we do *not* allow ourselves to create such a distance, relegating the darker side to what may have existed in some primitive past:

Here it appears as though it were only the hypothesis that gives the matter depth. . . . It is thus clear that what gives this practice depth is its *connection* with the burning of a human being. . . . The question is: Does this—shall we say—sinister character adhere to the custom of the Beltane fire in itself as it was practiced a

(as Frazer thinks)." Contrary to the British intellectualist tradition, primitive man is, in a sense, more right because he doesn't ascribe actions to beliefs.

But we fail to recognize this when, like Frazer, we fail to see them as rooted in common human inclinations. Hence, Wittgenstein's consistent move is to divorce rituals, ceremonies, and magical practices from the world of belief and doctrine and instead root them in the dispositions, inclinations, and sensibilities common to all humans. And divorce them as well from the world of chance, of haphazard occurrences, and of means-end activities in which humans alter the world for their benefit—using resources, for example, to build huts (#10). By so divorcing them, one can see them for what they are—spiritual matters. Spiritual matters that are shared by all humans, but perhaps more intensely so in primitive rituals, unobstructed by false ideas about doctrine.

In other words, if we assume the only human mode of being consists of making representations of the world and undertaking means-end activities to benefit ourselves, not only do we misunderstand primitive rituals, we also fail to see such inclinations playing out in our own lives.

But where would we find them in our own lives? Intriguingly, the modern examples that Wittgenstein uses to show similarities with "primitive" rituals are not the obviously religious ones—going to a church, for example. His modern examples on the contrary are the mundane ones where our emotions explode forth—people speaking sternly to one another (#43), hitting the ground with a cane (#31), being unsettled by love (#3). There are undoubtedly many reasons for this, including, obviously enough, the hope of demonstrating how universal the sentiments are: the ritual may seem bizarre, but we do the equivalent all the time. But there may be other reasons as well. The interesting depth of humanity, for Wittgenstein, is not to be found in the organized religions of the day, as they too are based on doctrines and theories. It is rather to be found in those activities that most elicit our basic human inclinations.

What we find in "primitive" rituals, therefore, are clear expressions of the ways that human inclinations play out in human practices—expressions that can be found in recent times in mundane activities (hitting the ground with a cane, someone speaking sternly to another), but are more difficult to find in distinctively religious contexts. This is why Wittgenstein is keenly concerned to rescue these practices from a Frazerian reading that would see them as simply errors based upon a misunderstanding of the workings of the world. But it is also why Wittgenstein is not terribly concerned with the rituals themselves, the contexts in which they were meaningful, or even much about the content of the rituals themselves. His concern is rather to line them up with other ritual actions that, while differing in form and content, nonetheless point toward similar human inclinations. Frazer's attempts to explain the happenings at Nemi entirely miss the point of what is interesting: the ritual emerges out of human dealings with the terribleness of death, and that is precisely why it is of interest to us.

This is what Wittgenstein means when he says, "A whole mythology is deposited in our language" (#24). A mythology that is present not as historical remnants from a previous period of human evolution but a mythology that is with us still, as it is in the Beltane ritual. That is with us still in all the complexities of being human, including our unsettledness and our sinister sides. But we miss it because of our emphasis on theory, explanation, means-end rationality.

Although he does not use the word, what interests Wittgenstein in the *Remarks* is sincere, authentic religious commitment: the authentic religious commitment that emerges from basic human experiences in the world, properly contemplated in depth. If Frazer operated in the realm of (bad and good) science, Wittgenstein operates in the realm of religious commitment—a commitment that is lost when we try to explain away the practices as based on mistaken representations, and a commitment that we have lost as well through our emphasis on reducing everything to theory. A commitment, then, that would be the same for any human who fully and authentically lives up to his or her experience. The thrust, in other words, is what we can learn from the practices once we see them as related to actions that we undertake ourselves. What ultimately interests Wittgenstein is the depth of contemplation that can come from seeing these inclinations laid bare, without the explanations and theories and doctrines that otherwise overlay that experience.

So what are the larger implications of this for anthropology?

I mentioned above that Wittgenstein says almost nothing about the larger contexts within which these rituals were practiced. But it is worth pausing a bit on the *almost*. With the Beltane ritual, Wittgenstein's call was to explore "the kind of people that take part in it, their usual way of behaving [on other occasions]—that is, their character—and the kind of games they play at other times" (#42). As we saw, the goal of the exercise for Wittgenstein was to demonstrate that the sinister sides of the ritual were also to be found in the daily lives of the people, and that the ritual was thus rooted in and emerged from their daily experience. And this was distinguished from other aspects of our lives, where we do use the sorts of means-end rationality that Frazer was emphasizing—working with wood to build a hut, for example. Wittgenstein gives the hut example to demonstrate that of course "primitives" perfectly well understand how the world operates, while ritual comes out of the inclinations that develop in our daily experience.

But the distinction between ritual and nonritual activity could perhaps be elaborated a bit more. And to do so, let's try one of the very things that Wittgenstein argues against: looking at indigenous discussions—let's even call them theories—of ritual.

In early China, one finds analyses of ritual that might at first glance seem similar to those offered by Wittgenstein. They are all about working with the complexities of human dispositions, most certainly including the darker sides. But the difference is that the activities, roles, and behaviors played out in the ritual sphere are not seen as expressions of our inclinations, nor are they rooted in our experience of the world. They are rather presented as "as if" worlds that work precisely because they are disjunct from and in tension with our nonritual experiences (Seligman et al. 2008: 28–34; Puett 2014). These as-if worlds are usually self-consciously counterintuitive to the worlds that we otherwise inhabit. They are not so much expressions of our deepest inclinations but rather the places where we work with and against those inclinations through imaginative play.

These as-if worlds are not repositories of beliefs. But they are also not repositories of the same inclinations that would govern our behavior when, for example, someone speaks sternly. Wittgenstein's goal in emphasizing the links between ritual activity and basic human inclinations was to force us to take ritual seriously. But, ironically, by creating too coherent a picture of this side of human behavior, by rooting ritual so tightly in the realm of basic human inclinations, Wittgenstein may lose precisely the complexity of human activity that interests him so deeply. If we follow these indigenous theories, then it is precisely the tension-filled *relationship* between ritual and nonritual activity that is of interest—the daily work of shifting between the different types of ritual and nonritual worlds that humans are constantly creating. This, perhaps, is where we really find the depths of humans.

PART II: COMMENTARIES

1. One must begin with error and transform it into truth.
   That is, one must uncover the source of the error, otherwise hearing the truth won't help us. It cannot penetrate when something else is taking its place.

To convince someone of what is true, it is not enough to state the truth; one must find the *way* from error to truth.

Again and again I must submerge myself in the water of doubt.

Frazer's representation of human magical and religious notions is unsatisfactory: it makes these notions appear as *mistakes*.

Was Augustine mistaken, then, when he called on God on every page of the *Confessions*?

But—one might say—if he was not in error, then surely so was the Buddhist saint—or whoever else—whose religion expresses entirely different notions. But none of them was in error except where he was putting forth a theory.

Already the idea of explaining the practice—say the killing of the priest king—seems to me wrong-headed. All that Frazer does is to make the practice plausible to those who think like him. It is very strange to present all these practices, in the end, so to speak, as foolishness.

But it never does become plausible that people do all this out of sheer stupidity.

When he explains to us, for example, that the king would have to be killed in his prime because, according to the notions of the savages, his soul would otherwise not be kept fresh, then one can only say: where that practice and these notions go together, there the practice does not spring from the notion; instead they are simply both present.

It could well be, and often occurs today, that someone gives up a practice after having realized an error that this practice depended on. But then again, this case holds only when it is enough to make someone aware of his error so as to dissuade him from his mode of action. But surely, this is not the case with the religious practices of a people, and that is why we are *not* dealing with an error here.

Commentary: Frazer's analysis, according to Wittgenstein, is focused upon demonstrating that earlier magical and religious ideas were simply hypotheses about the workings of the world—hypotheses that have since been corrected as humans have gradually developed better theories of how the world operates.

Wittgenstein's opening critique is precisely on this point. Magical and religious notions are not attempts to develop an accurate theory of the world, and religious practices are not attempts to apply these theories in acting upon the world. Frazer is misunderstanding them altogether. As Wittgenstein states, "All that Frazer does is to make the practice plausible to those who think like him."

From such a beginning, it might appear that Wittgenstein's call would be for a careful study of what the actors in the cultures in question were trying to do. And, to some extent, that will be true, but not in the ways that one might immediately expect.

Hints of Wittgenstein's primary concerns are clear almost immediately. "Again and again I must submerge myself in the water of doubt." One of the things that particularly bothers Wittgenstein about Frazer's approach is that the analyst becomes someone who is, in a sense, simply correcting the errors of those undertaking religious practice. The analyst learns nothing from the religious practices themselves.

And he goes a step further as well. Wittgenstein is not simply criticizing Frazer's attempt to see religious notions as errors. He is also arguing against any attempt to explain a practice by means of religious notions. In other words, Wittgenstein's critique is not aimed at saying that Frazer has failed to consider the indigenous notions underlying a given practice. The critique is rather aimed at any attempt to explicate a religious practice in terms of notions at all.

2. Frazer says it is very hard to discover the error in magic—and this is why it persists for so long—because, for example, a conjuration intended to bring about rain will sooner or later appear as effective. But then it is strange that, after all, the people would not hit upon the fact that it will rain sooner or later anyway.

I believe that the enterprise of explanation is already wrong because we only have to correctly put together what one already *knows*, without adding anything, and the kind of satisfaction that one attempts to attain through explanation comes of itself.

And here it isn't the explanation at all that satisfies us. When Frazer begins by telling us the story of the King of the Woods at Nemi, he does so in a tone that shows that something strange and terrible is happening here. However, the question "Why is this happening?" is essentially answered by just this [mode of exposition]: because it is terrible. In other words, it is what appears to us a terrible, impressive, horrible, tragic, etcetera that gave birth to this event [or process].

Commentary: If we cannot explain a practice according to a notion, then how should we understand it? Wittgenstein gives us one of our first clues here. What gave birth to this event is something terrible.

And this is precisely what "satisfies us." We can learn from this ritual not by placing it within an evolutionary context, running from mistaken, "primitive" representations of the world to correct, modern scientific ones. And not by analyzing it according to the notions that explain the ritual. The goal is rather to locate the emotions that generated the ritual—emotions that all humans share.

This is connected to the argument that Wittgenstein notes later:

> If one sets the phrase "majesty of death" next to the story of the priest king of Nemi, one sees that they are one and the same. The life of the priest king represents what is meant by that phrase. Whoever is gripped by the [idea of] majesty of death can express this through just such a life. —Of course, this is also not an explanation, it just puts one symbol for another. Or one ceremony in place of another. (#5)

The majesty of death underlies the ritual. We—and all humans—possess the same inclinations, even though we express the inclinations in different types of rituals. But by focusing on similar expressions of this same inclination, we can understand the "primitive" rite as well.

Why would this satisfy us? Wittgenstein does not elaborate, but hints can be seen in the ensuing note.

3. One can only resort to description here, and say: such is human life.
    Compared to the impression that what is so described to us, explanation is too uncertain.

Every explanation is a hypothesis.

But someone who, for example, is unsettled by love will be ill-assisted by a hypothetical explanation. It won't calm him or her.

Commentary: The proper context to understand these practices is in terms of human life in general.

As opposed to explanations, Wittgenstein is calling for descriptions—descriptions of what human life is like. The analogy is telling. "Unsettled by human love." Like the terribleness of death in the previous note.

What interests Wittgenstein are the most profound of human sentiments and the ways that these sentiments are expressed in human practices.

Explanations do not help us to get at these sentiments. And they may—as in the case of Frazer—prevent us from doing so.

But let us return to the analogy. Note that the person unsettled by love in the analogy is not just the ritual practitioner. It seems also to include the analyst. What concerns Wittgenstein so much here is that we are dealing with complex aspects of human life, yet Frazer's approach is a (failed) attempt to not be unsettled by them. Wittgenstein's call on the contrary is for descriptions that would deal with human life in all of its complexity, instead of displacing that complexity through distancing frameworks portraying rituals as a product of mistaken understandings of the world.

If these basic human emotions are what underlie religious practice, then a true description of them may give us a more profound understanding of human inclinations and the ways these inclinations are expressed.

6. A religious symbol is not grounded in an *opinion*.

Error only corresponds to opinion.

Commentary: Opinion operates on an axis of truth and error. By working exclusively on this axis, Frazer constructs an evolutionary framework running from "primitive" (mis)understandings of the world to modern science.

But religious symbols, like religious practices, operate on another axis altogether. They are not opinions about the world but rather expressions of human inclinations. Placing them on an axis of truth and error allows us to dismiss them. The goal on the contrary is to explore religion as a means of contemplating the depths of humans.

10. The same savage who, apparently in order to kill his enemy, pierces an image of him, really builds his hut out of wood, and carves his arrow skillfully and not in effigy.

The idea that one could beckon a lifeless object to come, just as one would beckon a person. Here the principle is that of personification.

Commentary: All humans—including those Frazer would call savages—are capable of working with the world in a way that demonstrates a full understanding of the nature of the world and of basic causative principles. They build with wood to makes huts, and carve wood to make arrows.

The fact that "primitives" will do this while at the same time piercing an image of an enemy they wish to kill demonstrates that ritual practice is not based upon a mistaken understanding of the workings of the world. Ritual should rather be thought of as a different sphere of human activity. The goal is then to see what human tendencies underlie the ritual action.

What underlies the ritual uses of effigy is the principle of personification. As Wittgenstein notes as well in remark #13, personification is a common human mode of being in the world. In remark #13, Wittgenstein links personification to a related human tendency to see resemblances and similarities.

As we will see, Wittgenstein's arguments for how one could connect ritual data is based upon this same mode of being—seeing resemblances across a seemingly disparate array of human activities across cultures and throughout history.

When looking at ritual, Frazer is using a means-end rationality—the sort of rationality that any human, savage or modern alike, is capable of using. But in misapplying this to ritual, Frazer incorrectly construes "savages" as misunderstanding the world. For Wittgenstein, the key is to recognize that ritual operates through a different human mode of being in the world, and—we shall see—even to utilize that different mode of being, rather than a means-end rationality, to study humanity.

11.   And magic always rests on the idea of symbolism and of language.
        The representation of a wish is, eo ipso, the representation of its fulfillment.
        But magic gives representation to a wish; it expresses a wish.
        Baptism as washing. —An error arises only when magic is interpreted scientifically.

When the adoption of a child is carried out in a way that the mother pulls the child through her clothes, then is it not crazy to think that there is an *error*, and that she believes to have born the child.

We should distinguish between magical operations and those operations that rest on false, oversimplified notions of things and processes. For instance, if one says that the illness is moving from one part of the body into another, or if one takes measures to draw off the illness as though it were a liquid or a state of heat, then one is entertaining a false, inappropriate image.

Commentary: Here again Wittgenstein insists on a distinction between actions that require accurate understandings of causation on the one hand, and magic on the other. Magic for Wittgenstein is not based upon an erroneous understanding of the world, and it is therefore not something that can be considered a mistaken representation of the world. Magic is not a representation *of* anything. It rather expresses a wish. And magic is immediately comprehensible if understood as such, since all humans have ways of expressing wishes.

The adoption ritual is not based upon a mistaken idea on the part of the mother that she has actually given birth to the child. It is rather a ritualized expression of basic human inclinations.

18. Frazer: ". . . That these operations are dictated by fear of the ghost of the slain seems certain . . ." [p. 212]. But why does Frazer use the word "ghost"? He thus evidently understands this superstition only too well, since he explains it with a superstitious term familiar to him. Or rather, he could have seen from this that there is something in us, too, that speaks in support of such observances on the part of the savages. —When I, who do not believe that there exist, anywhere, human-superhuman beings whom one can call gods—when I say: "I fear the wrath of the gods," then this shows that I can mean something with this [utterance], or can express a sentiment that is not necessarily connected with such belief.

Commentary: Frazer's use of the term "ghost" unwittingly reveals the very similarity between ourselves and "savages" that Frazer is intending to deny. "He could have seen from this that there is something in us, too, that speaks in support of such observances on the part of the savages." And the similarity again lies in the emotions. We are expressing the same sentiment when we say, "I fear the wrath of the gods." The issue is the expression of the sentiment, not a statement of a belief.

But Wittgenstein's chosen example here is telling, as is the nature of the critique. Wittgenstein's concern is not simply that Frazer has mistakenly read a belief into a common saying. What again bothers Wittgenstein is how Frazer's framework allows such distance between the analyst and the practice. Wittgenstein wants us to focus instead on the deep fear that wells in all of us when dealing with death or the capriciousness of life. Looking at ritual practice elsewhere should help us to contemplate this aspect of humanity sincerely.

20.   A historical explanation, an explanation in the form of a hypothesis of development is only *one* kind of summary arrangement of the data—of their synopsis. It is equally possible to see the data in their relation to one another and to gather them into a general picture without doing so in the form of a hypothesis concerning temporal development.

Commentary: Note again Wittgenstein's commitment to a religious sphere that would be treated on its own terms—not explained in terms of opinions or beliefs, and also not explained in terms of historical development. Historical development, just like analyses of notions or theories or opinions, only serve to remove us from seeing the common human sensibilities that underlie ritual activity.

Here we have one of Wittgenstein's clearest articulations of what he would like to see instead. Wittgenstein is calling for an approach that would organize rituals from throughout human history according to the emotional inclinations—the dispositions, sentiments, wishes, fears, horrors—inherent in human beings. What we would get would be a general picture of the complexity of human inclinations, including the dark sides.

31.   I read, among many similar examples, of a rain-king in Africa to whom the people appeal for rain *when the rainy season comes*. But surely this does not mean that they actually think he can make rain, for otherwise they would do it in the dry periods of the year when the land is "a parched and arid desert." For if one assumes that the people once instituted the office of the rain-king out of stupidity, it certainly still is clear that they would have previously made the experience that the rains commence in March, and they could have let the rain-king perform his work during the other parts of the year. Or again: toward morning, when the sun is about to rise, people celebrate rites of daybreak, but not at night, for then they simply burn lamps.

When I am angry about something, I sometimes hit the ground or a tree with my cane. But surely, I do not believe that the ground is at fault or that the hitting would help matters. "I vent my anger." And all rites are of this kind. One can call such practices instinctual behavior. —And a historical explanation, for instance that I or my ancestors earlier believed that hitting the ground would help is mere shadow-boxing, for these [*sic*] are superfluous assumptions that explain *nothing*. What is important is the semblance of the practice to an act of punishment, but more than this semblance cannot be stated.

Once such a phenomenon is brought into relation with an instinct that I possess myself, it thus constitutes the desired explanation; that is, one that resolves this particular difficulty. And further investigation of the history of my instinct now proceeds along different tracks.

Commentary: An explanation in terms of either a (mistaken) representation of reality or a historical analysis fails to do justice to the ritual. Rather, one finds the human instinctual behavior that corresponds in any given society to the ritual in question.

Rites come out of the instinctual behavior of humans—instincts that all of us share. "All rites are of this kind."

The goal is then to bring religious phenomena from "primitive" cultures into relation with instincts that we ourselves possess. This is all the explanation that is required. Further investigation would thus be properly focused on the instinct, rather than trying to further explain the ritual according to historical development or according to notions, theories, or doctrines, let alone the progressive rationalization of human life worlds.

Wittgenstein's example here is hitting the ground with a cane when one is angry. What is important is the semblance between this action and an act of punishment—not because one believes that one is punishing the ground but rather because the acts emerge from a common instinct of anger and rage. Based upon this semblance, one brings the activities in question in relation to each other. The inquiry can thus explore the nature of this instinct in more depth.

33. P. 168. (At a certain stage of early society the king or priest is often thought to be endowed with supernatural powers or to be an incarnation of a deity, and consistently with this belief the course of nature is supposed to be more or less under his control . . .)

It is of course not the case that the people believe that the ruler has these powers while the ruler himself very well knows that he does not have them, or does not know so only if he is an idiot or fool. Rather, the notion of his power is of course arranged in a way such that it corresponds with experience—his own and that of the people. That any kind of hypocrisy plays a role in this is only true to the extent that it suggests itself in most of what humans do anyway.

Commentary: The notion of divine rulership is not based upon a false belief regarding the supernatural powers of the ruler. The people can of course see as well as the ruler himself that he possesses no such powers. It is rather based upon the experience of power—an experience common to all humans.

Note again that for Wittgenstein, the key for a religious notion, like a religious practice, is that it "corresponds with experience." This is the genesis of both religious notions and rituals. And, since they are rooted in human experience, this is the basis by which we can contemplate them in depth.

But such a commitment to experience as the rooting principle behind religious notions and rituals has its dangers as well. What about religious notions and practices that work precisely because they are counterintuitive to experience? And could divine kingship be one such example?

36.   P. 171. ". . . a network of prohibitions and observances, of which the intention is not to contribute to his dignity . . ." This is both true and false. Of course not the dignity of the protection of the person but rather—as it were—the natural sacredness of the divinity in him.

Commentary: We can understand the rituals surrounding a ruler not by looking at belief or by looking at practical concerns but rather by focusing on sentiments. A natural sacredness inheres in figures of authority, and the prohibitions and observances that arise around him come out of such a sentiment.

37.   Simple though it may sound: The difference between magic and science can be expressed in the way that there is progress in science, but not in magic. Magic possesses no direction of development internal to itself.

Commentary: Frazer places magic and science on an evolutionary line. Magic is a result of "primitive" man's mistaken understanding of the workings of the world, whereas science is based upon a proper understanding.

In contrast, Wittgenstein argues, we should think of these as simply two different modes of being in the world. Science, from such a perspective, is a means-end rationality toward the world—the same mode of being that allows a so-called primitive to use wood to build a hut. Over time, one gets better at working with the world, and there is thus an inherent developmental tendency in such activities. As Frazer would put it (accurately enough, for this mode of being in the world), science is based upon developing theories about the world, and there is thus a development inherent to science as those theories are revised in response to the world. In contrast, magic (and religion) are based upon human sensibilities in the world—sensibilities rooted in experience. There is thus no inherent development in magic.

The move is thus to cordon off the sphere of magic and religion and argue that it makes sense within its own domain. It should not be seen as a theory (and thus a mistaken theory) of the world. And it is an inherent part of what all humans do.

REFERENCES

Puett, Michael. 2014. "Ritual Disjunctions: Ghosts, Philosophy, and Anthropology." In *The Ground Between: Anthropologists Engage Philosophy*, edited by Veena Das, Michael Jackson, Arthur Kleinman, and Bhrigupati Singh, 218–33. Durham, NC: Duke University Press.

Seligman, Adam, Robert Weller, Michael Puett, and Bennett Simon. 2008. *Ritual and its Consequences: An Essay on the Limits of Sincerity*. Oxford: Oxford University Press.

CHAPTER 8

Of Mistakes, Errors, and Superstition
Reading Wittgenstein's *Remarks on Frazer*

VEENA DAS

PART I: SOME OPENING THOUGHTS

Ludwig Wittgenstein made a departure from the *Tractatus Logico-Philosophicus* (1922) when he acknowledged that there was no single definition of a proposition that could provide a fit for the diverse forms it takes in the world.[1] Thus, the contact between language and reality is not a singular once-and-for-all achievement, which we either reach or fail to reach by the layering of a system of names against a system of objects. Yet, the question of the kind of contact between language and reality continues to be the single most pressing issue in what are called the second Wittgenstein and the third Wittgenstein (Moyal-Sharrock 2004, 2009). Departing from the *Tractatus*, our experience of how to

---

1. I am fascinated by the ongoing debates on continuity versus discontinuity between early and later Wittgenstein—the standard reading of the *Tractatus* and the austere reading—and although I have learned much from these debates, especially on the importance of the theme of nonsense in Wittgenstein, my point here is limited to a related but different register in his thought—namely, the place of superstition versus simple mistake in his comments on Frazer.

relate words to worlds in Wittgenstein's later work is one of disappointment, for we may succeed and then flounder repeatedly. This is a stance mirrored in the form of writing especially in *Philosophical Investigations* ([1958] 1973) and *On Certainty* (1974), when paragraphs come to an end abruptly and then begin again later as the same thought reappears with a new example or a different formulation. How, then, are specific (or singular) relations to be found between language and reality or in the way words are found to be world-bound?

My basic idea in this commentary is to depart from the many discussions that take Wittgenstein's *Remarks on Frazer* as giving us a *theory* of religion or ritual, emphasizing its expressive or symbolic dimension as against James Frazer's evolutionary or historical one (Bouveresse 2008) and to think, instead, of *Golden Bough* as providing to Wittgenstein a provocation to reflect on issues relating to the internal (as distinct from an external) relation between language and the world (or worlds). There is, of course, some risk in taking the *Remarks on Frazer* as forming a well-thought-out argument on the part of Wittgenstein. As Peter Hacker (1992) notes, these are a rough set of notes. "In commenting on them, it should be borne in mind that they are incomplete, unpolished, and not intended for publication. If one wants to learn from them, they should not be squeezed too hard" (Hacker 1992: 278). All this is true—and one must be cautious that even the device of treating these remarks as numbered—as in the present translation and my own comments—is nothing more than an editorial convenience: this device should not be equated with the apparatus of the numbered remarks as in *Tractatus* or in *Philosophical Investigations*.

Anthropologists might have something important to offer to this conversation. The trajectory of disavowal and occasional return to Frazer within anthropology (see Stephan Palmié's excellent introduction to this volume) attests to a deeper issue here than Frazer having simply confused the instrumental and the expressive dimensions of social action, or his having been mistaken in thinking that rituals in primitive societies mistook the nature of the world by attributing efficacy to ritual or magical action. Anthropologists, after all, have been deeply engaged with the issues of how to think of language, gesture, and performance in rituals (and religion) as not simply evidence about how mistaken primitive societies were about the nature of the world but about something else—be that society, cosmology, concept formation, or efficient (as opposed to material) causation as found, respectively, in Émile Durkheim ([1912] 1971), Claude Lévi-Strauss (1966), Eduardo Viveiros de Castro (1992), and E. E. Evans-Pritchard ([1937] 1976). More generally, we might ask how to think of the real in relation to what some call semantic opacity of rituals (Severi [2007] 2015) and others call the braiding of the ordinary and the extraordinary in the form of miracles (de Vries 2001)?

The concepts that I signal in the title of this essay—mistake, error, and superstition—have some resemblance to each other, but there also subtle differences between them, of which Wittgenstein gives us a detailed geography. The cases that interest him most, though, are those in which we are misled by our language either because it captures us within a given picture of the real or because it goes idling. How are such cases to be brought to the surface of our thought? What is the harmony between language and the world that is implied here? When is a statement to be seen as a mistake, when an error, when superstition, and what might be the stakes in distinguishing them?[2] I do not discuss here the notion of shadows that are always present as the potential of a word, allowing it to move to new contexts, for they do not play exactly the same role that errors and superstitions do. Instead, they block the notion of a straightforward or obvious way in which words or gestures might be aligned to the world through aspects of reference. In *Philosophical Investigations* (the therapeutic voice?), Wittgenstein says: "My aim is to teach you to pass from a piece of disguised nonsense to something that is patent nonsense" (Wittgenstein [1958] 1973: §465).[3] What is the nature of the disguised nonsense in Frazer as Wittgenstein sees it?

Let us first consider how Wittgenstein makes a distinction between mistake (or error) and superstition (see Travis 2009).[4] As distinct from a mistake, Wittgenstein seems to suggest, superstition is something produced through

---

2. I leave for the moment the intriguing discussion of nonsense that would take us to the difficult questions of not only sense and reference but also whether meaning resides in words or sentences, and the distinction between nonsense as gibberish versus patent nonsense, which is illuminating. In the latter case, as for instance when a sentence is not a syntactic mess—it looks as if it could make sense but on close examination is revealed to be nonsense—we need to examine each sentence for its alignment with the world in a different way than in cases of pure gibberish (see Conant and Diamond [2004] and Williams [2004] for a very interesting debate on the status of nonsense in the *Tractatus*). I have elsewhere examined how the question of words in and out of sentences is engaged in grammatical and ritual theory in Sanskrit—the echoes of some of that discussion resonate here (see Das 2016).

3. The distinction between disguised nonsense and patent nonsense is interesting because Frazer's sentences are not quite gibberish—so finding why they make no sense is a task one sets oneself—it is not obvious.

4. One could make finer distinctions—for instance, error refers to opinions whereas mistakes might be made due to misunderstandings or because, in the case of language, one is not master of one's expressions. See the distinction J. L. Austin makes between abuses and misfires (Austin 1962: 16, 18) as two different ways in which a performative utterance can fail.

grammatical illusions (grammar in the sense of philosophical grammar or criteria that are grown within a form of life), leading to the feeling that something that is quite banal or commonplace is really exciting and in need of explanation. One example Charles Travis (2009) gives from *Philosophical Investigations* (hereafter PI) is of the child amazed that a tailor could sew a dress, imagining that he had nothing else to work with except his hands and pieces of thread. Thus, a casual expression—a tailor made me this dress—becomes the cause of excitement, if (mis)interpreted as the extraordinary event of the dress being produced by sewing, adding one thread on another without the materiality of the cloth (see PI: §195). Wittgenstein then seems to fault Frazer not simply because he read expressive acts as statements of fact but also because he wrongly added excitement to ritual acts without seeing what kind of geography of description could provide the scaffold that supports them. I submit that much is at stake here because it misleads Frazer into a direction that turns out to be fatal for understanding how to render cultural difference and context-saturated meaning into a problem for anthropological thought. One of the paragraphs in *Philosophical Investigations* concludes by saying, "When we do philosophy, we are like savages, primitive people, who hear the expressions of civilized men, and then draw the queerest conclusions from it" (PI: §194). Frazer's superstition then consists in having taken a routine, commonplace occurrence within a ritual complex and added false excitement to it. We shall see what is the source of this excitement a little later—for now I want to draw out a little more of what it means to think of ritual actions as expressions that are both set apart from the mundane and are yet commonplace. As Michael Lambek (2007) has observed, religious utterances, although different from extraordinary utterances or everyday acts, are not extraordinary either since they entail nothing more than slight shifts and reframing of ordinary speech and ordinary acts. He suggests that we might regard such acts as parasitical on ordinary acts, producing what he calls the mystery of the ordinary in that it can produce this newness, this something other than itself.

Let me suggest here a slightly different inflection, taking an example from the conflict of interpretations around a simple ritual gesture for the fulfillment of a wish and the argument and counterargument that follows between the critics and defenders of the *mimamsa* school of Indian philosophy (see Das 1983, 2016). The critics ridicule the proponents of mimamsa for countless injunctions, such as the one in which someone desirous of sons should boil bits of gold, much as one boils grains of rice, as an offering to be made in the sacrificial ritual. The critics say that everyone knows that grains of rice can be boiled to cook them and they will satisfy hunger, but not pieces of gold. The reply from the defenders of the mimamsa is a calm assertion that indeed, that criticism holds true for action in the mundane world, but the injunction pertains to sacrificial action and thus has no relevance for action in the mundane world. What the defenders of the mimamsa achieve here is to restore calm to what otherwise might have become an argument about the truth or falsity of such ritual actions. I suggest that though we know that the sacrificial arena is a bounded one in which actions and expressions are imbued with heightened intensity, they do not necessarily challenge the common background of our everyday life.

Consider the following remark that Wittgenstein offers in his criticism of Frazer:

> I would like to say: nothing shows our kinship to those savages better than the fact that Frazer has at hand a word as familiar to us as "ghost" or "shade" to describe the views of these people.
>
> (For this surely is something different from what it would be if he were to describe, say, how the savages imagined that their heads would fall off when they have slain an enemy; in this case, *our description* would have nothing superstitious or magical about it.)
>
> Yes, the strangeness of this relates not only to the expressions "ghost" and "shade," and far too little is made of the fact that we count the words "soul" [*Seele*] and "spirit" [*Geist*] into our own civilized vocabulary. Compared to this, it is a minor detail that we do not believe that our soul eats and drinks. (#23)

What I take from this remark is that the familiar word "ghost" gestures to the fact that an understanding derived from the common background of our lives as humans is implicated in the description of "savage" customs. The fact that Frazer can use such words at hand as "ghost" and "shade" connects our life to that of the so-called savages, gives us a footing in that life—their customs can be imagined within our form of life as a "human" form of life. If, on the other hand, someone had reported that the savage belief is that their own heads simply fall off the body when they kill an enemy (and are put back when the need arises), we would not know how to relate to such a description and would consider that we were, perhaps, not of the same flesh, or that their ideas of what are heads and where they belong on the body are perhaps in need of a completely different description. The mimamsa scholars were able to preserve the integrity of the everyday when they desisted from saying that boiled pieces of gold were a perfect substitute for cooked rice. In that case, it would have been perfectly right to add excitement to what was commonplace in the way rituals were enacted. Let us take one more example of what Wittgenstein means by the harmony between language and the world, and in what way Frazer seems to him to have violated a much more important aspect of what we might mean by thinking than simply to have committed an error by mistaking symbolic expressions for factual statements.

Consider: "The agreement, harmony, of thought and reality consists in this: if I say falsely that something is *red*, it nonetheless isn't *red*. And if I want to explain to someone the word "red" in the sentence 'That isn't red,' I point to something red" (PI: §429; see Travis 2009 for a detailed discussion of this example). The point here is that the issue is not if the statement is *true* or *false* according to whether the thing pointed to is red or not but, rather, if it *could have* been red or not-red (Travis 2009). In other words, in speaking of shoes being red, there should be at least the possibility that they could be red. In this sense, the truth of a statement and the falseness of a statement are not states that completely exclude each other. Statements and facts, so to say, are not simply made for each other as gloves and hands are—as J. L. Austin said, there are different dimensions and degrees of success that statements achieve—part of this depends on whether a space has been prepared for a particular kind of statement or not (Austin 1950). In the context of the fire festivals, Frank Cioffi ([1987] 1998) takes Wittgenstein to be saying that when we consider the sinister character attributed to these festivals in their contemporary enactment, it is the space that the story finds already prepared for it that has to be scrutinized and not only the space that the events themselves might occupy.[5] So what Frazer fails to understand is not so much this or that fact about the fire festivals but the nature

5.   Frank Cioffi's (1990) later discussion on "Wittgenstein and Obscurantism" charges Wittgenstein with methodological obscurantism, for passing his epistemic preference for a methodological one in refusing to entertain any historical explanation for the feeling of dread that the contemplation of the fire festival evokes. Speaking up for the relevance of such explanations, Cioffi states that Catholic confession, for instance, can be explained by Catholic dogma, but in a counterargument one may say, surely, Catholic dogmas about apostolic succession, priestly ordination, and the power to absolve the sinner belong to the same practice of confession, the conditions of its emergence within this form of life—they are not "explanations" of the confessional practices (see Hacker 1992).

of the problem he is supposed to be resolving. (Consider also Wittgenstein's discussion of pain: I have no pain in my arm, to ask, in what sense does my present painless state contain the possibility of pain [PI: §448]? Elsewhere he asks, Does what is ordinary always make the impression of ordinariness [PI: §600]? And now we can understand the importance Wittgenstein attributes to the fact that Frazer uses words like "ghost" or "shade"—words that might suggest the uncanny but in a way that gestures to their already having a home in our language.)

A second important theme that makes a considerable impression on Wittgenstein is the deep (and sinister) character of magic. What makes magic deep, he asks? Why do we get the sensation of something deep and sinister in the contemplation of human sacrifice? For Frazer, the traces of human sacrifice are particularly clear and unequivocal in the Beltane Fire Festival, which involves the mock threat of burning a human victim selected arbitrarily by the ritual use of a cake prepared for this very purpose. For Wittgenstein, such an evocation of human sacrifice that is supposed to lie at the origin of the festival explains nothing in itself—in order to understand why a deep and sinister feeling is created we would have to look at present practices and not the putative origin of the offering in the fire festival. Similarly, the explanation that the priest-king must be "killed in his prime because according to the notion of the savages, his soul would not be kept fresh otherwise" (#1), which impresses Frazer, cannot be made to do much work here. As Thomas Zengotita (1989) says of this explanation, "What should we make of it? According to Wittgenstein, nothing much." Instead, we should ask what kind of experiences did such thoughts evoke in Frazer himself? Let us listen to Wittgenstein once again:

> What I want to say is this: what is sinister, deep [about all this] does not lie in how the history of this practice actually went, for perhaps it did not go that way at all; nor that it maybe or [even] probably went that way, but in what gives me reason to assume so. What makes human sacrifice so deep and sinister in the first place? For is it only the suffering of the victim that impresses us thus? All manners of illnesses bring about just as much suffering, and yet do not evoke this impression. No, this deep and sinister aspect does not become self-evident just from our knowledge of the history of the external actions; rather, we impute it to them [reintroduce it into them] on the basis of an inner experience of our own. (#43)

I think there are two remarkable things Wittgenstein achieves here. First, he redefines depth not as vertical, inward depth (Zengotita 1989) but as spread out into the context. Second, he turns Frazer's interpretations to reflect on what these can tell us about English society through the various incipient rituals we construct every day, such as addressing our illness or hitting a rock to "punish" it. In other words, the reflexive gesture that many anthropologists made by asking what the interpretation of a ritual tells us about the discursive power or desire of the observer (see, for example, Scott 1994; Povinelli 2002) is evoked here not only to fault Frazer for his interpretation of these rituals but also to illuminate an aspect of our form of life as a human form of life.

Returning to the first point, take the concluding sentences of Remark #42. Wittgenstein states:

> The question is: Does this—shall we say—sinister character adhere to the custom of the Beltane fire in itself as it was practiced a hundred years ago, or only if the hypothesis of its origin were to be confirmed. I believe that what appears to us as sinister is the inner nature of the practice as performed in recent times, and the facts of human sacrifice as we know them only indicate the direction in which we ought to look at it. When I speak of the inner nature of the practice, I mean all of those circumstances in which it is carried out and that are not included in the report on such a festival, because they consist not so much in particular actions that characterize the festival than in what one might call the spirit of the festival that would be described, for example, if one were to describe the kind of people that take part in it, their usual way of behaving [on other occasions]—that is, their character—and the kind of games they play at other times. And then one would see that what is sinister lies in the character of these people themselves. (#42)

The remarkable point here is that experience is not located in the vertical depth of the subject but in the dispersal of activities—the saturation of meaning by a recounting of what constitutes "context." Note that Wittgenstein is not picking up only certain features of language (e.g., the use of indexicals) as connecting language to the world; instead, he is positing the character of worldliness or context-saturated character of language as a whole (see Moyal-Sharrock 2009). If further support was needed for this point, we could read *Philosophical Investigations*, in which Wittgenstein takes the sentence, "He measured him with a hostile glance and said . . ." (PI: §652) and asks how a reader of a narrative in which this sentence appears guesses at or supplies the meaning of this sentence. After all, the narrative might show the hostile glance later to be a pretense, or the reader may be kept in suspense about whether or not these words are pretense—so the reader is challenged to guess at a possible interpretation. "But then the main thing he guesses at is context." In other words, ordinarily we just take the words to mean what they say but when planted with a doubt (were these two men friends or enemies?), what we have to guess is not the meaning of the words but their context. In order to discern why the fire festivals create a feeling of dread in their modern enactments, we would have to discern the spirit of the festival and not simply particular ritual gestures.

The second point regarding the similarity between our customs and theirs is well illustrated in the examples Wittgenstein gives of kissing a picture of the beloved not because we are in error in thinking that the picture *is* the loved one but because it satisfies a wish:

> Burning an effigy. Kissing the picture of a loved one. This is *obviously not* based on a belief that it will have a definite effect on the object that the picture represents. It aims at some satisfaction, and does achieve it, too. Or rather, it does not *aim* at anything; we act in this way and then feel satisfied. (#9)

I cannot pursue the theme of what "feeling satisfied" tells us about the relation between, say, a wish and its satisfaction; an expectation and its fulfillment; or an order and its execution—except to state that no further evidence as to the truth or falsity of such statements is asked for. Wittgenstein gives us whole range of examples in which it would be absurd to say that an error was committed, since these are not, in the first place, matters of opinion and thus cannot be true of false. In drawing connections between our practices and those that Frazer evokes as evidence of primitive mentality, Wittgenstein's aim is to arrive at what he calls a perspicuous arrangement. He makes the case that, "A perspicuous representation produces just that understanding which consists in 'seeing connexions.' Hence the importance of finding and inventing *intermediate* cases" (PI: §122).

The effort that Wittgenstein makes in arranging the cases in a way that we can see connections (see also Sachs 1988) has the effect of taking away the excitement that superstition adds to what might be banal actions or those expressions produced through grammatical illusions. Moreover, his further achievement is to suggest that there is a background of common sense that we might identify as part of the human way of life—but we must pause and ask what notion of human informs him here? The best guide for making our way through this question is not the "universalism versus relativism" debate but the frequent references to the natural history of mankind, which are related equally to our being embodied creatures and creatures who have a life in language. Wittgenstein says, "commanding, questioning, recounting, chatting, are as much a part of our natural history as walking, eating, drinking, playing" (PI: §25). Thus what we do as embodied creatures (walking, eating) and as creatures who have a life in language (recounting, questioning) are not laid along the axis of nature and culture but rather along the axis of a "natural history" of mankind.

Finally, consider one of the last three passages in *Philosophical Investigations*:

> If the formation of concepts can be explained by facts of nature, should we not be interested, not in grammar, but rather in that in nature, which is the basis of grammar? —Our interest certainly includes the correspondence between concepts and very general facts of nature. (Such facts as mostly do not strike us because of their generality.) But our interest does not fall back upon these possible causes of the formation of concepts; we are not doing natural science; nor yet natural history—since we can also invent fictitious natural history for our purposes. (PI 230ᵉ)

The ideas here are of rightness, fitness, of our expressions carrying greater natural weight in a way that we might come to feel that our language and world are in harmony with each other. Thus, how we choose and value words is not about (or not only about) having a common framework for interpreting the meaning of what is said but what the person means in saying them—the sense in which one's words are an expression of what matters to one and of the rightness in relation to context. "The whirl of organism" that Wittgenstein alludes to in reference to forms of life refers in part to what Austin characterized as made possible by our ordinary language: It "embodies all the distinctions men have found worth drawing and the connections they have found worth marking in the lifetimes of many generations" (Austin 1957: 8). It is also made possible partly because we share a sense of the natural, as in Austin's example that one cannot say, "I stepped on the baby inadvertently." It is not that the sentence is not grammatical in terms of linguistic rules or that the sentence does not make sense treated just as a sentence; it is that the sense of one's natural attitude to how your body is in relation to that of a baby lying on the floor or on the grass perhaps, makes no sense when one uses the term "inadvertently," for it takes us to regions of life one does not normally inhabit (humans, we might say, don't inadvertently step on a baby). If one had said instead, "I stepped on the child accidentally," that would be a possible construction, for such accidents do happen. Here Austin shows the intimacy between language and the world by bringing expression in harmony with action that alludes to distinctions (inadvertently and accidentally) as natural to our way of being in the world. As Sandra Laugier (2018) puts it, for Austin, the statement fits the facts in different ways, on different occasions, for different intents and purposes—"fits" does not carry any sense of correspondence or even correctness but, rather, it designates the character of the utterance in particular circumstances, for particular interests. Does this mean that there are no overarching norms for rightness of usage? The point is that such norms are context bound and hence no general theory can be offered that would cover all situations.

My goal here has not been to give a chronological account of what I think are seminal concepts that link our understanding of different forms of life to our form of life as humans, but instead to say that Frazer provided an important provocation to Wittgenstein as to how we might see other forms of life as both ours and theirs, much as our own forms of life fold the natural and the social, modes of living and modes of dying into each other. In my own remarks on specific paragraphs in *Remarks on Frazer*, I will try to say how attunement and absorption in the world through our agreements in our forms of life does not exclude the idea that we might have been otherwise than we are. This register of the subjunctive mood is particularly appropriate to think of the domains of rituals and myths through bringing Wittgenstein into anthropology (see Das 1998).

PART II: REMARKS ON FRAZER

I was encouraged to comment on the following remarks: 27, 28, 29, 30, 32, 34. And though initially I felt a sense of panic because I could not get a handle on them, I found, to my surprise, that they opened up another region of Wittgenstein's thought that connected to the anthropological mode of thinking. However, it is important to note that these remarks seem to stand as reflections that show our familiarity with many of the rituals and highly formalized gestural languages in other forms of life. Yet they begin by asking, How might I make these actions significant to myself?

27. I could imagine that I might have had to choose some being on earth as my soul's dwelling place, and that my spirit had chosen this unsightly creature as its seat and vantage point. Perhaps because the exception of a beautiful dwelling would repel him. Of course, for the spirit to do so, he would have to be very sure of himself.

Commentary: Zengotita (1989) makes the point that in suggesting that depth is not about inward depth but about connections, Wittgenstein spreads out subjectivity into context, which results in the radical move of dissolving the Protestant or Cartesian subject. Similar to the imagination that my pain could be in another body (Das 2007), Wittgenstein is also provoking us to imagine that the boundaries of our body are not the boundaries of our subjectivity for our existence is always capable of being more, or other, than its present realizations. For all our worldliness, then, we might never be fully at home in any particular world. Might one then think of ritual as one way of imagining: What if the world was otherwise? In my reading, then, this thought could morph into the deep skepticism that might destroy my everyday life or, conversely, it might show that the ability to imagine a different everyday (or eventual everyday) is part of the actual everyday.

How have anthropologists addressed this problem of the subjunctive mood? A promising move is made by Adam Seligman, Robert Weller, Michael Puett, and Bennett Simon (2008: 17–42), who start a substantive chapter on "Ritual and the Subjunctive" by declaring that ritual creates a shared and conventional world of human sociality but that "such a world is always subjunctive, just one possible alternative" (2008: 17). An important example of such a subjunctive world that Seligman, Weller, Puett, and Simon give is that of creating certain social illusions by our everyday practices of politeness, for instance. Rituals of politeness, they suggest, posit a possible world of activity that pulls its practitioners outside the Hobbesian world of war of each against all. One problem with this interpretation is that the authors seem to posit the world of polite interactions as "illusory," since the sense of options created for a child who may be pleased to pass the salt in everyday domestic interactions is illusory—for can't we *command* her to pass the salt or grab the salt cellar from her, making the "please" a fiction? However, the authors slip into a position in which they seem to implicitly attribute "reality" to the Hobbesian world of war of each against all rather than treating it as part of the mythical world of the state of nature, a fiction created to authorize a certain form of sovereignty. Then there are two forms of fiction circulating as part and parcel of the actual world, rather than the world created through ritual being illusory and the other world of conflict or power being real.

In Wittgenstein's account, possibility was the space prepared for a particular statement or story to find a footing, not simply an alternative to actuality. How might such a story as imagining a myth of origin for oneself, in which one's decaying or unsightly body was what one's spirit had chosen as the best picture or the best dwelling place for itself, find a footing in the world? Are the senses of the subjunctive different in Wittgenstein's "I could imagine" remark versus what Seligman, Weller, Puett, and Simon describe? Both accounts address the issue of how the inner and the outer are stitched together but take us in fairly different directions.

28.   One could say "every view has its charm," but that would be wrong. What is correct is that every view is significant for whoever sees it so (but that does not mean one sees it as something other than it is). Indeed, in this sense every view is equally significant.

Yes, it is important that I must make my own even any one's contempt for me, as an essential and significant part of the world seen from my vantage point.

Commentary: The theme here relates to how one might make one's life significant to oneself, or in Stanley Cavell's signature idea, What is it to find one's voice in one's own culture? Laugier (2011) argues that whereas for Wittgenstein the central question was the common use of language, Cavell makes a new question arise from that problematic—the question of the relation between an individual speaker and the linguistic community. "For Cavell, this leads to a reintroduction of the voice into philosophy and to a redefinition of subjectivity in language precisely on the basis of the relationship of the individual voice to the linguistic community: the relation of a voice to voices" (Laugier 2011: 633). In Remark 28, the issue is not only establishing the relation of my body and my soul or the alignment between them alone but also seeing singularity within the domain of culture. Every view to be found in a given form of life acquires significance as it is made part of one's own disposition, or one's vantage point on one's culture (see Hage 2015), but not when seen as if in a catalogue of beliefs testifying to the internal pluralism or internal heterogeneity of a culture. What is at stake here is not a parabolic insistence on the significance of one's existence or the uniqueness of one's experience, as in Cavell's (1976) famous discussion: "But surely you cannot be having THIS pain," pointing to one's chest and thumping it. Rather, the insistence is on the work of making my voice *count*, on taking the facts of my existence upon myself. In saying that taking someone else's contempt for myself as part of how the world is for me, I attest to my singular vantage point on the world.

I am particularly interested here in pursuing the idea of what it means to take the facts of my existence upon myself through aligning myself to ritual performances, whether religious or secular. One way we could approach this question is by asking what is it for one to be attached to the words one utters, the gestures one makes, and thus taking an external performance as attesting to an internal state? Austin (1962) famously saw a promise as the outward and visible sign (initially read so for convenience or for some similar reason) that was read as indicative of an inward and spiritual act. From there, he said, it is a short step to assume that the outward utterance is a description, true or false, of the occurrence of an inward act. Thus, for instance, we begin to ask if the person who promised to come back tomorrow meant his words or not. Austin's point, of course, was that at least as far as illocutionary force of an utterance was concerned, the officiating priest did not have to be sincere in declaring someone man and wife. The external performance was not stitched to an inner state of sincerity—if all the conventions were in place for the marriage to be accomplished, his words would accomplish it. If such utterances, such as making a promise, were to be regarded as the prototype of all ritual utterances, then collective performances do not have to be translated into any evidence of inner attachment. Then, the kind of pressure Wittgenstein is putting on "making my own" the viewpoints I encounter would not carry weight. But matters are, of course, more complicated.

First, as Cavell (1994) brilliantly demonstrated, there are different moments in the performance of such ritual enactments as a marriage ritual. It may be sufficient for the presiding priest to utter the correct formulas without raising issues of sincerity or attachment to those words, but the man who says "I do" had better not be a bigamist who intends to cheat the bride of her inheritance. Thus, the issues of how one makes the collective words one's own: the relationship between the third-person statements of belief and the first-person statements of belief becomes an urgent issue. After all, I do not come to know my belief in the same way as I get to know the beliefs of others—nor do I have to examine myself to see if I am in pain. These are all matters that call for attention to our singular relations to the world and cannot be derived from generalized descriptions.

An intriguing aspect of Wittgenstein's remarks is his insistence that my view of the world must also include the viewpoint of those who have contempt for me. It makes me think of the anthropological studies of certain castes or sects that were despised for either the lowly tasks they performed (Parry 1994) or for their transgressive practices (Suri and Pitchford 2010). Parry, for instance, describes how the Mahabrahmans, a caste of funeral priests who make their living on the funeral gifts they receive, feel that their work of absorbing the death pollution of others makes them open to misfortunes and feelings of ill-being. The ritual acts of eating the sins of others makes them wealthy but also makes their bodies heavy, slothful, unlike the bodies of those who earn their living with the sweat of their brow. The Aghoris, a sect known for its transgressive and even repulsive practices (such as eating corpses, living in cremation grounds), on the other hand, seem to convert their intimacy with death as life giving to others, much as Lord Shiva made the gods immortal by taking poison that had emerged in the churning of the sea upon himself. Such research on the ways in which individuals might integrate the contempt of others into their own perspective on the world still remains fragmentary, since anthropologists have not given sustained attention to the relation between the absorption of the third-person perspective on one's ritual role and the first-person account of how this provides a vantage point for singular individuals.[6]

29. If a human being were free to choose to be born in a tree in the forest, then there would be some who would seek out the most beautiful or highest tree for themselves, some who would choose the smallest, and some who would choose an average or below-average tree, and I do not mean out of philistinism, but for just the reason, or the kind of reason for which someone else chose the highest. That the feeling we have for our

---

6. Although the theme of religion and emotion has received attention in the work of Saba Mahmood (2005) and Charles Hirschkind (2006), exemplary for some purposes, these authors take subjectivity to be the same as the process of subjectivation—hence the individuals cited in their accounts all speak as generalized subjects representing "typical experiences" rather than as singular ones. For an account of the general theme of religion and emotion, see François Berthome and Michael Houseman (2010)

life is comparable to that of a being that could choose its standpoint in the world has, I believe, its basis in the myth—or belief—that we choose our bodies before birth.

Commentary: My remark here is based on my somewhat shaky and intermittent understanding that Wittgenstein is using a philosophical allegory to contest the Cartesian allegory, in which I am able to doubt if my body is mine but not if my mind is mine. The fate of the human body in philosophy appears in many places in *Philosophical Investigations* and in *On Certainty* (Wittgenstein [1958] 1973, 1974 respectively). I offer the suggestion that we could learn something about how Wittgenstein's remark about the human body being the best picture of the human soul (PI: §178) might be illuminated through a comparison with the intimate relations he posits between a word and its meaning. Elsewhere, he speaks about imagining a language in which use of the idea of "soul" of the words plays no part. "In which, for example, we had no objection to replacing one word by another arbitrary one of our invention" (PI §530). But this paragraph immediately draws comparison with Wittgenstein's evocation of a people who are "soul blind" and to Wittgenstein's pointing us to the feeling we have for the physiognomy of words. Our relation to our body, then, is not simply that of imagining it as an arbitrary relation—any more than we can simply replace one word by another by consulting a dictionary, almost as if our words did not matter to us—what then shall we make of the last line of Remark 29? I believe what is being suggested here is that our feelings about the rightness of our bodies as somehow fitting for us is similar to our feelings for our life as a whole—not simply the rightness of this or that action that we perform (see Das 2015).

What about the fact, then, that in many cases techniques of the body are about our bodies being able to give expression to other bodies, such as bodies of animals or bodies of plants, as in many yoga postures (Alter 2004)? Or the fact that in Amerindian mythologies, humans might make their home in human bodies or in animal bodies (Descola 1992, 2009; Vilaça 2005)? Of course, if our relation to our body might be that of having to contain or release the animal that is housed in it—as in all the talk of "animal spirits"—then there should be no difficulty in imagining that there are also humans in animal skins. What might distinguish a café skeptic's formulations on all these possibilities of human and animal bodies from the range of practices encountered, say, in the life of a yogi or a family with a jaguar brother-in-law is the fact that the feeling we have of our life as a whole comes not from one or another myth or item of belief but from the sense of what it is to live *this* life and not another? Of course, it is also true that one might not simply have the feel for the kind of life that one's culture requires of one, like the young head of a farm family in the Bocage who must learn to vanquish the claims of others on the land but may have no inclination for violence and hence must be brought into it through practices of, say, witchcraft (see Favret-Saada 2015). This is the stuff of the tragedy of having a body, unless of course, you can find its comedy—of which, too, Wittgenstein offers many examples.

30.   I believe the characteristic feature of primitive man is that he does not act on the basis of *opinions* (as Frazer thinks).

Commentary: Let us pair this remark with *Philosophical Investigations*:

> So you are saying that human agreement decides what is true and what is false?"
> —It is what human beings *say* that is true and false; and they agree in the *language* they use. This is not agreement in language but in form of life. (PI: §241)

And now consider:

> My attitude toward him is an attitude toward a soul. I am not of the *opinion* that he has a soul. (PI: §178)

Did Frazer think primitive man acted on the basis of opinions? I believe what Wittgenstein is identifying as "opinion" is the form of argumentation Frazer often resorts to, in which a custom is explained by citing a participant's view of what he or she is doing when following a custom. Thus, early on in *Golden Bough*, Frazer explains: "The notion that a person can influence a plant homeopathically by his act or condition comes out clearly in a remark made by a Malay woman. Being asked why she stripped the upper part of her body naked in reaping the rice, she explained that she did it to make the rice-husks thinner, as she was tired of pounding thick-husked rice. Clearly, she thought that the less clothing she wore the less husk there would be on the rice" (Frazer [1922] 2004: 32). In many ways, anthropology has moved far beyond this mode of "explaining" the meaning of a ritual with our advances in semiotic or hermeneutic interpretation of the ritual complex. Yet, Wittgenstein seems to me to discern an important question—namely, when and how do we know that what is being said is an indicative statement, an order, a proposition, the expression of a wish, or something else? It is the nature of our agreements that tell us the difference between these forms of talk, and yet this agreement is not simply over a particular speech act but over criteria grown within a form of life. The methodological imperative to bring context centrally into the analysis of speech acts by attention to metapragmatic signaling grew in response to some of these issues. However, it is worth asking how much the emphasis on what is formulaic (e.g., speech acts with illocutionary force) or what can be elicited in speech by way of explanation of what is happening orients our analysis toward certain objects of analysis (e.g., declarations of sovereign subjects in ritual, witchcraft accusations) as compared to other things (discursive and nondiscursive) that are going on both within a ritual or ceremonial occasion and outside it.[7]

32.   It could have been no insignificant reason—that is, no *reason* at all—for which certain races of man came to venerate the oak tree other than that they and the oak were united in a community of life, so that they came into being not by choice, but jointly, like the dog and the flea (were fleas to develop a ritual, it would relate to the dog).

One might say, it was not their union (of oak trees and humans) that occasioned these rites, but, in a certain sense, their separation.

For the awakening of intellect goes along with the separation from the original *soil*, the original ground of life. (The origin of *choice*.)

(The form of the awakening mind is veneration.)

Commentary: There are two thoughts here—one relates to the community of life, and the second to the picture of thought. A community of *life*, suggests Wittgenstein, is a community made up of what sustains life. Here, rituals seem to relate not to arbitrary constructions but to expressions of this mutuality of human and nonhuman in making up the community of life. There is a whole trajectory of anthropological thought we could trace in this connection made between animals and totemic symbols and rites. Are animals chosen because

---

7.   For an acute criticism of the tendency in Anglo-American anthropology to settle on, say, witchcraft accusations as the most important in the understanding of witchcraft because these have the appearance of facts that can be immediately grasped, see Jeanne Favret-Saada (2015).

they are good to eat (Radcliffe-Brown [1929] 1952)[8] or because they are good to think (Lévi-Strauss1966)? Body or Mind? Interestingly, we might go back to a classic such as Durkheim's ([1912] 1971) *Elementary Forms of Religious Life* and discover that while he says somewhat lamely that animals are chosen as totems because they are easy to represent, he also insists that the totemic sign has to be painfully inscribed on the body as a means of making future memory (Das 1995).

And then there is that pretense of community as in sacrificial rituals, the illusions with which we cover our forms of cruelty. "You do not want to kill, O judges and sacrificers until the animal has nodded? Behold, the pale criminal has nodded: out of his eyes speaks the great contempt" (Nietzsche 1961: 35).

In the second part of Remark 32, Wittgenstein gives us a picture of thought that lies in the moment of our separation from the original ground: a picture that takes the moment of detachment as the sign of the awakening mind. This is resonant of how Michael Jackson (2015) formulates his own process of thinking. Yet it seems to me that later, in *Philosophical Investigations*, Wittgenstein has vastly complicated the relation between thinking and awakening of intellect. For example, Wittgenstein asks us to consider what relation solving a mathematical problem has to the context and ground of its formulation (PI: §334). And this is followed by the question as to what happens when we try to find the right expression for our thoughts? Does the thought exist before the expression? And if we say that thinking is an incorporeal process, that makes sense only when we are trying to distinguish thinking from eating—otherwise it is only the picture of things going on in our head that leads us to the idea that thinking can be separated from its context and its ground (see PI: §339). Awakening to my life, I suggest, has a different modality than that of thinking; here, it is helpful to be in company with Cavell on the difference between knowing and acknowledging, and to be mindful of the horror that might come with

---

8. The sharp opposition between "good to eat" and "good to think" that Claude Lévi-Strauss proposed, might be, as he himself acknowledges, softened by tracing what he calls the "evolution" in Radcliffe-Brown's thought. The functionalist explanation, which Lévi-Strauss refers to as his first theory, is summarized as follows: "According to Radcliffe-Brown's first theory, as for Malinowski, an animal only becomes 'totemic' because it is 'good to eat'" (Lévi-Strauss 1964: 62). However, he also acknowledges that for Radcliffe-Brown, as for Durkheim, the problem of totemism was to be placed within the larger issue of the way in which nature was incorporated within the social. See also Milton Singer (1984).

the success of knowledge, as when reason itself becomes demonic (see Cavell 1976; Das 2015).

While I do not have the space to elaborate this distinction in greater detail, I point to the discussion on the fatality of the "success of knowledge" as discussed by Cavell through the figure of Faust. "If there were a drama of pure knowledge, it seems that Faust must be its protagonist. But is Faust a tragic figure? Is he to be understood in terms of the light of skepticism? Skepticism, after all, has to do with the absolute *failure* of knowledge, whereas what Faust lived was the absolute *success* of knowledge. But apparently what he is to have discovered about this success is that it is not humanly satisfying. He is the Midas of knowledge" (Cavell 1979: 455).

In other words, the success of knowledge is that if I allow myself to trust only that which I have come to know through the application of rational procedures, then I am bound to turn reason against itself much as Midas was bound to turn his golden touch against his own children. One instance of the application of the idea of reason turning demonic is that it blocks us from accepting such things as the humanity of the other on trust—demanding evidence where none should be needed; or, it asks for proof for the love of my partner, or the fact (for a man) that my children are mine, or that the groan I hear is, indeed, an expression of pain. The point is not that such doubts might not arise in the weave of life but that they cannot be settled by the production of more and more evidence. The fatal consequences of the success of knowledge can only be mitigated by accepting the other in his or her concrete reality. Wittgenstein, in asking, "How can I prove the existence of the other?" is inclined to turn to the existence of the concrete other in such quotidian scenes as children playing in the street. From the perspective of the one demanding hard evidence, such scenes are not enough to settle the problem of existence—for one who is willing to accept that our agreements are fragile but that these agreements are all we have, doubts are not absolutely extinguished but a way is found to live with them.

34.   (In ancient times he was obliged to sit on the throne for some hours every morning, with the imperial crown on his head, but to sit altogether like a statue, without stirring either hands or feet, head or eyes, nor indeed any part of his body, because, by this means, it was thought that he could preserve peace and tranquility in his empire . . .)

When someone in our (or at least my) society laughs too much, I press my lips together in an almost involuntary fashion, as if I believed I could thereby keep his lips closed.[9]

Commentary: In order to interpret this remark, it is helpful to insert an earlier remark in which Wittgenstein says, "At a certain stage of early society the king or priest is often thought to be endowed with supernatural powers or to be an incarnation of a deity, and consistently with this belief the course of nature is supposed to be more or less under his control" (#33) and then goes on to remark that, "It is of course not the case that the people believe that the ruler has these powers while the ruler himself very well knows that he does not have them, or does not know so only if he is an idiot or fool. Rather, the notion of his power is of course arranged in a way such that it corresponds with experience—his own and that of the people. That any kind of hypocrisy plays a role in this is only true to the extent that it suggests itself in most of what humans do anyway" (#33). The excitement around the idea that the king wrongly believes that sitting still like a statue will ensure peace and tranquility of the empire is taken away by juxtaposing it with the quotidian example of pressing your lips together to block the loud or vulgar laughter of someone in your vicinity, not because you *believe* that it will block this offensive laughter but because a response is drawn out of you. With this perspicuous arrangement, the excitement is removed, and disguised nonsense gives way to patent nonsense.

REFERENCES

Alter, Joseph S. 2004. *Yoga in Modern India: The Body between Science and Philosophy*. Princeton, NJ: Princeton University Press.

Austin, J. L. 1950. "Truth." *Aristotelian Society Supplementary Volume* 24 (1): 111–28.

———. 1957. "A Plea for Excuses: The Presidential Address." *Proceedings of the Aristotelian Society*, n.s., 57: 1–30.

---

9.   Surprisingly, Peter Hacker (1992) takes this involuntary action as an example of an instrumental, albeit naturalized, action. He misses the "as if" and also the fact that an expression may be simply drawn out of us!

————. 1962. *How to Do Things with Words*. Cambridge, MA: Harvard University Press.

Berthome, François, and Michael Houseman. 2010. "Ritual and Emotions: Moving Relations, Patterned Effusions." *Religion and Society* 1: 57–75.

Bouveresse, Jacque. 2008. "Wittgenstein's Critique of Frazer." In *Wittgenstein and Reason*, edited by John Preston, 1–21. Oxford: Blackwell Publishing.

Cavell, Stanley. 1976. *Must We Mean What We Say? A Book of Essays*. Cambridge: Cambridge University Press.

————. 1979. *The Claim of Reason: Wittgenstein, Skepticism, Morality, and Tragedy*. Oxford: Oxford University Press.

————. 1994. *A Pitch of Philosophy: Autobiographical Exercises*. Cambridge, MA: Harvard University Press.

Cioffi, Frank. [1987] 1998. "Wittgenstein and the Fire Festivals." In *Wittgenstein on Freud and Frazer*, 80–106. Cambridge: Cambridge University Press.

————. 1990. "The Inaugural Address: Wittgenstein and Obscurantism." *Proceedings of the Aristotelian Society, Supplementary Volumes* 64: 1–23.

Conant, James, and Cora Diamond. 2004. "On Reading the Tractatus Resolutely: Reply to Meredith Williams and Peter Sullivan." In *Wittgenstein's Lasting Significance*, edited by Max Kolbel and Bernhard Weiss, 46–99. London: Routledge.

Das, Veena. 1983. "Language of Sacrifice." *Man*, n.s., 18 (3): 445–62.

————. 1995. *Critical Events: An Anthropological Perspective on Contemporary India*. Delhi: Oxford University Press.

————. 1998. "Wittgenstein and Anthropology." *Annual Review of Anthropology* 27: 171–95.

————. 2007. *Life and Words: Violence and the Descent into the Ordinary*. Berkeley: University of California Press.

————. 2015. *Affliction: Health, Disease, Poverty*. New York: Fordham University Press.

————. 2016. "Ritual Action and Grammatical Action: Life Lived in Language." Invited Public Lecture. Amherst College, Amherst, MA, March 24.

Das, Veena, Michael Jackson, Arthur Kleinman, and Bhrigupati Singh. 2015. "Introduction: Experiments Between Anthropology and Philosophy: Affinities and Antagonisms." In *The Ground Between: Anthropologists Engage Philosophy*, edited by Veena Das, Michael Jackson, Arthur Kleinman, and Bhrigupati Singh, 1–26. Durham, NC: Duke University Press.

de Vries, Hent. 2001. "Of Miracles and Special Effects." *Issues in Contemporary Philosophy of Religion* 50 (1–3): 41–56.

Descola, Philippe. 1992. "Societies of Nature and the Nature of Society." In *Conceptualizing Society*, 107–26. New York: Routledge.

———. 2009. "Human Natures." *Social Anthropology* 17 (2): 145–57.

Durkheim, Émile. (1912) 1971. *The Elementary Forms of the Religious Life*. Translated by Joseph Ward Swain. London: George Allen and Unwin.

Evans-Pritchard, E. E. (1937) 1976. *Witchcraft, Oracles and Magic Among the Azande*. Oxford: Clarendon Press.

Favret-Saada, Jeanne. 2015. *The Anti-Witch*. Translated by Matthew Carey. Chicago: HAU Books.

Frazer, James. (1922) 2004. *The Golden Bough*. Sioux Falls, SD: NuVision Publications, LLC. eBook.

Hacker, Peter. M. S. 1992. "Developmental Hypotheses and Perspicuous Representations: Wittgenstein on Frazer's 'Golden Bough.'" *Iyyun: The Jerusalem Philosophical Quarterly* 41: 277–99.

Hage, Ghassan J. 2015. "Eavesdropping on Bourdieu's Philosophers." In *The Ground Between: Anthropologists Engage Philosophy*, edited by Veena Das, Michael Jackson, Arthur Kleinman, and Bhrigupati Singh, 138–58. Durham, NC: Duke University Press.

Hirschkind, Charles. 2006. *The Ethical Soundscape: Cassette Sermons and Islamic Counterpublics*. New York: Columbia University Press.

Jackson, Michael. 2015. "Ajala's Heads: Reflections on Anthropology and Philosophy in a West African Setting." In *The Ground Between: Anthropologists Engage Philosophy*, edited by Veena Das, Michael Jackson, Arthur Kleinman, and Bhrigupati Singh, 1–26. Durham, NC: Duke University Press.

Lambek, Michael. 2007. "On Catching up with Oneself: Learning to Know That One Means What One Does." In *Learning Religion: Anthropological Approaches*, edited by David Berliner and Ramon Sarró, 65–82. Oxford: Berghahn.

Laugier, Sandra. 2011. "Introduction to the French Edition of *Must We Mean What We Say?*" *Critical Inquiry* 37 (4): 627–51.

———. 2018. "The Vulnerability of Reality: Austin, Normativity, and Excuses." In *Interpreting J. L. Austin: Critical Essays*, edited by Savas Tsohatzidis, 119–41. Cambridge: Cambridge University Press.

Lévi-Strauss, Claude. 1964. *Totemism*. Translated by Rodney Needham. London: Merlin Press.

———. 1966. *The Savage Mind*. London: Weidenfeld and Nicolson.

Mahmood, Saba. 2005. *Politics of Piety: The Islamic Revival and the Feminist Subject*. Princeton, NJ: Princeton University Press.

Moyal-Sharrock, Danièle, ed. 2004. *The Third Wittgenstein: The Post Investigations Works*. Aldershot, UK: Ashgate.

———. 2009. "Introduction." *Philosophia* 37 (4): 557–62.

Nietzsche, Friedrich. 1961. *Thus Spoke Zarathustra: A Book for Everyone and No One*. Translated by R. Hollingdale. London: Penguin Classics

Parry, Jonathan. 1994. *Death in Banaras*. Cambridge: Cambridge University Press.

Povinelli, Elizabeth A. 2002. *The Cunning of Recognition: Indigenous Alterities and the Making of Australian Multiculturalism*. Durham, NC: Duke University Press.

Radcliffe-Brown, A. R. (1929) 1952. "The Sociological Theory of Totemism." In *Structure and Function in Primitive Society*, 117–33. London: Cohen & West.

Sachs, David. 1988. "On Wittgenstein's *Remarks on Frazer's Golden Bough*." *Philosophical Investigations* 11 (2): 147–50.

Scott, David. 1994. *Formations of Ritual: Colonial and Anthropological Discourses on the Sinhala Yaktovil*. Minneapolis: University of Minnesota Press.

Seligman, Adam B., Robert P. Weller, Michael J. Puett, and Bennett Simon. 2008. *Ritual and Its Consequences: An Essay on the Limits of Sincerity*. New York: Oxford University Press.

Severi, Carlo. (2007) 2015. *The Chimera Principle: An Anthropology of Memory and Imagination*. Translated by Janet Lloyd. Foreword by David Graeber. Chicago: HAU Books.

Singer, Milton. 1984. "A Neglected Source of Structuralism: Radcliffe-Brown, Russell, and Whitehead." *Semiotica* 48 (1–2): 11–96.

Suri, Rochelle, and Daniel B. Pitchford. 2010. "The Gift of Life: Death as Teacher in the Aghori Sect." *Transpersonal Studies* 29 (1): 128–33.

Travis, Charles. 2009. *Thought's Footing: A Theme in Wittgenstein's Philosophical Investigations*. Oxford: Oxford University Press.

Vilaça, Aparecida. 2005. "Chronically Unstable Bodies: Reflections on Amazonian Corporealities." *Journal of the Royal Anthropological Institute* 11 (3): 445–64.

Viveiros de Castro, Eduardo. 1992. *From the Enemy's Point of View: Humanity and Divinity in an Amazonian Society*. Chicago: University of Chicago Press.

Williams, Meredith 2004. "Nonsense and Cosmic Exile: The Austere Reading of the Tractatus." In *Wittgenstein's Lasting Significance*, edited by Max Kolbel and Bernhard Weiss, 6–31. London: Routledge.

Wittgenstein, Ludwig. 1922. *Tractatus Logico-Philosophicus*. London: Kegan Paul.

———. (1958) 1973. *Philosophical Investigations*. Translated by G. E. M. Anscombe. Oxford: Blackwell.

———. 1974. *On Certainty*. Edited by G. E. M. Anscombe and G. H. Von Wright. Translated by Denis Paul and G. E. M. Anscombe. Oxford: Basil Blackwell.

Zengotita, Thomas. 1989. "On Wittgenstein's *Remarks on Frazer's Golden Bough*." *Cultural Anthropology* 4 (4): 390–98.

CHAPTER 9

Remarks on Wittgenstein's *Remarks on Frazer's Golden Bough*: Ritual in the Practice of Life

Michael Lambek

In the course of his life, Ludwig Wittgenstein shifted from writing nested propositions to discrete remarks. These remarks are condensed pictures, intended to show something or present an obvious or hard-won insight, not to construct an argument or provide an explanation. Isadora Duncan is reputed to have responded when asked the meaning of her dance that if she could put it into words she wouldn't have to dance it.[1] I have something like the same apprehension in commenting on Wittgenstein. Had he felt he could express himself (or be understood) in a more discursively elaborated form, he would have done so—and this is also one way to take what he is saying about ritual.

A respectful response to Wittgenstein's remarks is one of emulation, adding further aphorisms that repeat or re-present, or that follow from his own. That is to understand there is no final explanation or hidden code. It is, as Clifford Geertz (1973a: 28–9) has retold the Indian story, turtles all the way

1. To this Stephan Palmié adds, "I think it was Schumann who, when asked what a certain piano concerto meant, sat down and played it again." My thanks to Palmié for a careful reading of the essay. Thanks also to Giovanni da Col and Veena Das for inspiration, to Michelle Beckett for excellent advice, and to the Canada Research Chairs for support.

down. Despite the fact that my commentary fails to reach the density of the aphorism, I would like it to be understood, however immodestly, as "Remarks on Wittgenstein's Remarks on Frazer."

Aphorisms are not syllogisms and they don't link up in the form of an argument. Nor are they necessarily to be taken literally. Instead they show by saying or say by showing, and they pile up on one another, like turtles. They work much as, Wittgenstein argues, magic or religion works—one image, symbol, or ceremony after another. The aphorism, like the rite, exemplifies, pictures, or points rather than explains, theorizes, or hypothesizes. It does not present itself as a correspondence or logical truth, hence the sort of statement that can be evaluated as true or false.

And yet the concept of truth does recur, both in Wittgenstein's language (e.g., in pointing to Frazer's errors) and frequently in religion (that is, in the language games we have come to call religion). Stating the truth, Wittgenstein says, is not sufficient to convince someone who is in error; they need to "find the *way* from error to truth." In this thicket, aphorisms serve as signposts or stepping-stones.

The form of the aphorism approximates iconically the substance of its thought. As Hans Sluga has summarized Wittgenstein's eventual message, what we come up with is not "truths for which our words fail us . . . not unsayable truths but certain practices of life in which we resolve or fail to resolve the problem of the meaning of our existence" (2011: 55). "The meaning of life reveals itself only in the practice of life" (2011: 58).

Stanley Cavell seems to suggest even that the aphorism is no mere language game but a position outside ordinary language games, speaking of the "struggle . . . between the ordinary and the aphoristic (the desire for the transcendental, for a satisfaction out of the ordinary that is not provided by the provision of language games, that indeed will eventually be disappointed by the correction in language games)" (2005: 170).

***

My commentary draws little from Wittgenstein's larger body of work, from either the first, propositional writing, in which there might be unspeakable truths, or from the later, aphoristic writing, in which "truth" disappears in favor of what simply is there to see. My hermeneutic strategy is to move outward and forward in time, to contextualize Wittgenstein's remarks with respect to an anthropology of religion that has long departed from Frazer, in some respects in Wittgenstein's footsteps, albeit his influence on subsequent anthropological work has never been consistent or complete and has been rarely acknowledged directly.[2]

The point is not to use anthropology to empirically validate Wittgenstein's insights, a tactic that would transform and reduce them to hypotheses, which they patently are not, and that might equally distort what it is that anthropology does.

And just what is it that anthropology does? How is it that anthropologists celebrate the brilliance of Godfrey Lienhardt's (implicitly Wittgensteinian) *Divinity and Experience: Religion of the Dinka* (1961) but cannot build on it and too often forget to teach it?

I write as an anthropologist on the subject (it is not an object) of what some-times gets called "religion," or here "magic." Like Wittgenstein and unlike either Frazer or some commentators on Wittgenstein, I do not trouble to distinguish religion from magic, at least not along some kind of hierarchy or linear trajecto-ry of ethics, rationality, or progress. A main difference between "magic" or "rites" (in the sense of Wittgenstein and other writers of his period) and "religion" is that the latter has become objectified, not only as a type but in various histori-cally located holistic tokens—"Christianity," "Hinduism," etcetera. Following Wittgenstein, we could speak more clearly of a series of practices or language games with family resemblances to one another. We could also speak about the historical and political effects of (category) errors (Ryle 1949) when they are committed en masse, as it were.

I take Wittgenstein to be less a social evolutionist than a (limited) kind of relativist, acknowledging cultural difference without placing value judgments. The only exception—obviously a significant one—is that if magical practices are not in error, certain intellectualizing ones are. Wittgenstein is arguing—or rather, showing—that religious and ritual practices persist not in order to explain the world but to many other ends, responses, satisfactions, or inten-tions, such as veneration or wonder,[3] to acknowledge majesty, beauty, fear, the

---

2. An exception is Rodney Needham, starting with his book on belief (1972). Clifford Geertz (1973a) is also deeply informed by Wittgenstein; see Richard Bell (1984) for a useful comparison. A more recent attuned anthropological reading is that of Veena Das (2012).

3. Wittgenstein writes in his Lecture on Ethics that "wonder at the existence of the world" is central to his own experience (Sluga 2011: 54).

inexpressible, and so forth. Yet surely some practitioners (local intellectuals, lay participants, priests, theologians) make the same mistake as Frazer; "primitive man" *does* sometimes act on opinions (#30). Then how are anthropologists to understand such attempts to offer an explanation or assumptions that there must be an explanation? Is this "mistake" itself a mistake (as Frazer saw magic) or simply something else that human beings do (as Wittgenstein saw rites)?[4]

There is something odd or at least paradoxical about this. Whether or not religious practices are the result of an error in reasoning, how are we to think about local theories of practice, justifications, and rationalizations? Whether we see them as containing surface errors or more deeply as the products of a category mistake, do we not approximate again Frazer?

Wittgenstein is open to the entire range of human cultural expressions without a sense of hierarchy, yet he himself is first and foremost a thinker, indeed a fierce one. If knowing, explaining, and philosophizing are not our only relations to the world, surely they still count among the practices of life and are language games connected in various ways to other language games. Wittgenstein himself does not only point to practices like veneration; he demonstrates frustration with his own tendency to argue, and he does argue against the narrow-mindedness of Frazer and of his (Wittgenstein's) fellow philosophers.

Contemporary anthropologists who think they are wiser than Frazer might still ask what Wittgenstein has to teach us not only about the practices we write on but also about our own practices. Do we evade scientism or transcend the divide between rationalism and relativism? Are we empiricists, intellectualists, skeptics, or fervent identifiers in multiple and complex ways with worshippers, shamans, hunters, and harvesters of last sheaves? Do we recognize, any differently than those whom we study, what it is we do?

To put this all another way, we might acknowledge widespread practices of intellectualization with the same open mind Wittgenstein takes to "magic," even as we leave open to question "the cost of our continuous temptation to knowledge" (Cavell 1979: 241).

There is debate whether Wittgenstein holds a position of fideism; that is, that faith is independent of and possibly superior to reason. I suggest a nonfideist reading of the *Remarks*. Wittgenstein shows that ritual is ordinary and panhuman. Moreover, he appears to challenge or ignore any distinction between the natural and the cultural or conventional. Learning language, being brought into

4.   Palmié suggests: secondary rationalizations all the way down.

language and hence into ritual, happens to all human infants in the natural course of events. And ritual action can be a response to environmental phenomena, like thunderstorms or eclipses; sometimes (but not always!) he makes it appear almost an instinct. To be responsive to the majesty of life is the antithesis not of the animal but of the complacency of Wittgenstein's foil, the English parson.

Questions that arise include the following: How distinctive is ritual from other forms of acting or speaking? Is ritual fundamentally parasitic upon—or is it formative of, or a condition for—other forms of speaking and acting? Is ritual intrinsic to social being or is it somehow at arm's length? Is there anything more ordinary than greeting the sunrise or the neighbors, the rainy season (#31) or a new infant—or parting from the deceased? Is this not how human beings live?

Moreover, what is the nature of the boundaries between language games and how are the boundaries crossed? How orderly is the separation of ritual qua language game from other language games? Is it a single game or a series of games holding family resemblances to one another? Does the metaphor of the game not reach its limits for understanding the relationship *between* sets of practices or games, in what is a complex field of relatively unrationalized (in Weber's sense) commensurable and incommensurable relations? Do games not interpenetrate and draw upon one another logically, recursively, practically, referentially, and metaphorically? Is it possible outside of the classroom on logic to distinguish purely rational from metaphorical or poetic speech or to distill purely rational acts from ones of much more complex (or simpler) formation?

Wittgenstein himself recontextualizes his remarks on veneration when he says, "That any kind of hypocrisy plays a role in this is only true to the extent that it suggests itself in most of what humans do anyway" (#33). I would only replace "hypocrisy" in this fine remark with "irony."

Indeed, countering the view that Wittgenstein offers an account of fideism, Richard Amesbury (2012) argues that Wittgenstein

> suggests that the result of "looking" is that "we see a complicated network of similarities overlapping and criss-crossing" ([1953] 1958, I, §66). A metaphor to which he returns periodically is of language as an ancient *city*: "a maze of little streets and squares, of old and new houses, and of houses with additions from various periods; and this surrounded by a multitude of new boroughs with straight regular streets and uniform houses" ([1953] 1958, I, §18). Remarks such as these seem to militate against the balkanized view of language implied by Wittgensteinian Fideism.

I think the question could be better addressed if Wittgenstein were a little clearer on when (or if)[5] he is attributing ritual practice to direct or spontaneous affective responses and when he is acknowledging what is or could be intrinsic to ritual as a *form* of action, irrespective of stimulus, such as the requirement for repetition or imitation or formality or the fact that in ritual what are elsewhere the double functions of the verbs "to act" and "to perform"—as matters respectively of accomplishing or taking action and of pretending or presenting action—appear as a single whole. Thus ritual iteration equally indicates and enacts an action (including acknowledgement, acceptance, commitment, deference, subjection) and expresses what is internal to, or generative from, its particular symbolic matrix and not necessarily what is in the hearts of its performers.[6] And this is also why to take ritual as the unthinking symbolic expression or representation of the social (which in 1960s social anthropology was considered the only alternative to intellectualism) is no better than intellectualism.

Here it is difficult to respond to Wittgenstein's remarks without drawing from hindsight on ideas of category mistakes, illocutionary function, and performative truth that were developed from foundations he established. In particular, J. L. Austin's elucidation of illocutionary acts and functions ([1955] 1965) decisively transcends the opposition between instrumentalism and expressivism in which a number of interpreters of Wittgenstein have been entangled.[7]

Wittgenstein is congenial for anthropologists, first, because whereas many philosophers are stuck in a discourse about "belief" and rationality (attempting thereby either to legitimate or to attack religion), he treats faith not as belief but as a kind of practice, as what we *do*. But then so too is "reason" another kind of practice. Rather than independent, mutually exclusive or contradictory alternatives, the question is how these practices are linked in ordinary life and at their limits.

---

5. Avishai Margalit (1992: 309) claims that Wittgenstein argues that ritual does not respond with wonder but rather produces it.

6. Wittgenstein's argument against private language, and hence for meaning as public, has been developed by Paul Ricoeur (1971) and Geertz (1973a) on action as text and Roy Rappaport (1999) on the canonical dimension of ritual.

7. Discussion of category mistakes is underdeveloped in anthropology, but see Lambek (forthcoming); on performativity see Bloch (1989, 2005), Rappaport (1999), and Tambiah (1985). Rappaport develops distinctions among correspondence, axiomatic, poetic, and performative truths.

Second, unlike most philosophers, Wittgenstein embraces the practices of all humanity, seeing no radical differences between Christians, or for that matter Frazer, and the people about whom Frazer writes or among whom Christians proselytize.

I conclude these brief general remarks with a Wittgensteinian caveat, as expressed by Cavell.

> That the justifications and explanations we give of our language and conduct, that our ways of trying to intellectualize our lives, do not really satisfy us, is what, as I read him, Wittgenstein wishes us above all to grasp. . . . If philosophy is the criticism a culture produces of itself . . . then Wittgenstein's originality lies in having developed modes of criticism that are not moralistic, that is, that do not leave the critic imagining himself free of the faults he sees around him, and which proceed not by trying to argue a given statement false or wrong, but by showing that the person making an assertion does not really know what he means, has not really said what he wished. (Cavell 1979: 175)

Philosophy qua understanding ourselves, and anthropology qua understanding others, and the two combined—understanding others by means of better understanding ourselves; understanding ourselves by means of better understanding others—are forms of therapy that are interminable.

***

5. If one sets the phrase "majesty of death" next to the story of the priest king of Nemi, one sees that they are one and the same.

The life of the priest king represents what is meant by that phrase.

Whoever is gripped by the [idea of] majesty of death can express this through just such a life. —Of course, this is also not an explanation, it just puts one symbol for another. Or one ceremony in place of another.

One symbol for another. This is the chain of metaphor, the complex of metonymy, the constellations that have been described so well in structuralism, nowhere more than in Claude Lévi-Strauss's metaphorical musical scoring of Amerindian mythological transformations ([1964–71] 1969–81). Conversely, symbolic anthropologists have asked, why *this* symbol rather than another? What makes a *compelling* symbol, a compelling ceremony?

The majesty of death does not *explain* the story or ceremony of the priest king any more than the story or ceremony of the priest king explains (the majesty of) death. Nor, avers Wittgenstein, were they intended to do so. Some things cannot be explained. Not that they are simply mysterious but that they are the kinds of things for which explanation is an inappropriate response, a kind of category error. As an anthropologist you shouldn't try to explain the symbol or ceremony, you interpret it and try to locate its power.

Poetic truth differs from correspondence truth or logical truth and is not falsifiable. It is true as a line is true. You either grasp it or you do not.

Insofar as Frazer mistakes a poetic response for an intellectual one, he is in error. And insofar as he then intellectualizes that intellectual response, offering it as a metaexplanation, he is caught in a kind of double error.

Frazer is in error. But there is no reason not to assume that many people throughout history have been Frazerian, seeking explanations for matters where no explanation is either required or possible, where intellectualizing, asking why or how, are the wrong kinds of responses to make. There are many attempts to rationalize poetic responses. Insofar as humans err, this propensity should be as much the subject of philosophical or anthropological inquiry (and not just correction or therapy) as the fact that they acknowledge the majesty of death. In other words, we should be no more dismissive of human error or attempt to reduce it by means of explanation than we are or do of any other human activity. We have to ask (as Wittgenstein does) where the attribution of error is itself an error, where—that is, in what provinces of human life or activity—truth and falsity are not valid or appropriate criteria.

Death is a fact of life whose "majesty" (of a kind) is available even to a non-believer in religion or an afterlife. The majesty of death is not an abstraction but something that grips us. Yet death so frequently passes unnoticed, like a hit-and-run or a drone aircraft, another homeless person or occupant of a hospital bed. Who is there to observe the majesty of these deaths, of death in its singularity? And conversely, who is there to acknowledge the majesty of death in the obscenity of its mass form, in the midst of war or the sinking of a ship overloaded with refugees? Do Frazer or the priest king (or Jesus) step in or is there something intrinsic to human being that is suppressed in such circumstances?

Wittgenstein himself is not making a normative point; he is free of the kind of moralizing I have just indulged in. He is not saying *how* we should respond to death or even *that* we should respond to it. He is saying that as human beings we *do* respond to death and that some of us sometimes respond in a manner that could be called "gripped by the majesty of death" or manifest as the story of the priest king.

***

14. In magical healing one *indicates* to the illness that it should leave the patient. After the description of such a magical cure one wants to say, If the illness doesn't understand *that*, then I don't know *how* else to tell it [to do so].

Action is a form of speaking. The point is to understand it.

Wittgenstein emphasizes that the cure *indicates* something. Such indicating or pointing is linked to the indexical function in Peircean semiotics, but a full curing ritual embraces iconic and symbolic functions as well. Indeed, the poetic aspect of ritual or magic is the subject of many of Wittgenstein's other remarks. Healing rituals include a perlocutionary dimension—persuading the illness to leave—but also carry illocutionary force.[8] Acts of healing also assign or acknowledge responsibility; if the cure is felicitously enacted, improvement will be understood as due to its effects.

Wittgenstein anticipates much anthropological writing on curing rituals, with respect to the rhetorical effects of tropes, narrative, drama, and aesthetics (e.g., Turner 1967; Fernandez 1982; Kapferer 1983; Tambiah 1985; Severi 1987; Boddy 1989; Werbner 2015), and discussions of the placebo effect in biomedicine. What is most distinctive in Wittgenstein's remark is that he depicts the addressee as the illness rather than the patient, healer, or community.[9]

Wittgenstein's remark suggests that the cure works on the moral level, or simultaneously on moral and material levels (mind and body). It addresses the material by means of moral exhortations and the moral by means of material objects and techniques—formal speeches, medicines, sculpted icons, and bodily manipulations. (Whether this is dualism or a function of monism is another matter.)

To illustrate briefly, the cure for sorcery in Mayotte (western Indian Ocean) entailed the dramatic manifestation of harm in the form of a small packet of

---

8.   On illocutionary force in ritual see Bloch (1989); Rappaport (1999). For a mapping of Austin's functions of speech with Peirce's categories of signs see Lambek (2013).

9.   Compare the following, attributed to Voltaire: "The art of medicine consists in amusing the patient while nature cures the diseases."

dirt, broken glass, etcetera that the healer forcibly removed from the patient's body (Lambek 1993).[10] The healer presented the packet to the patient as direct materialization of the sorcery but privately understood it to signify the spirit who had been deployed to harm the patient. Following a successful extraction, and unbeknownst to the patient, the healer struggled with the spirit in his sleep. The cure thereby addressed and persuaded through different registers the patient, the healer, and the cause—working to ensure, in Wittgenstein's terms, that the vehicle of sorcery *understood*.

Sorcery was not the material illness itself—which subsequently could be treated by local herbal remedies or a biomedical doctor—but the moral force inhibiting a straightforward material cure. In the end, it signified the ill will of the sorcerer, his intention that the patient remain unwell, and his acceptance of moral responsibility, whatever the material cause. Illocutionary force is central to understanding what is entailed in both the act of committing sorcery and the act of committing its removal.

Further matters concern the relationship (fit, tension, confusion?) between causes and reasons, the role of performative action and persuasive passion in mediating between them, and whether healing is construed as grammatically transitive or intransitive, finite completed actions or manifest in the doing.[11] Given the inextricable connection of the instrumental and the rhetorical that is characteristic of any cure, is one function understood to have precedence?

We might distinguish between recognizing the availability of certain practices or genres of action (a particular kind of ritual or expression) within a given tradition or form of life, their enactment *in general*, and understanding their use in particular instances, within a given social field (*this person* enacting *this* ritual *now*). This is the difference between accounting for a specific act of prayer for the recovery of one's sick child and accounting for prayer qua canonical text, genre, practice, or language game. The form cannot be explained simply by the function of the instance, as perhaps Bronisław Malinowski tried to do. Thus, the explanation for a given instance of spirit possession does not account for the existence of, or possibility for, possession qua genre of meaningful action. It does not account for possession as a form of life nor what is at stake to live with or

---

10. These observations are based on fieldwork conducted in Mayotte beginning in 1975.

11. See the discussion of transitivity and intransitivity in Said (1975; cf. Lambek 2007).

adjacent to intransigent or irritable beings who can take active possession at any moment. It does not account for spirit possession as an art of living.

* * *

21. Identification of one's own gods with the gods of other peoples. One convinces oneself that the names have the same meaning.

This highly condensed remark could be interpreted along several lines.[12] I will take it as a particularly sharp instance of the translation problem, indeed what Barbara Cassin has called an "untranslatable" in the sense that "to speak of untranslatables in no way implies that the terms in question . . . are not and cannot be translated: the untranslatable is rather what one keeps on (not) translating" ([2004] 2014: xvii).

Translation requires the plowing over of language in order to realize we are not simply replacing one signifier for another. Otherwise translation serves covertly to constitute the objective nature of the signified (perhaps its status, in Ian Hacking's [1999] terms, as a "natural kind"). Thus, the identification of one god with another presupposes and reinforces the existence of such a kind, just as when we translate the word "dog." In the latter case we point to specific instances of the species and can discuss whether dachshund and Doberman fall equally into the category

Are the words for God or gods proper names or simple nouns?[13] Must they be nouns at all? In a language like Malagasy, in which there is no necessary distinction of gender or number, it is less obvious than in English or French that deity is nominalized as a singular or particular being. Indeed, deity could be constituted deictically, with material referents as innumerable as those of "here" and "there" in English (Lambek 2008). That is to say, in some worlds or language games "deity" might serve less as a fixed referent or a discrete entity or person, than as an indexical signifier pointing to something recursive, like the

---

12. In the *Tractatus*, Wittgenstein states:
    3.142   Only facts can express a sense, a set of names cannot.
And:
    3.221   Objects can only be named. Signs are their representatives. I can only speak about them: I cannot put them into words. Propositions can only say how things are, not what they are.

13. Note the capitalization of Doberman but not dachshund.

English word "home," or diffuse, like "power." This could describe the grammatical function of Nuer *Kwoth* (Evans-Pritchard 1956; cf. Lienhardt 1961). "God" in this sense would likely be less transcendent than immanent and less a discrete being than a reminder of being itself.

This is a controversial argument, not least insofar as it suggests that certain societies have no God in the sense we understand that term. While that could be a delight for anthropologists, it has been perceived as a scandal by practitioners of monotheistic religion, who speak of infidels or heathens and who assume, incorrectly, that the absence of a singular (paternal) God indicates an absence of morality, hence a target of disparagement or strenuous efforts at conversion. Anthropologists move between the Scylla of exoticizing people ostensibly "without" God and the Charybdis of painting them ethnocentrically and unimaginatively according to a Christian template of religion.

The puzzle of identification to which Wittgenstein points can be internal to a given tradition as much as between traditions. Arguments about the nature of the trinity have been central to the history of Christianity, while Hinduism is characterized by a multitude of names and materializations of and for deities that are complex refractions of one another.

How could we ever translate ultimate sacred postulates? These are the phrases Roy Rappaport (1999) identifies at the core of religion, whose utterance forms the most elemental yet powerful act and that are characterized as deeply meaningful yet carrying no informational content; an argument, I think, that is in line with the direction of Wittgenstein's remarks. It is true that ultimate sacred postulates can be transliterated, as in "There is no God but God," from the Arabic, but they cannot readily be *translated* between liturgical orders; one cannot simply substitute the Muslim phrase in a Christian or Buddhist ritual.

The translation problem looks different under the distinct semiotic ideologies of different religious and philosophical traditions. For Islam, translation is a nonissue insofar as the Qur'an and the name or names for God are to be uttered in the original. Here the sound is a salient component of the meaning and indeed it is the *act* of utterance, not the reference that is important, entirely in line with Rappaport's argument. Muslims recite the Qur'an in its original form and may never learn the semantic content of phrases whose utterance has so much import for them. By contrast, Christianity has a long history of translating the Bible, including the names of God, hence the postulated identification of gods of which Wittgenstein speaks, like the virgin of Guadalupe whose veneration may replicate or continue that of an Aztec goddess (Wolf 1958). There are compelling accounts of the paradoxes that ensue from the partial identification (or conversely, diabolicization) of strange gods—for example, in the *longue durée* of the Christian encounter with southern Africans (Comaroff and Comaroff 1991) or Biblical translation in Yucatan (Hanks 2010) or Goa (Henn 2014). Spirit possession in both the western Indian Ocean and the Afro-Atlantic worlds (Lambek 1993; Johnson 2014) situates identification as embodied, passionate, ironized performances in a manner that Wittgenstein might have found congenial.

Perhaps one of the factors that makes the charismatic form of Christianity so compelling is that the intellectual problems of identifying or translating God are circumvented by the forceful presence of the Holy Spirit.

***

25. Casting out death or slaying death; but on the other hand he is also represented as a skeleton, as if he were in some sense dead himself. "As dead as death." "Nothing is so dead as death; nothing is so beautiful as beauty herself." Here the image used in thinking of reality is that beauty, death, etcetera are the pure (concentrated) substances, and that they are present in a beautiful object as an admixture. —And do I not recognize here my own observations on "object" and "complex"?

I am not competent to speak of the language of substance and complex from the *Tractatus*, but aside from the chemistry of signs and substances, the point here is very similar to that of #5 above, namely that one symbol replaces or interprets another, with the addition that some representations are particularly salient. A particularly effective illustration of Wittgenstein's point is to be found in Geertz's (1973b: 114–18) depiction of the Balinese witch Rangda, whose hideous masked presence strikes terror in the audience. What constitutes the witch? Looking closely at her dress and mannerisms, it becomes evident that the frightful witch is herself afraid. Geertz cites the observation by Gregory Bateson and Margaret Mead (1942: 36) that "the Witch is not only a fear inspiring figure . . . she is Fear [itself]."

This insight is both ethnographically generalizable and psychologically realistic. An aggressive acquaintance who strikes fear in others is often someone who is deeply paranoid, and one of the frightening things about paranoia is the way it spreads. In Bali, however, the fearful witch is confronted with the comic dragon, who dances playfulness and nonchalance in counterpoint to fear.

The elaborate composition of the performance along with its dramatic (but in Bali, unresolved) trajectory produces an even more complex admixture than Wittgenstein perceives in a single object, or perhaps a recursive and structurally imbricated hierarchy of objects. Such ceremonies enable the deployment of complex ideas, not in the form of rational argument but through juxtaposing moving images. Much as death and beauty can be synthesized (recall Richard Wagner's *Liebestod*), so is comedy often combined with tragedy or fear, low comedy with the high seriousness Protestants attribute to religion. These are not always stable mixtures but highly catalytic. As Geertz says, in such dramas people "attain their faith as they portray it" (1973b: 114).

***

35. (The power of giving or withholding rain is ascribed to him, and he is lord of the winds . . .)

    What is nonsensical here is that Frazer presents it as if these people had an entirely wrong (indeed, insane) notion of the course of nature, while they really only entertain a somewhat peculiar interpretation of the phenomena. That is, if they wrote it down, their knowledge of nature would not be *fundamentally* different from ours. Only their *magic* is different.

Wittgenstein's point that, appearances to the contrary, people have a clear knowledge of "the course of nature" has been rediscovered by many anthropologists. E. E. Evans-Pritchard (1937) noted that Azande know that granaries fall because termites eat the posts; the attribution of witchcraft is relevant only when they collapse while someone is sitting beneath them. The two forms of explanation are not opposed to one another but combine to explain a given event. Azande speak of this with the image of two spears needed to down an elephant.

    Lévi-Strauss (1966) describes the exquisite observational powers of Amerindians with respect to plant and animal species. Philippe Descola (2013) likewise explores Achuar relations with their environment but ends up rejecting—or rather, attempting to transcend—the kind of dualism represented as nature and culture, or as Wittgenstein presents it, knowledge and magic.[14]

---

14. Wittgenstein is evidently not a simple dualist either.

Descola's argument is not specifically monist but discerns four types of ontology from which an understanding of the world takes place. Moreover, dualism is not restricted to the West or to modernity, any more than reason itself is.

We could ask whether one of the advantages of poetic (symbolic) representation over abstract reason—what is created or performed over what is intellectualized—is that it evades or circumvents dualism. Of course, even to phrase things this way is to make recourse to dualism. The trick is to acknowledge and understand the prevalence of *both* dualism and nondualism in human practice and the way they interpenetrate (Lambek 1998, forthcoming).

Wittgenstein is rejecting not simply explanation but explanation in the form of reduction. In Frazer, the reduction is twofold. First, magic serves a function in the absence of something better (a better explanation). Second, action is the direct product or expression of a (faulty) belief or theory. Wittgenstein, by contrast, points to rites as they are—enacted, performed, practical, poetic, and embodied. There is no reduction with respect to function or cause.

And yet perhaps it is not always quite so easy to understand what people are doing or think they are doing with the directness and insightfulness of Wittgenstein's aphorisms. Understanding is realized by tracking the complexity of language to which the *Philosophical Investigations* point, or the multiple layers of contextualization that anthropology raises to theoretical significance and that only sustained ethnography can provide.

One of the attractive features of Wittgenstein's remark is that it implies not only that other societies have a comprehensive knowledge of nature but that "we" too have our magic. At least that is what the wonderful last sentence invites us to discover and acknowledge.

REFERENCES

Amesbury, Richard. 2012. "Fideism." In *The Stanford Encyclopedia of Philosophy (Winter 2012 edition)*, edited by Edward N. Zalta. http://plato.stanford.edu/archives/win2012/entries/fideism/.

Austin, J. L. (1955) 1965. *How to Do Things with Words*. Oxford: Oxford University Press.

Bateson, Gregory, and Margaret Mead. 1942. *Balinese Character*. New York: New York Academy of Sciences.

Bell, Richard H. 1984. "Wittgenstein's Anthropology: Self-understanding and Understanding Other Cultures." *Philosophical Investigations* 7 (4): 295–312.

Bloch, Maurice. 1989. *Ritual, History and Power*. Oxford: Berg.

———. 2005. "Ritual and Deference." In *Essays on Cultural Transmission*, 123–38. Oxford: Berg.

Boddy, Janice. 1989. *Wombs and Alien Spirits*. Madison: University of Wisconsin Press.

Cassin, Barbara, ed. (2004) 2014. *Dictionary of Untranslatables: A Philosophical Lexicon*. Translated by Emily Apter, Jacques Lezra, and Michael Wood. Princeton, NJ: Princeton University Press.

Cavell, Stanley. 1979. *The Claim of Reason: Wittgenstein, Skepticism, Morality, and Tragedy*. New York: Oxford University Press.

———. 2005. "Responses." In *Contending with Stanley Cavell*, edited by Russell Goodman, 157–76. Oxford: Oxford University Press.

Comaroff, Jean, and John Comaroff. 1991. *Of Revelation and Revolution*, vol. 1. Chicago: University of Chicago Press.

Das, Veena, 2012. "Ordinary Ethics." In *A Companion to Moral Anthropology*, edited by Didier Fassin, 133–49. Boston: Wiley-Blackwell.

Descola, Philippe. 2013. *Beyond Nature and Culture*. Translated by Janet Lloyd. Chicago: University of Chicago Press.

Evans-Pritchard, E. E. 1937. *Witchcraft, Oracles and Magic among the Azande*. Oxford: Clarendon.

———. 1956. *Nuer Religion*. Oxford: Clarendon.

Fernandez, James. 1982. *Bwiti: An Ethnography of the Religious Imagination in Africa*. Princeton, NJ: Princeton University Press.

Geertz, Clifford. 1973a. "Thick Description." *The Interpretation of Cultures*, 3–32. New York: Basic Books.

_____ 1973b. "Religion as a Cultural System." *The Interpretation of Cultures*, 87–125. New York: Basic Books.

_____ 1973c. "Deep Play: Notes on the Balinese Cockfight." *The Interpretation of Cultures*, 412–54. New York: Basic Books.

Hacking, Ian 1999. *The Social Construction of What*. Cambridge, MA: Harvard University Press.

Hanks, William. 2010. *Converting Words: Maya in the Age of the Cross*. Berkeley: University of California Press.

Henn, Alexander. 2014. *Hindu-Catholic Encounters in Goa: Religion, Colonialism and Modernity*. Bloomington: Indiana University Press.

Johnson, Paul Christopher, ed. 2014. *The Work of Possession(s)*. Chicago: University of Chicago Press.

Kapferer, Bruce. 1983. *A Celebration of Demons*. Bloomington: Indiana University Press.

Lambek, Michael. 1993. *Knowledge and Practice in Mayotte: Local Discourses of Islam, Sorcery, and Spirit Possession*. Toronto: University of Toronto Press.

———. 1998. "Body and Mind in Mind, Body and Mind in Body: Some Anthropological Interventions in a Long Conversation." In *Bodies and Persons: Comparative Perspectives from Africa and Melanesia*, edited by Michael Lambek and Andrew Strathern, 103–23. Cambridge: Cambridge University Press.

———. 2007. "Sacrifice and the Problem of Beginning: Reflections from Sakalava Mythopraxis." *Journal of the Royal Anthropological Institute* 13 (1): 19–38.

———. 2008. "Provincializing God? Provocations from an Anthropology of Religion." In *Religion: Beyond a Concept*, edited by Hent de Vries, 120–38. New York: Fordham University Press.

———. 2013. "Varieties of Semiotic Ideology in the Interpretation of Religion." In *A Companion to the Anthropology of Religion*, edited by Janice Boddy and Michael Lambek, 137–53. Boston: Wiley-Blackwell.

———. Forthcoming. "Concepts and Persons." The Tanner Lecture in Human Values. Department of Philosophy, University of Michigan, January 2019.

Lévi-Strauss, Claude. 1963. "The Effectiveness of Symbols." In *Structural Anthropology*, translated by Claire Jacobson and Brooke Grundfest Schoepf, 186–205. New York: Basic Books.

———. (1964–71) 1969–1981. *Mythologiques I–IV*. Translated by John Weightman and Doreen Weightman. Chicago: University of Chicago Press.

———. 1966. *The Savage Mind*. Chicago: University of Chicago Press.

Lienhardt, Godfrey. 1961. *Divinity and Experience: The Religion of the Dinka*. Oxford: Clarendon.

Margalit, Avishai. 1992. "Sense and Sensibility: Wittgenstein on 'The Golden Bough.'" *Iyyun: The Jerusalem Philosophical Quarterly* 41: 301–18.

Needham, Rodney. 1972. *Belief, Language and Experience*. Oxford: Blackwell.

Rappaport, Roy. 1999. *Ritual and Religion in the Making of Humanity*. Cambridge: Cambridge University Press.

Ricoeur, Paul. 1971. "The Model of the Text: Meaningful Action Considered as a Text." *Social Research* 38 (3): 529–62.

Ryle, Gilbert. 1949. *The Concept of Mind*. Harmondsworth, UK: Penguin.

Said, Edward. 1975. *Beginnings: Intention and Method.* New York: Basic Books.

Severi, Carlo. 1987. "The Invisible Path: Ritual Representation of Suffering in Cuna Traditional Thought." *Res—Anthropology and Aesthetics*, no. 14. Peabody Museum, Harvard University: 66–85.

Sluga, Hans. 2011. *Wittgenstein.* Malden, MA: Wiley-Blackwell.

Tambiah, Stanley, 1985. *Culture, Thought, and Social Action.* Cambridge, MA: Harvard University Press.

Turner, Victor. 1967. *The Forest of Symbols.* Ithaca, NY: Cornell University Press.

Werbner, Richard. 2015. *Divination's Grasp: African Encounters with the Almost Said.* Bloomington: Indiana University Press.

Wittgenstein, Ludwig. (1922) 1961. *Tractatus Logico-Philosophicus.* Translated by D. F. Pears and B. F. McGuinness. London: Routledge.

———. (1953) 1958. *Philosophical Investigations.* Translated by G. E. M. Anscombe. Englewood Cliffs, NJ: Prentice Hall.

Wolf, Eric. 1958. "The Virgin of Guadalupe." *Journal of American Folklore* 71: 34–39. Reprinted in *A Reader in the Anthropology of Religion*, edited by Michael Lambek, 160–66. Malden, MA: Wiley Blackwell, 2008.

CHAPTER 10

Explanation as a Kind of Magic

Michael Taussig

Actually, we could write my title several ways, but first let's acknowledge what fun it is—how refreshing—to have an outsider examine our discipline of anthropology.

In regard to my title, we could refer to Ludwig Wittgenstein's style—trenchant, explosive, and aphoristic—as a kind of magic. And this to such an extent that thoughts, as Wittgenstein says, become persons (and not just like persons) pushing forward, wedged in the doorway. Franz Kafka's diaries come to mind, this same Kafka who Wittgenstein dismissed after a weekend reading him, telling Elizabeth Anscombe that here was a man with severe problems.

> #4. The crowding of thoughts that will not come out because they all try to push ahead and are wedged at the door.

Then there is metaphysics as a kind of magic, the kind we have trouble without, something Wittgenstein wished to show, as did Friedrich Nietzsche and Gilles Deleuze. Not that history of philosophy was Wittgenstein's forte. He was even more into philosophy as a "pickup game" than Deleuze was, but Deleuze was a scrupulous student of the history of philosophy.

And is not language itself a kind of magic, especially the movement in language? We say "movement" rather than a confusion or multiplicity of meanings so as to get across the inner surge we ride every time we speak. Wittgenstein's text reads that "a whole mythology is deposited in our language" (#24), and gives by example the different yet combined meanings of the belief in the corn-wolf as (1) what is hidden in the last sheaf of corn (i.e., the wolf); (2) the sheaf itself; and (3) the person who binds it (#26). Let it be noted immediately that language is a delightful if rarely acknowledged puzzle. It weighs on us, it must be perused and, as with the water of doubt, we must plunge into it again and again. A whole mythology does not mean our language is stable; note, for example, the corn-wolf. But James Frazer's language (held up as one model of fine English prose) gives no hint of that.

#26. What we have in the ancient rites is the use of a highly cultivated gestural language.

And when I read Frazer, I keep wanting to say at every step: All these processes, these changes of meaning are still present to us in our word language. If what is called the "corn-wolf" is what is hidden in the last sheaf, but [if this name applies] also to the last sheaf itself and the man who binds it, then we recognize in this a linguistic process with which we are perfectly familiar.

#1. One must begin with error and transform it into truth.

That is, one must uncover the source of the error, otherwise hearing the truth won't help us. It cannot penetrate when something else is taking its place.

To convince someone of what is true, it is not enough to state the truth; one must find the *way* from error to truth.

Again and again I must submerge myself in the water of doubt.

Frazer's representation of human magical and religious notions is unsatisfactory: it makes these notions appear as *mistakes*.

Was Augustine mistaken, then, when he called on God on every page of the *Confessions*?

But—one might say—if he was not in error, then surely was the Buddhist saint—or whoever else—whose religion expresses entirely different notions. But none of them was in error except where he was putting forth a theory.

Already the idea of explaining the practice—say the killing of the priest king—seems to me wrong-headed. All that Frazer does is to make the practice plausible to those who think like him. It is very strange to present all these practices, in the end, so to speak, as foolishness.

But it never does become plausible that people do all this out of sheer stupidity.

When he explains to us, for example, that the king would have to be killed in his prime because according to the notions of the savages, his soul would otherwise not be kept fresh, then one can only say: where that practice and these notions go together, there the practice does not spring from the notion; instead they are simply both present.

It could well be, and often occurs today, that someone gives up a practice after having realized an error that this practice depended on. But then again, this case holds only when it is enough to make someone aware of his error so as to dissuade him from his mode of action. But surely, this is not the case with the religious practices of a people, and that is why we are *not* dealing with an error here.

Frazer has a lot to say about corn (which is not maize from the New World, but cereals such as wheat or rye from the Middle East). In our time of the ultimate domination of nature by means of agribusiness, Frazer's two volumes on corn magic deserve close attention (see Mannhardt 1868), just as does Frazer's organic outlook tying any and everything to the passage of the seasons, an approach I find congenial, especially in our time of Global Warming. As a frustrated theater person, I keep trying to figure out how we could today use ritual and magic in agri/culture so as to turn around the impoverishment of our earth/birthright.

Such a project could use Wittgenstein's remarks on Frazer to alert us to the magical absence of magic in mainstream academic writing, which I call "agribusiness writing," meaning that which uses magic to deny it. Quite a feat, the antidote to which is a shamanic performance of the skilled revelation of skilled concealment, which is what Wittgenstein, the ultimate enigma of clarity, supplies in spades.

#9. Burning in effigy. Kissing the picture of a loved one. This is *obviously not* based on a belief that it will have a definite effect on the object that the picture represents. It aims at some satisfaction, and does achieve it, too. Or rather, it does not *aim* at anything; we act in this way and then feel satisfied.

One could also kiss the name of the loved one, and here the representation through the name [as a place-holder] would be clear.

Indeed, this strategic lack of awareness as to the magical—or what Nietzsche called metaphorical basis of language—is what makes it magical. (See Nietzsche's *On Truth and Lies in a Nonmoral Sense* [1873].)

Frazer's mistake—according to Wittgenstein—is that he thinks of magic as an impoverished science, whereas for Wittgenstein, magic is ritual and esthetics, poetry and theater, affect and empathy. Magic "dissolves" into the "ether" of culture, the unknown and the unknowable of custom and body-language forever prone to contradiction and doubt, like language itself. It is a puzzle and always will be, both for us and the people involved. In this regard, I like to think back to the Australian anthropologist W. E. H. Stanner's insistence that Daly River religion in the 1930s could not be reduced to a practical function other than the evocation of the mysteriousness of the mystery, "a joyous thing with maggots at its centre."

Nevertheless, many of the rites and charms considered by Frazer do in fact exist so as to achieve an immediate physical effect such as cure an illness, kill someone through sorcery, make someone fall in love, abate the mystically destructive envy of a neighbor or sibling, and so forth, which raises a problem. For there is a practical concern on the part of the magician and those who suffer misfortune.

Our problem is how to bring the ritualistic and the pragmatic together, which in turn means using magic to deny it. It is an old problem.

Here Wittgenstein raises the issue of understanding another culture. Is it possible to explain strangeness without explaining it away?

Wittgenstein's response is radical. "We can only describe and say, human life is like that." Well! That puts most of us out on the street. Isn't "explanation" the sine qua non of a card-holding academic?

#12. What narrowness of spiritual life we find in Frazer! Hence the impossibility of grasping a life different from the English one of his time!

Frazer cannot imagine a priest who is not basically an English parson of our times, with all his stupidity and shallowness.

#13. Why should it not be possible for someone's own name to be sacred to himself? On the one hand, it surely is the most important instrument given to him, and, on the other, it is like a jewel hung around his neck at birth.

How misleading Frazer's explanations are becomes clear, I think, from the fact that one could very well invent primitive practices oneself, and it would only be by chance if they were not actually found somewhere. That is, the principle according to which these practices are ordered is a much more general one than [it appears] in Frazer's explanation, and it exists in our own soul, so that we could think up all the possibilities ourselves. —We can thus readily imagine that, for instance, the king of a tribe becomes visible for no one, but also that every member of the tribe is obliged to see him. The latter will then certainly not occur in a manner more or less left to chance; instead, he will be *shown* to the people. Perhaps no one will be allowed to touch him, or perhaps they will be *compelled* to touch him. Think how after Schubert's death his brother cut Schubert's scores into small pieces and gave to his favorite pupils these pieces of a few bars. As a gesture of piety, this action is *just* as comprehensible that that of preserving the scores untouched and accessible to no one. And if Schubert's brother had burned the scores, this could still be understood as a gesture of piety.

The ceremonial (hot or cold) as opposed to the haphazard (lukewarm) is what characterizes piety.

Yes, Frazer's explanations would not be explanations at all if they did not, in the end, appeal to an inclination in ourselves.

Eating and drinking have their dangers, not only for the savage but also for us; nothing more natural than wanting to protect oneself against them; and we could think up such protective measures ourselves. —But what principle do we follow in confabulating them? Clearly that of formally reducing all dangers to a few very simple ones that are ready to see for everyone. In other words, according to the same principle that leads uneducated people in our society to say that the illness is moving from the head to the chest, etcetera, etcetera.

In these simple images personification will, of course, play a great role, for everyone knows that people (hence [also] spirits) can become dangerous to others.

That a human shadow, which looks like a human being, or one's mirror image, that rain, thunderstorms, the phases of the moon, the change of seasons, the likeness or difference of animals to one another and to human beings, the phenomenon of death, of birth and of sexual life, in short, everything that a human being senses around himself, year in, year out, in manifold mutual connection—that all this should play a role in the thought of human beings (their philosophy) and in their practices is self-evident; or, in other words, it is what we really know and find interesting.

How could the fire or the fire's resemblance to the sun have failed to make an impression on the awakening mind of man? But not perhaps "because he can't explain it to himself" (the stupid superstition of our time)—for does an "explanation" make it less impressive?—

The magic in *Alice in Wonderland*, trying to dry out by reading the driest thing there is.

Actually, the vast bulk of *Golden Bough*—for which it is criticized as much as praised—is description. The celebrated section on sympathetic magic runs some 150 pages, but only the first two pages could be called "explanatory." Moreover, if we read Wittgenstein's description of a hypothetical reader's reaction to Frazer's descriptions of the Beltane Fire Festival, we see that description/explanation gets wonderfully muddled, which I take to be Wittgenstein's point. The mind grapples with words and pictures as presented. The mind explains, so to speak, the description and does so through empathy. In reading Wittgenstein reading Frazer we are subject to a theatrical display of a theatrical display ad infinitum. We have become theater critics, something that would find ready agreement from Deleuze and from Nietzsche, author of *The Birth of Tragedy*. It's as if description needs explanation as "theory" but theory dissolves itself into de-territorializing /re-territorializing tidal flows plunging us into the water of doubt.

Nietzsche provides tantalizing arguments about confronting strangeness, pointing out that while we tend to domesticate the strange by reducing it to our normal so as to explain it, this not only dilutes the strange but diverts attention from the strangeness of the normal to which we reduce the strange. Wittgenstein never forgets the strangeness of the normal nor the everydayness of the strange.

What then of "explanation"—and its fellow traveler, "theory"—as the currency of academic power? Where is the anthropologist who will write "Remarks on Academe" alongside "Remarks on Frazer's *Golden Bough*"?

REFERENCES

Mannhardt, Wilhem. 1868. *Die Korndämonen: Beitrag zur germanischen Sittenkunde*. Berlin: Ferd. Dümmler's Verlagsbuchhandlung.

Nietzsche, Friedrich. (1873) 2010. "On Truth and Lie in a Nonmoral Sense." In *On Truth and Untruth: Selected Writings*. New York: Harper.

Stanner, W. E. H. (1959) 1989. *On Aboriginal Religion*. Preface by Francesca Merlan and Les Hyatt. Sydney: University of Sydney Press, The Oceania Monograph.

CHAPTER 11

On an Anthropological Tone in Philosophy

Sandra Laugier

> *One can only describe here, and say: such is human life.*
> —Ludwig Wittgenstein, *Remarks on Frazer's* The Golden Bough

PART I: PHILOSOPHY'S ANTHROPOLOGY

Ludwig Wittgenstein's *Remarks on Frazer's Golden Bough* represents a crucial stage in the evolving relationship between philosophy and anthropology. This work changed that relationship as radically as Wittgenstein transformed philosophy itself. However, for the most part, it has been philosophers who have studied and written on the *Remarks*, where they have found either an angle of approach for reading Wittgenstein or else evidence of an anthropological turn in his later philosophy (Chauviré 2005). But, too often, they have also used Wittgenstein's work to evaluate James Frazer's anthropology, and hence anthropology in general, or to judge what constitutes good ethnographic method and what does not (see, for example, Bouveresse 1977; Hollis and Lukes 1982; Sperber 1982; etc.). In short, they have used the *Remarks on Frazer* to once again arrogate for philosophy a superordinate, even supervisory position over anthropology—an ironic inversion, considering that Wittgenstein always sought to destroy philosophy's privilege and to bring it back down to the "rough ground" of ordinary life: "Where does our investigation get its importance from, since it seems to destroy everything interesting, all that is great and important? What we are destroying is nothing but houses of cards [*Luftgebäude*]" (Wittgenstein 1953: §118).

It is for this reason that the publication of this volume is an important intellectual event—in particular, because of the decisions by the authors and editors to showcase some of the most important contemporary anthropological perspectives on this text. This will perhaps be taken as a provocation by philosophers, but for me, the strength of this project lies both in its *teaching* and in its *content*—in the same way that Wittgenstein's *Tractatus* is important for the way it forces us to examine our position as well as for its content. The impression that it is provocative is highly revealing: after all, many contemporary philosophers, including Wittgenstein, have had no problem expressing their opinion of anthropology or proclaiming that they themselves are doing anthropology. It is now anthropology's turn—as an established discipline in its own right—to take on this text and assess its significance and provocation for it.

Taking an anthropological perspective makes it possible to do away with the idea that Wittgenstein is simply critiquing Frazer (and thus, anthropology, or a certain form of anthropology) by demonstrating his errors (see Lambek, this volume). It becomes clear that this is *not* what he is doing when we look at the passage where he reproaches Frazer for attributing erroneous "opinions" to the natives and suggests that it is he, Frazer, who is mistaken rather than the natives. The right way to read Wittgenstein is to grasp instead to what extent the very attribution of beliefs, opinions, or theories is a trap: we are as "mistaken" as Frazer if we attribute to Wittgenstein an opinion on Frazer (that is, the opinion that Frazer is mistaken). Thus, Wittgenstein teaches his readers (in what is sometimes called his therapeutic tone) to realize that we ourselves, as philosophers with anthropological pretentions, have been mistaken and have gone astray.

In fact, it is somewhat astonishing that philosophers who read the *Remarks on Frazer*—even those who are experts on Wittgenstein—do so as if Wittgenstein were a "traditional" philosopher who criticizes points of view or data on the basis of a theory. On this point there is a similarity between how Wittgenstein's reading of Frazer and his "critique" of Sigmund Freud have been used. In both cases, a denunciation of "mythologies" is invented and ascribed to Wittgenstein. This is often done for ideological or scientistic purposes, by ignoring or bypassing Wittgenstein's typical method, which is to make us understand, or see, what we really mean. In the case of Frazer, such mistaken interpretations are coupled with an ignorance of the very notion of "mythology." The first thing we must acknowledge (and which this volume teaches us) is that the aim of the *Remarks* is *not* to criticize anthropology or to do "philosophical" anthropology but rather for the reader to be transformed by the anthropological point of view, which is not the same as "playing anthropologist."

That said, *Remarks on Frazer's Golden Bough* is a significant text from Wittgenstein's crucial "middle" period. It is frequently discussed in Wittgenstein scholarship, even if many studies have focused on his philosophy of religion rather than on his view of anthropology or non-Western cultures. Furthermore, Wittgenstein is often treated with a kind of reverential if anxious distance, or even distrust, by philosophers and anthropologists. But among those who approach Wittgenstein with erudition and familiarity, there has been an attempt to push back and ask what *meaning* references to and citations of Wittgenstein have within anthropological literature—as if there were something incongruous about anthropologists citing Wittgenstein, although philosophers do not hesitate to make references to, say, Lucien Lévy-Bruhl, Marcel Mauss, Bronisław Malinowski, Margaret Mead, Philippe Descola, or Tim Ingold. Of course, here I have intentionally listed anthropologists with philosophical backgrounds, whose work has contributed to such intertextualities. Yet there is a form of tacit domination at work here, such that philosophy is always placed over and above anthropology—even if there is, at the same time, a relation of mutual fascination between the two disciplines.

This peculiar relationship between the two disciplines deserves to be studied at length. Here, however, I would like to examine how Wittgenstein's philosophy constitutes a true *account* of anthropology, not a cynical or critical use of it. Given that philosophy has long claimed to take up the task of anthropology, this leads to the question of how anthropology can in a sense claim to be philosophy—not through a kind of upgrading of its status but rather because it illustrates the philosophical method Wittgenstein proposes: attention to ordinary human forms of life in their unity and diversity; that is, attention to forms of life and lifeforms. It is for that reason that this afterword does not claim to add another element to commentaries on the *Remarks*, either those of Wittgenstein scholars or the remarkable works by anthropologists gathered and masterfully presented by Stephan Palmié in this volume.[1] These essays represent high-quality, careful Wittgensteinian scholarship, and have much to offer readers of

---

1.   For earlier work by anthropologists on the later Wittgenstein, see Needham (1985); James (2005); Das (2006); and Lambek (2015).

all backgrounds. They do not need to be complemented by philosophy, as I will now explain.

PART II: FROM A PRAGMATIC POINT OF VIEW

Within the recent history of anthropology, the relationships between this discipline and philosophy have been rearranged in various ways. It is no insult to anthropology to say that (as a discipline) it was born out of a philosophical concern. The difficulty is that philosophy and anthropology came to be related (they are "cousins," as Wittgenstein says about "agreement" and "rule" [1953: §224]) ever since philosophy began to attend to *the human* in general, as part of the "modern" turn represented by Immanuel Kant; they grew apart precisely because philosophy, when it takes an anthropological tone, speaks of the human *in general*—without paying attention to the various ways of being human or to the various ways in which humans may be living beings.

Anthropology, in its Kantian version, emerges when the question of the human is no longer only metaphysical (let alone theological) but comes to comprise its own domain of philosophy. Of course, this does not mean that concern with the human did not exist prior to modernity; rather, it existed as a non-autonomous domain of the moral sciences. Anthropology emerges within the framework of a philosophy freed of (or at least critical of) metaphysics, where the question of "the being of man" had previously been subordinated to the question of metaphysics (that is, the question of the foundation of all being and becoming). This, however, did not set the stage for an independent field of inquiry. It only cleared the ground for reflections on the human as an ethical and political—thus, *practical*—being who lives in society: what in the West has traditionally been referred to as the "moral sciences."

In fact, it was with Kant's reversal of traditional metaphysics and his separation of knowledge from moral theology that anthropology claimed its title. Kant's critique of metaphysics necessitated a reformulation of the question of the human, of its place and method of investigation. In his *Anthropology from a Pragmatic Point of View* (2006), Kant distinguishes between anthropology from a "physiological" point of view (the science of humans as natural beings; the science of "what nature makes man") and anthropology from a pragmatic point of view, that of man "as a freely acting being"; the science of humans as social and political beings, or of shared forms of human life. Modernity centered the philosophical question raised by this "anthropology from a pragmatic point of view" as the study of the behavior befitting the human as a citizen of the world. But this anthropology was understood in conformity with the delimitation of traditional "practical" disciplines that took the human as an ethical and sociopolitical being as their subject.

Kant effected the break from metaphysics that was necessary for the emergence of this anthropology and reshaped the question of the human. The most radical passage can be found in his *Introduction to Logic* ([1800] 1885): if "philosophy is the science of the relation of all cognition to the ultimate and essential aims of human reason," then it boils down to the following famous questions:

1. What can I know?
2. What must I do?
3. What may I hope for?
4. What is man?

"Metaphysics answers the first question," Kant writes, "morality the second, religion the third"—hence the three *Kritiken*—and the fourth, Kant says, is answered by anthropology. And he continues, "In reality, however, all these might be reckoned under anthropology, since the first three questions refer to the last" (Kant [1800] 1885). This amounts to placing philosophy within the frame of anthropology, and thus appears to reinvent the relations between the two disciplines. Except that anthropology is not here conceived of as a proper domain of knowledge, so its mission is still a matter of philosophy, as the study of the human per se. From "anthropology from a pragmatic point of view" was born the whole domain of "philosophical anthropology" (ranging, in German thought, from Wilhelm von Humboldt to Martin Heidegger, Arnold Gehlen, Helmuth Plessner, or Jürgen Habermas), which reverses Kant's discovery—anthropology as *the* question because it is the question of the human—and instead establishes the monopoly of philosophy over anthropology.

Given this philosophical background, one of Wittgenstein's goals in his *Remarks on Frazer's Golden Bough* was to subvert precisely this kind of philosophical anthropology: his immediate curiosity about *The Golden Bough*, which Maurice O'Connor Drury describes, was certainly due to the intuition that ethnographic material could offer a response to the mounting anthropological pretensions of philosophy. Rather than presenting a mere critique of Frazer and deriving whatever normative consequences might follow for anthropology, we can say that Wittgenstein takes the critique of the kind of metaphysics impeding the autonomization of anthropology a step further.

To understand this step, we need to consider that to affirm the existence of anthropology as a discipline was to affirm its autonomy in relation to philosophy, and especially in relation to "philosophical anthropology." This was not an easy task in a consensual universe of fascination and reciprocal *claims* that ethnologists and philosophers made upon each other; a universe of discourse where modern philosophy saw itself as anthropology, and where anthropology aimed at a kind of generality beyond that achievable by a single discipline. The result is a form of rivalry or equivalence that still structures contemporary thought. Superseding this historical disjuncture requires philosophers to stop claiming that they are doing anthropology by mere philosophizing, and instead—as Wittgenstein clearly recommends in the *Philosophical Investigations*— that they aim to grasp the proximity between the results and methods of the two disciplines that becomes inevitable once philosophy attends to ordinary life. It is necessary, moreover, for it to renounce "philosophical anthropology" for good. In other words, the desire regularly expressed for philosophy to provide "foundations" for the social sciences and the recurrent question, "What can philosophy draw from anthropology today?" need to be put on hold.

For Wittgenstein, neither logic nor mathematics nor social science required a foundation in the sense usually meant by philosophers—that is, in the sense that these fields would risk collapse or, in any case, appear totally arbitrary, if philosophers failed to logically found them. In the twentieth century, the connection between anthropology and Wittgenstein's thought has, for the most part, been drawn by philosophers or social scientists who deliberately chose to do philosophy. Here the French case may be instructive. French anthropology derived much of its prestige, particularly with Claude Lévi-Strauss and *L'Homme*, from a dialogue with French philosophy (Jean-Paul Sartre, Michel Foucault, Jacques Derrida, etc.), as opposed to Anglophone analytical philosophy. Wittgenstein's thought was not available in France until it was discovered by Pierre Hadot, Jacques Bouveresse, and later by Pierre Bourdieu, Luc Boltanski, and others. In France, Wittgenstein has largely been explored by sociology (see Salgues 2008 for an insightful analysis). Anthropology left Wittgenstein to the Wittgenstein specialists. In fact, the first French publication of Wittgenstein's *Remarks on Frazer's Golden Bough* was in the famous journal *Actes de la recherche en sciences sociales* in 1977, where it was followed by Bouveresse's now-classic commentary. The lasting friendship and theoretical alliance between Bourdieu and Bouveresse undoubtedly played a major role in Wittgenstein's reception in French sociology: he was essentially ignored by anthropologists, perhaps because of his "official" connection to analytic philosophy and the lasting influence of Louis Althusser on French anthropology. This is especially clear from use of the *Remarks* to rationalize ethnography through the recurrent use of select passages focusing on beliefs, rites, and ceremonial practices (Bouveresse 1977; de Lara 2005). Note here that none other than Bourdieu, in an intervention shortly before his death, presented himself as an actual Wittgenstein scholar defending rational procedures and Wittgenstein as a "serious" author:

> One of the philosophers who ranks among the most demanding and rigorous can thus . . . sometimes find himself converted into a kind of philosopher for non-philosophers, allowing sociologists or historians with philosophical claims to situate themselves in an indefinable place, halfway between philosophy and sociology, where they can escape the jurisdictions and sanctions of both disciplines. (Bourdieu 2002: 346–47)

As if "philosopher for non-philosophers" were a kind of insult—and as if it were necessary to prevent Wittgenstein from being used by anyone but those "good" philosophers and philosophically inclined sociologists! This normative use of Wittgenstein, and especially of the *Remarks on Frazer*, has been characteristic of twentieth-century analytic angst (see Quine [1953] 1980, 1960; Geertz 1984; Laugier 1992, 1996; see also chapters by Kwon, Severi, and Taussig, this volume), as if "postanalytic" philosophy, after Willard van Orman Quine and Donald Davidson, after the thesis of the indeterminacy of translation and the idea of a conceptual scheme, had created the risk of radical pluralism and skepticism, which would bar any understanding between (however) divergent human forms of life. The *Remarks* were brandished against the relativist scarecrow—even though, as Lévi-Strauss had quite early indicated, anthropology was precisely (as Wittgenstein also advocated) a matter of *paying attention* to people's thinking, avoiding both *reading* absurdities into them ("imputing properties to indigenous thought"; see Quine [1953] 1980) and conforming to a sanitized version of "our" common sense.[2] As Lévi-Strauss once put it, apropos an imaginary "here,"

---

2.   See Severi's discusssion of Sperber (this volume). See also Kwon (this volume); Quine (1960); Lévi-Strauss (1962); Needham (1972). For a discussion of Quine's anthropological tone, see Laugier (1992, 2013: ch. 4).

Mana really is Mana here. But one wonders whether their theory of Mana is anything other than a device for imputing properties to indigenous thought which are implied by the very peculiar place that the idea of mana is called on to occupy in their own thinking. Consequently, the strongest warning should be sounded to those sincere admirers of Mauss who would be tempted to halt at that first stage of his thinking; their gratitude would be not for his lucid analyses so much as for his exceptional talent for rehabilitating certain indigenous theories in their strangeness and their authenticity. (Lévi-Strauss 1950: 57)

Here, the relevance of Wittgenstein's irony in the *Remarks* is obvious:

Frazer is far more *savage* [English in the original] than most of his *savages* [English in the original], for these savages will not be as far removed from an understanding of spiritual matters as an Englishman of the twentieth century. His explanations of primitive practices are much cruder than the meaning of these practices themselves. (p. 44; emphasis mine)

Still, for Lévi-Strauss, the question—central to ethnography through today—of the risk of resorting to "mere description" remains, and he wants to prevent readers of Mauss from feeling encouraged by the latter's "exceptional talent for rehabilitating certain indigenous theories in their strangeness and their authenticity." He writes:

We would risk committing sociology to a dangerous path: even a path of destruction, if we then went one step further and *reduced social reality to the conception that man—savage man, even—has of it.* That conception would furthermore become empty of meaning if its reflexive character were forgotten. Then ethnography would dissolve into a verbose phenomenology, a falsely naïve mixture in which the apparent obscurities of indigenous thinking would only be brought to the forefront to cover the confusions of the ethnographer. (Lévi-Strauss 1950: 57–8; emphasis mine)

Here we may compare the notion of description proposed by Lévi-Strauss and Veena Das (*Textures of the Ordinary*, unpublished ms). Das introduces a concept taken from the later Wittgenstein: *forms of life*, which require description—and even an "excess of description" (perhaps even a "verbose phenomenology")—because what must be described is no longer belief or opinions but rather what life is *like*.

> If culture is a matter of shared ways of life as well as of bequeathing and inheriting capabilities and habits as members of society, then clearly it is participation in forms of sociality (Wittgenstein's forms of life) that define simultaneously the inner and the outer, that allow a person to speak both within language and outside it. Agreement in forms of life, in Wittgenstein, is never a matter of shared opinions. It thus requires an excess of description to capture the entanglements of customs, habits, rules, and examples. (Das 1998: 179)

Here again the question is the boundary between philosophy and anthropology. "Between the fundamental absurdity of primitive practices and beliefs, proclaimed by Frazer, and their specious validation by the evidence of a supposed common sense, invoked by Malinowski, there is room for a whole science and a whole philosophy" (Lévi-Strauss 1962: 99).

But what is the philosophy Lévi-Strauss calls for? One way to avoid or clarify these discussions about describing (still present today) would be, as this book allows us to do, to go back to the letter of Wittgenstein's text. As all the comments gathered here show, this calls upon us to turn to description as well as to revisit the question of common sense, which is not transparent to ourselves. Wittgenstein's main discovery, especially in the *Remarks on Frazer* but also throughout the 1930s, is of the uncanny character of common sense or ordinary life, hence of description.

> Are mathematical proposals anthropological proposals that say how we human beings infer and calculate? —Is a collection of laws a book of anthropology that says how the people of this people treat thieves, etc.? —Could we say: "The judge consults a book of anthropology and then sentences the thief to a prison sentence"? Fine, but the judge doesn't use the collection of laws as an anthropology manual. (Wittgenstein 1954: §65)

PART III: THE UNCANNINESS OF THE ORDINARY

Wittgenstein's later approach, as a philosophical method attentive to ordinary uses, is the most powerful subversion of philosophy's craving for an anthropological monopoly. This subversion can only be achieved in a reversal of metaphysics, and a return to ordinary life (see Laugier 2008, 2009). The ordinary is not *given*; rather, it pertains to the idea that "a whole mythology is deposited in our language" (p. 48). Ordinary language is "highly cultivated" and also contains everything that matters to the human ("in this sense every view is equally significant" [p. 52]). Wittgenstein explicitly states that "our" own language (by which he means the language he shares with his interlocutor) is "primitive" (1953: §5; 1958: 17).

> And when I read Frazer, I keep wanting to say at every step: All these processes, these changes of meaning are still present to us in our word language. (p. 50) Frazer's representation of human magical and religious notions is unsatisfactory: it makes these notions appear as *mistakes*. Was Augustine mistaken, then, when he called on God on every page of the *Confessions*? (p. 32)

Frazer, Augustine, Freud, Fyodor Dostoyevsky all provide, Wittgenstein suggests, views we are able to *make sense of* even if they may be strange—or terrifying. Anthropology's task is to give sense to thought and words—which would be "dead signs" were we not able to give them meaning, significance, and importance.

> One could say "every view has its charm," but that would be wrong. What is correct is that every view is significant for whoever sees it so (but that does not mean one sees it as something other than it is). Indeed, in this sense every view is equally significant. (p. 50f)

Here, the matter of error and common sense becomes the matter of significance and self-reliance, and of your capacity to put yourself in someone else's place. In "The Difficulty of Reality and the Difficulty of Philosophy," the moral philosopher Cora Diamond (2003) examines our moral capacity to put ourselves in the place of an animal, whether this is Kafka's monkey speaking to the Academy or an animal being killed in a slaughterhouse. Diamond cites an essay by J. M. Coetzee (2004), "The Life of Animals" (included in his novel *Elizabeth Costello*), in which a network of texts—Kafka's *Report to an Academy*, Wolfgang Köhler and his account of experimenting on apes, Thomas Nagel's bat, René Descartes's *cogito*—are gathered around the character of an Australian writer, Elizabeth

Costello, who is coming to the United States to address a conference on animal rights. Coetzee and Diamond both investigate our ability to understand the other, however strange. Diamond shows that Kafka's text—by giving voice to a monkey, Red Peter—allows one to place oneself in the position of a radically different other. Costello claims that the experience granted by literature is that of sympathy, the possibility of imagining what it would really mean to be in a strange being's position. Why not imagine that one is Red Peter, a monkey?

> There are people who have the capacity to imagine themselves as someone else, there are people who have no such capacity (when the lack is extreme, we call them psychopaths), and there are people who have the capacity but choose not to exercise it. There is no limit to the extent to which we can think ourselves into the being of another. There are no bounds to the sympathetic imagination. (Coetzee 2004: 79–80)

Anthropology becomes a name for this capacity, as illustrated often in Wittgenstein at the very moment when he discovers the concrete sense of the limits of language posited in the *Tractatus*. For example, Wittgenstein imagines in the *Remarks*

> that I might have had to choose some being on earth as my soul's dwelling place, and that my spirit had chosen this unsightly creature as its seat and vantage point. Perhaps because the exception of a beautiful dwelling would repel him. Of course, for the spirit to do so, he would have to be very sure of himself. (p. 50)

Few Wittgenstein scholars have pointed to this poetic passage about being born in a tree in the forest:

> If a human being were free to choose to be born in a tree in the forest, then there would be some who would seek out the most beautiful or highest tree for themselves, some who would choose the smallest, and some who would choose an average or below-average tree, and I do not mean out of philistinism, but for just the reason, or the kind of reason for which someone else chose the highest. That the feeling we have for our life is comparable to that of a being that could choose its standpoint in the world has, I believe, its basis in the myth—or belief—that we choose our bodies before birth. (p. 52)

As Bouveresse notes (at a moment when he is not obsessed with telling us what's wrong with Frazer):

> What Wittgenstein reproaches Frazer with is a total lack of comprehension or consideration for certain foundational images, whose strangeness seems to him to require an explanation at all costs. It doesn't occur to him that the "aberrations" that he condemns and whose presence he would like to explain as far as possible could correspond to things whose sense is quite simply inaccessible to him because of his own limitations. (Bouveresse 2007: 373)

He reminds us of something Wittgenstein said to Drury:

> The Cathedral of St Basil in the Kremlin is one of the most beautiful buildings I have ever seen. There is a story—I don't know whether it is true but I hope it is—that when Ivan the Terrible saw the completed Cathedral he had the architect blinded so that he would never design anything more beautiful. (Drury 1981: 178)

Wittgenstein explained his reaction, by saying, "What a *wonderful* way of showing his admiration!" To this, Drury replied it was "a *horrible* way." This suggests a reconception of ritual violence (see Puett, this volume), a mutation through the concepts of violence, of wonder, and of the ordinary, of the separation between "barbarity" and the "modern" vision of humanity (which is at the core of Das's vision [2007]).

One could also relate this whole discussion to understanding what is apparently nonsensical—better yet, as Diamond (2000) explains, understanding someone who speaks nonsense (which is not the same as understanding a nonsensical proposition). Wittgenstein says in his "Lectures on Religious Belief":

> Suppose someone, before going to China, when he might never see me again, said to me: "We might see one another after death"—would I necessarily say that I don't understand him? I might say [want to say] simply, "Yes. I *understand* him entirely." . . . No, it's not the same as saying "I'm very fond of you'"—and it may not be the same as saying anything else. It says what it says. (Wittgenstein 1966: 70–71)

To understand *someone* is not like understanding sense. In 1931—at the moment of his discovery of Frazer's work and his writing the first set of notes—at the end of his famous "Lecture on Ethics," Wittgenstein made some observations in an anthropological tone, concerning expressions that are apparently nonsensical, such as "I wonder about the existence of the world":

> I see now that these nonsensical expressions were not nonsensical because I had not yet found the correct expressions, but that their nonsensicality was their very essence. For all I wanted to do with them was just *to go beyond* the world and that is to say beyond significant language. My whole tendency and I believe the tendency of all men who ever tried to write or talk Ethics or Religion was to run against the boundaries of language. This running against the walls of our cage is perfectly, absolutely hopeless. Ethics so far as it springs from the desire to say something about the ultimate meaning of life, the absolute good, the absolute valuable, can be no science. What it says does not add to our knowledge in any sense. But it is a document of a tendency in the human mind which I personally cannot help respecting deeply and I would not for my life ridicule it. (Wittgenstein 1965: 12)

PART IV. ANTHROPOLOGY OF THE ORDINARY AND AGREEMENT IN LIFEFORMS

In her contribution to this volume, Das explains why it is wrong to talk about such expressions as *opinions*. She refers to a passage from Part II of the *Philosophical Investigations* on opinions: "My attitude toward him is an attitude toward a soul. I am not of the *opinion* that he has a soul" (PI: §178). This passage is central to Stanley Cavell's reading of Wittgenstein (Cavell 1979): our interactions with others are not based on any *opinion* about their being human but in our acknowledgement of them, of our sharing a texture of life.

This strongly suggests the need for an ethics within Wittgenstein's anthropological tone. Here the same criticism that I have applied to the concept of "philosophical anthropology" could be applied to "moral anthropology" as a way to dispense with the ordinary ethics that emerges from the descriptions of life.

Agreement *in* language is not in opinions but in form of life (Wittgenstein 1953: §242). By replacing opinions or beliefs with the concept of form of life in what we may call his anthropological picture,[3] Wittgenstein destroys the

---

3.   See the excellent presentation of the concept of form of life and the concept of language-games by Myrhe (this volume). See also Laugier (2018).

idea of attributing beliefs—that is, the core of traditional epistemology (and anthropology). Here, his strongest interpreter is Cavell, for whom the *availability* of Wittgenstein's philosophy is conditioned by recognition of forms of life and lifeforms—the whirl of organism—as the objects of philosophical and anthropological description. The anthropological method in philosophy (what J. L. Austin calls "fieldwork"; [1962] 1975: 185) does not turn philosophy into anthropology, but still outlines a common task shared by anthropology and philosophy, the attention to the ordinary.

> We learn and teach words in certain contexts, and then we are expected, and expect others, to be able to project them into further contexts. Nothing insures that this projection will take place (in particular, not the grasping of universals nor the grasping of books of rules), just as nothing insures that we will make, and understand, the same projections. That on the whole we do is a matter of our sharing routes of interest and feeling, modes of response, senses of . . . when an utterance is an assertion, when an appeal, when an explanation—all the whirl of organism Wittgenstein calls "forms of life." (Cavell 1969: 52)

Cavell takes inspiration from Wittgenstein when he defines "the uncanniness of the ordinary" inherent to the anthropological tone. In his foreword to Das's *Life and Words*, Cavell (2006) defines the ordinary as our ordinary language in so far as we constantly render it foreign to ourselves, which brings up the Wittgensteinian image of the philosopher as explorer of a foreign tribe, moved to "philosophical wonder by their strangeness to themselves, therefore of himself to himself"; this tribe is ourselves, for it is *we* who are foreigners and strangers to ourselves—"at home perhaps nowhere, perhaps anywhere" (Cavell 2007: x). This intersection of the familiar and the strange is the location of the ordinary and of Wittgenstein's philosophy of culture:[4] "Wittgenstein's anthropological perspective is one puzzled in principle by anything human beings say and do, hence perhaps, at a moment, by nothing" (Cavell 1989: 170).

Parallel to the mystery of ethnography and translation (see James, this volume), there is the enigma of speaking the same language—of the child being capable of learning language, the uncanniness of the use of ordinary language. It is crucial for Cavell that Wittgenstein says that we agree *in* and not *on* language:

---

4.   "Wittgenstein as a Philosopher of Culture" is the subtitle to "Declining Decline," Part I of Cavell's *This New Yet Unapproachable America* (1989).

language precedes this agreement as much as it is produced by usage. The transition from social life forms to human life forms is not the return to a human universal but rather crosses two dimensions of the life form, natural and social (see, for example, Pitrou 2017). This concept of lifeform is probably the most promising concept to be born out of the new alliance between philosophy and anthropology: it is not only social and biological but also inseparably ethnological and ethological.

Attention to the everyday is attention to what is before our eyes. From a different stance, Michel Foucault was acutely aware of this:

> We have long known that the role of philosophy is not to discover what is hidden, but to render visible what precisely is visible—which is to say, to make appear what is so close, so immediate, so intimately linked to ourselves that, as a consequence, we do not perceive it. (Foucault [1978] 1994: 540–41)

If "a whole mythology is deposited in our language," the philosopher's work is then to unearth "the great treasure deposited deep down the tree of language" (see Kwon). Which means that *describing* is not seeing: it's *plowing*. "We must plow over language in its entirety" (p. 44). Heonik Kwon reminds us that Wittgenstein briefly worked as a gardener. Still, there is also violence in the very idea of plowing, as in Emerson's 1844 *Address on the Anniversary of Emancipation in the British West Indies*: "Language must be *raked*."[5]

The editors of *Philosophical Occasions* note that the exact words of what became §415 of Wittgenstein's *Philosophical Investigations* can be found at the very beginning of a manuscript (MS 119) dated from 1937: "What we are supplying are really remarks on the natural history of human beings; we are not contributing curiosities, however, but observations which no one has doubted, but which have escaped remark only because they are always before our eyes" (Klagge and Nordmann in Wittgenstein 1992: 369).

Here, then, we have the gist of Wittgenstein's later ethnographic method, formulated as such soon after his curious discovery of *The Golden Bough*: an anthropology of our forms of life as ordinary language users. The present volume offers a perspicuous view on how twenty-first-century anthropologists

---

5.   "Language must be raked, the secrets of the slaughter-houses and infamous holes that cannot front the day, must be ransacked, to tell what negro-slavery has been" (Emerson [1844] 1919). Wittgenstein was a reader of Emerson.

have come to appreciate and to read this ethnographic gesture on the part of Wittgenstein.

ACKNOWLEDGEMENTS

I am very grateful to Daniela Ginsburg for her translation, and to Andrew Brandel for his help in writing this essay.

REFERENCES

Austin. J. L. (1962) 1975. *Philosophical Papers*. Oxford: Clarendon.

Bourdieu, Pierre. 2002. "Wittgenstein, la sociologie et le sociologisme." In *Wittgenstein, dernières pensées*, edited by Jacques Bouveresse, Sandra Laugier, and Jean-Jacques Rosat, 345–53. Marseille: Agone.

Bouveresse, Jacques. 1977. "L'animal cérémoniel." *Actes de la Recherche en Sciences Sociales* 16: 43–54.

———. 2007. "Wittgenstein's Critique of Frazer." *Ratio*, n.s., 20 (4): 357–76.

Bouveresse Jacques, Sandra Laugier, and Jean-Jacques Rosat, eds. 2002. *Wittgenstein, dernières pensées*. Marseille: Agone.

Cavell, Stanley. 1969. *Must We Mean What We Say? A Book of Essays*. Cambridge: Cambridge University Press.

———. 1979. *The Claim of Reason: Wittgenstein, Skepticism, Morality, and Tragedy*. Oxford: Oxford University Press.

———. 1989. *This New Yet Unapproachable America: Lectures after Emerson after Wittgenstein*. Albuquerque, NM: Living Batch Press.

———. 2007. "Foreword." In *Life and Words: Violence and the Descent into the Ordinary*, by Veena Das, ix–xiv. Berkeley: University of California Press.

Chauviré, Christiane. 2005. *Le moment anthropologique de Wittgenstein*. Paris: Kimè.

Coetzee, J. M. 2004. *Elizabeth Costello: Eight Lessons*. New York: Vintage.

Crary, Alice, and Rupert Read, eds. 2000. *The New Wittgenstein*. London: Routledge.

Das, Veena. 1998. "Wittgenstein and Anthropology." *Annual Review of Anthropology* 27: 171–95.

—————. 2007. *Life and Words: Violence and the Descent into the Ordinary*. Berkeley: University of California Press.

Davidson, Donald. 1984. *Inquiries into Truth and Interpretation*. Oxford: Clarendon.

De Lara, Philippe. 2005. *Le rite et la raison, Wittgenstein anthropologue*. Paris: Ellipses.

Diamond, Cora. 1991. *The Realistic Spirit, Wittgenstein, Philosophy, and the Mind*. Cambridge, MA: MIT Press.

—————. 2000. "Ethics, Imagination, and the Method of the *Tractatus*." In *The New Wittgenstein*, edited by Alice Crary and Rupert Read, 149–73. London: Routledge.

—————. 2003. "The Difficulty of Reality and the Difficulty of Philosophy." *Partial Answers* 1 (2): 1–26.

Drury, Maurice O'Connor. 1981. "Conversations with Wittgenstein." In *Ludwig Wittgenstein: Personal Recollections*, edited by Rush Rhees, 97–171. Totowa, NJ: Rowman and Littlefield.

Emerson, Ralph Waldo. (1844) 1919. "Essays and Addresses: Address on the Anniversary of Emancipation in the British West Indies." *American Transcendentalism Web*. http://transcendentalism-legacy.tamu.edu/authors/emerson/essays/emancipation.html.

Foucault, Michel. (1978) 1994. "La philosophie analytique de la politique." In *Dits et Ecrits*, vol 3. Paris: Gallimard.

Geertz, Clifford. 1984. "Anti Antirelativism." *American Anthropologist*, n.s., 86 (2): 263–78.

Hollis, Martin, and Steven Lukes. 1982. *Rationality and Relativism*. Cambridge, MA: MIT Press.

James, Wendy. 2005. *The Ceremonial Animal*. Oxford: Oxford University Press.

Kant, Immanuel. (1800) 1885. *Introduction to Logic*. Translated by Thomas Kingsmill Abbott. London: Longman, Green. https://archive.org/stream/kantsintroductio00kantuoft/kantsintroductio00kantuoft_djvu.txt.

—————. 2006. *Anthropology from a Pragmatic Point of View*. Edited and translated by Robert B. Louden. Cambridge: Cambridge University Press.

Lambek, Michael. 2015. *The Ethical Condition: Essays on Action, Person, and Value*. Chicago: University of Chicago Press.

Laugier, Sandra. 1992. *L'anthropologie logique de Quine*. Paris: Vrin.

———. 1996. "Relativité linguistique, relativité anthropologique." *Histoire Épistémologie Langage* 18 (2): 45–73. https://www.persee.fr/doc/hel_0750-8069_1996_num_18_2_2460.

———. 2008. "L'ordinaire transatlantique." *L'Homme* 187–88 (3–4): 169–99.

———. 2009. "Transcendentalism and the Ordinary." *European Journal of Pragmatism and American Philosophy* 1 (1–2): 53–69.

———. 2013. *Why We Need Ordinary Language Philosophy*. Chicago: University of Chicago Press.

———. 2018. "Ordinary Language as Lifeform." In *Language, Form(s) of Life, and Logic: Investigations after Wittgenstein*, edited by Christian Martin, 277–304. Berlin: de Gruyter.

Lévi-Strauss, Claude. 1950. *Introduction à l'œuvre de Marcel Mauss*. Paris: Presses Universitaires de France.

———. 1962. *La pensée sauvage*. Paris: Plon.

Needham, Rodney. 1972. *Belief, Language, and Experience*. Chicago: University of Chicago Press.

———. 1985. *Exemplars*. Berkeley: University of California Press.

Pitrou, Perig. 2017. "Life Form and Form of Life within an Agentive Configuration: A Birth Ritual among the Mixe of Oaxaca, Mexico." *Current Anthropology* 58 (7): 360–80.

Quine, Willard van Orman. (1953) 1980. *From a Logical Point of View*. Cambridge, MA: Harvard University Press.

———. 1960. *Word and Object*. Cambridge, MA: MIT Press.

Rhees, Rush, ed. 1981. *Ludwig Wittgenstein: Personal Recollections*. Totowa, NJ: Rowman and Littlefield.

Salgues, Camille. 2008. "Un nouveau Wittgenstein encore inapprochable: Le rôle et la place du philosophe dans l'anthropologie." *L'Homme* 3 (187–188): 201–22.

Sperber, Dan. 1982. "Apparently Irrational Beliefs." In *Rationality and Relativism*, edited by Martin Hollis and Steven Lukes, 149–80. Cambridge, MA: MIT Press.

Wittgenstein, Ludwig. 1922. *Tractatus Logico-Philosophicus*. London: Kegan Paul.

———. 1953. *Philosophische Untersuchungen–Philosophical Investigations*, Edited by G. E. M. Anscombe. Oxford: Blackwell.

————. 1954. *Bemerkungen über die Grundlagen der Mathematik*. Edited by G. E. M. Anscombe, G. H von Wright, and Rush Rhees. Frankfurt: Suhrkamp.

————. 1958. *The Blue and Brown Books*. Edited by Rush Rhees. Oxford: Blackwell.

————. 1965. "A Lecture on Ethics." *Philosophical Review* 74 (1): 3–12.

————. 1966. *Lectures and Conversations on Æsthetics, Psychology and Religious Belief*. Edited by Cyril Barrett. Oxford: Blackwell.

————. 1969. *On Certainty*. Edited by G. E. M. Anscombe and G. H. von Wright, translated by D. Paul and G. E. M. Anscombe. Oxford: Blackwell.

————. 1992. *Philosophical Occasions: 1912–1951*. Edited by James Klagge and Alfred Nordmann. Indianapolis: Hackett.

Remarks on Wittgenstein and Ritual

Rodney Needham

The Master said, Ritual, Ritual! Does it mean no more than presents of jade and silk?
—Confucius

I

The influence of Ludwig Wittgenstein on the comparative analysis of social facts has been late, little, and slow. When it has not been flippantly dismissed, as though not even calling for counterargument (for example, Augé 1979: 93n.), it has had scarcely any effect on the practice of the great majority of social anthropologists.

Nevertheless, deliberate attempts have been made to demonstrate the radical importance of Wittgenstein's thought for the working concepts of comparativism. It has been argued, for instance, that the stock terms in the study of systems of descent and affinity are so defective as to be incapable of framing reliable scientific results (Needham 1974, chap. 1); that the psychological term "belief" does not have the value, as the index to a natural resemblance among mankind, that could justify its continued use as a concept of universal application (Needham 1972); and that the discrimination of inner states is crucially affected by inappropriate taxonomic premises (Needham 1981, chap. 3). These critiques are based on Wittgenstein's exploitation of the idea of "family resemblances," and their main intended effect is to extend into comparativism a recognition of the principle of polythetic classification (Needham 1975; 1983, chap. 3). Thus it is contended that terms such as "descent," "incest," "belief," or "anger" are vitiated because they are taken to denote monothetic classes of social facts, whereas actually they are highly polythetic and cannot therefore have the uses that are normally ascribed to them. A consequence of accepting this kind of critique is that the comparison of social facts must at first become far more difficult, if it is at all feasible in such terms; but the immense potential benefit that can follow is the attainment of a more "perspicuous representation" (Wittgenstein 1967a, sec. 122) of what is really at issue when we try to understand human nature and social action.

In the cases just mentioned, Wittgenstein's influence has been exerted through the criticism of individual concepts, and for the most part this is the way he did his own work in linguistic philosophy. While he certainly urged that "forms of life" should be taken into account in the analysis of expressions in German and in English, he did not make it his concern to set his findings against the ethnographic descriptions of more alien social forms. Even in his allusions to the value of an acquaintance with many languages, he does not resort to the abundant materials on natural languages (Needham 1972: 132–34). When he wants an example outside German or English, he makes up an imaginary language; and when he needs a different social setting, he asks us to imagine a primitive tribe that behaves in a way we should find strange. In these respects Wittgenstein himself behaves in the way that philosophers as a tribe usually do; and naturally enough this method does not answer directly to the concerns of those whose scientific objective is instead to study concrete similarities and differences throughout a global range of civilizations. If "the common behaviour of mankind is the system of reference by means of which we interpret an unknown language" (Wittgenstein 1967a, sec. 206), it is the task of the comparativist to determine empirically what the common features actually are. If we are to establish no more than a "natural history of mankind" (sec. 415), then we cannot just "invent natural history" (p. 230); we have to come to terms with factual accounts of what mankind really does.

We cannot reproach Wittgenstein for not making this his constant practice in relation to his philosophical interests (cf. Needham 1972: 186), but his normal method attracts all the more interest when he does apply himself to social facts. This he did in his "Bemerkungen über Frazers *Golden Bough*." These remarks fall into two sets: the first were notes that he made over a period of a few weeks in 1931; the second set of remarks dates from not earlier than 1936 and probably from after 1948 (Rush Rhees, in Wittgenstein 1979: v, vi). They were published, in German as they stood, in *Synthese* (Wittgenstein 1967b), and then in an English translation, omitting several concluding passages (1967b: 251–53), in *The Human World* (Wittgenstein 1971), with a long introductory note by Rhees. Eventually the German text, with corrections, and the translation, with revisions, were brought together in a single volume (1979). In the interim the remarks had also appeared in a French translation (1977b).

It cannot be said that Wittgenstein's remarks on *The Golden Bough* made any great impression on anthropologists. Apart from citations in certain predecessors to the present essay (Needham 1972, 1973b, 1976, 1980, 1981, 1983), they attracted in fact almost no professional attention. Rudich and Stassen published a critical paper on "Wittgenstein's implied anthropology" (1977), and Rhees has commented at some length on Wittgenstein's treatment of language and ritual (Rhees 1982). But anthropologists appear in general to have ignored what Wittgenstein found to say about a classical work in anthropology and about topics such as religion, magic, ritual, and symbolism which are central to their discipline. It is possible to conjecture probable reasons for this neglect, but a more useful course is to examine what is to be gained from a consideration of Wittgenstein's genius when, for once, it is applied to the explication of social facts.

To this end we shall rely on the bilingual edition of the "Remarks/Bemerkungen" (1979) and also on the passages in *Synthese* that were not included in that volume. At certain points, it should be observed, there are omissions and more or less consequential misrenderings in the translation from the German; these will be noticed explicitly only if they affect the present argument. (Page references followed by "e" cite the published translation; without this letter the passages quoted are direct translations from the German, and they differ from the English version.) Also, there are many connections to be made between the "Remarks" and one or another of Wittgenstein's other publications (cf. Bouveresse 1977); to take these up would result in a very extended and more philosophical commentary, so the investigation that follows will concentrate almost exclusively on the "Remarks" themselves and on their implications for the study of ritual.

Wittgenstein's "Remarks" are not only in two parts, written at an interval of perhaps as much as seventeen years, but neither part is composed as a sequential argument. There are connections, expectably enough, between some adjacent passages, but there is no overall development of a case. It is necessary therefore to jump from one place to another in the text and to collocate scattered remarks in order to bring out their effect in combination. This procedure may or may not result in a pattern of exposition that Wittgenstein would have been prepared to recognize; but the present commentary is not in any event intended as a re-ordered exposition of what we already have from Wittgenstein himself and, in the original, in the characteristic idiom that makes his writings so exciting. The object of the examination is instead one that he would surely have approved, namely to make what we can of his ideas in order to effect some advance in our own thoughts.

II

Wittgenstein's premise is that it is possible to distinguish, by observation, ritual actions from "animal activities" such as taking food. Certain actions bear a "peculiar character" and could be called ritual (1979: 7; the translation has "ritualistic," which is inexact).

We are not told what it is that gives this peculiar character to certain actions and sets them apart from animal activities, but only that it can be seen when "we watch the life and behaviour of men all over the earth." What exactly can we "see" that would make this differentiation? Formality is perhaps the attribute that will come most readily to mind. But all types of social action, if they are to be recognizable as social and as the type that any of them is, must to some degree be formalized. The prescribed forms of good manners, such as standing at the entrance of a woman or a superior, certainly and deliberately have this character, and so do other and more corporate actions such as soldiers executing parade-ground drill or the fellows of a college conducting a meeting of the governing body. We cannot distinguish the ritual from the merely formal by the degree of punctilio demanded, for in that event the minutiae of everyday etiquette would have to be placed at the ritual end of the scale. And even an innovation in collective behavior can be formalized in a coercive manner; for example, British soccer players kissing and cuddling and mounting one another after they have scored a goal. On the other hand, religious ceremonies which ought to be performed in set and careful observances may in the event be lacking in due formality (cf. Needham 1981: 83). And then there are activities, such as the transportation of the bier at a Balinese funeral, the formality of which consists in an appearance of boisterous informality.

Another conventional criterion of ritual is to be looked for in the inner state of the participants; for instance, reverence, awe, inspiration, grief, and so forth, according to what the ritual is about. It is often feasible to elicit a description of the inner state that is thought appropriate to a given case; but there is no certain way of being sure that a performer or assistant in a form of action is in that state (cf. Needham 1972: 98–101; 1981, chap. 3). Even when the prescribed inner state does obtain, and is certainly in consonance with the declared aim of the action being carried out, there is still the possibility that the subject will also be occupied by another emotion that is inconsistent with what is prescribed; Descartes gives the example of a man weeping over his dead wife when he would be put out if she were to be resuscitated (1649, art. 147). There is no doubt, however, that certain inner states are enjoined upon those who take part in what are customarily called rituals, and if such states cannot be seen perhaps it will serve as criterion that they should be displayed or simulated. But then there are two difficulties: first, that it is hard to exhibit even a genuine inner state, such as reverence, and harder still to interpret by simple observation what state it is; second, that a prescribed expression or posture is part of the action itself, and not a clue to an inner state that defines the action as a ritual.

There are of course other criteria that might contribute to the definition of ritual; for instance, it might be contended that rituals were significantly associated with boundaries and points of transition, so that the criterion would be, let us say, structural. But a social or symbolic structure cannot be seen, and we could not therefore directly identify ritual, in this sense, by considering the "life and behaviour of men." Various further criteria attract additional objections, and in the end there seems no secure defense of the presumption that there is a peculiar (*eigentümlich*) aspect of social action that provides an observable index to the ritual. Wittgenstein, at any rate, does not say what it is. He does, however, say that ritual can be seen apart from "animal activities," and perhaps these can help us to draw a line around ritual. The only example he cites is that of taking food, but this activity surely will not serve. The Eucharist involves the taking of food, as bread and wine, yet in the Christian tradition it is supremely a ritual; moreover, it rests on an ancient symbolic ideology, in Judaic tradition, in which dietary rules play a dominant role in the definition of status and action and in the relationship of men to God (Feeley-Harnik 1981). It is an anthropological commonplace, too, that all over the world food is far more than a merely animal concern; it is a fundamental vehicle for symbolizing incorporation, boundaries, sympathies, enmities, and much else in human relations. As for other animal activities, such as copulation or excretion or hunting, these also are never simply animal in human society; always they are governed by rules and symbolic usages which again make it not feasible to distinguish them, on the basis of their animal character alone, from what would then stand apart as ritual. If "we must begin with the mistake and transform it into what is true" (1e), the unargued premise that ritual has a peculiar character that can be observed is a prime candidate for transformation.

There is in fact another recourse in coming to terms with ritual. Instead of continuing to try to isolate the peculiar or special character of the activity, we can adopt another approach that Wittgenstein also mentions. Writing about the fire festivals of Europe, he says that what strikes him most apart from the similarities of all these rites is the dissimilarity among them. He compares them to a wide variety of faces with common features that repeatedly appear in one place and another. "And one would like to draw lines joining the parts that various faces have in common" (13e); more literally, lines that connect the common components. Now this is precisely the method for determining "family resemblances," and specifically that of Francis Galton, who in 1879 made composite portraits in order to bring out the typical characteristics of sets of individuals (cf. Needham 1972: 110–13). In other words, what Wittgenstein is doing in the comparison of fire festivals is to suggest a polythetic delineation of ritual.

In accordance with this procedure, we can say then that "ritual" is an odd-job word; that is, it serves a variety of more or less disparate uses, yet we are tempted to describe its use as though it were a word with regular functions (cf. Wittgenstein 1958: 43–44). It cannot be relied upon for any precise task of identification, interpretation, or comparison—as it could be if it were the monothetic concept that it is usually taken for—but this does not mean that it can have no serious use. What follows, rather, is that it has a range of uses, not one strict application corresponding to some peculiar character in the phenomena that it denotes. As a polythetic concept, "ritual" variously combines certain characteristic features, and the task of the comparativist is to identify these features and to register the patterns into which they combine.

This task is made more manageable by subsuming ritual under the more general heading of symbolic action, for we have a fair command of the vehicles, modes, and relations of symbolism. These components of symbolic classification and its social expression are marked by parsimony, regular concatenation, and a global distribution (Needham 1979; 1981: 85–88). Wittgenstein suggests that in ritual practices we can see something that is similar to the association of ideas and related to it: "we could speak of an association of practices" (13e). This impression, it can now be responded, is created by the recurrence of features from among a steady repertory of such components. What we isolate as "ritual," in one or another form or context, is no more than the expression in social action of symbolic features which are by no means peculiar to it—whatever it may be.

III

To approach ritual as a polythetic concept and as a variety of symbolic action makes a useful beginning, but the identification of characteristic features does not in itself constitute interpretation or explanation.

In trying to understand ritual, a standing inclination among anthropologists is, reasonably enough, to look for the reasons behind it; either the reasons that led to its inception or those that sustain its continued performance. Wittgenstein repeatedly contends that this is a mistake. "What makes the character of ritual action," he asserts, "is not any view or opinion, either right or wrong" (7). More generally yet, he holds that "the characteristic feature of primitive man . . . is that he does not act from *opinions* he holds about things (as Frazer thinks)" (12). If this is correct, the explanation of ritual cannot consist in discovering the reasons for which the participants, at any point in its development or in the course of its practice, carry it out.

The topic of rationality has received much sociological attention, and various approaches to it have most usefully been brought together by Wilson in a collaborative volume under that title (Wilson 1970), but the basic issues have nevertheless proved very recalcitrant. On the one hand, the topic is clearly philosophical, yet on the other hand certain philosophical treatments have proved rather divagatious from the analysis of social facts. Since the problems arise typically in attempts to understand exotic forms of behavior, it seems better in this case to begin, not with the scrutiny of our own conceptual predispositions, but directly, so far as this may be done, with reports of the phenomena in question. These are voluminous, and different ethnographers have stressed different aspects and from different points of view, but certain common findings can be discerned. The most general, it seems, is that those who take part in ritual can give no reasons for it; they say that it is their custom (*adat*, as is said in Indonesia, or some such word) or that it is what they are enjoined to do by their ancestors; or else they react in such a way as to show that for them there is no comprehensible question in the ethnographer's query (cf. Needham 1983, chap. 4). In other instances an acknowledged local authority, such as a priest or some other celebrant of the ritual, gives a traditional reason, and other participants acquiesce; in that case, the reason is to be regarded as being itself part of the ritual, not as an independent excogitation providing a rational explanation for the performance of the ritual. In yet other instances, different participants may give conflicting reasons; in such a case there can sometimes be acceptable evidence of cogitation, but there is no means of deciding which explanation is the correct one, and there are certainly no grounds to presume that the most rational explanation (if that can be isolated) will provide the real reason for the behavior. Also, Sir Thomas Browne asserted quite long ago, about the ancient Gentiles, that "in severall rites, customs, actions and expressions, they contradicted their own opinions" (Browne 1658, chap. 4); and, while it is difficult to decide, without begging the question, what is to count as a contradiction between rite and opinion, in some sense or another this is a real contingency with which in the ordinary way we are quite familiar.

All of these possibilities can be demonstrated by reference to a rite that we know especially well, and on which there is a superabundance of historical and theological evidence, namely the Eucharist. This paradigmatic rite of the Christian faith has been excellently analyzed, from a point of view made feasible only by comparativism, by Feeley-Harnik (1981). She has uncovered numerous factors that enable us to comprehend better the inception of the rite, but it is out of the question that any significant number of communicants today could know anything of these determinants. If communicants are asked their present reasons for partaking in the rite, it is sure that these will be various, even in the most strictly disciplined of churches. Ultimately, moreover, the inquirer will come up against the sophisticated response that what is in question is a mystery and hence ineffable. This does not prevent different exponents of the Christian faith from offering divergent accounts of the real significance of the rite and hence different reasons for its celebration.

The objection might be raised that Christianity is an exceptionally complex and disputatious religion, and that therefore the Eucharist is too idiosyncratic an example to rely on. But Christianity is also exceptional in the extent to which it has elaborated reasons for its tenets and their symbolic expression, and in this regard the Eucharist makes in fact an exceptionally instructive test case. Taken as such, it can readily be adduced as testimony against any theory that would explain the enactment or the form of a rite by reference to the opinions of those who participate in it. Indeed, Feeley-Harnik's analysis tends to show in another way that concomitant opinions cannot provide an explanation; for to the extent that she isolates factors which enable us to comprehend the rite more clearly, these are characteristics of symbolic ideation which are far too general, in their incidence among other traditions and rites as well, to account for the particularities of this individual rite.

If it should be thought that these characteristic features of ritual, such as the symbolism of sacrifice, contain in their turn more fundamental explanations of the rite, then the response must be that such features are not rational constructs and that they bear only contingent relations to the opinions of those who subscribe to this form of ritual. Whereas the Christian liturgy is indeed a privileged case for fundamental analysis, an enterprise in which Yarnold's study of its rites of initiation (1971) would occupy an advanced place, the conclusions to be derived are likely only to confirm what Waley wrote in connection with Confucian practices: "The truth . . . is that there is no 'real reason' for ritual acts" (1938: 57).

IV

Wittgenstein contends that the very idea of trying to explain a practice, say the killing of the priest-king, is a mistake (2e). The particular case that he takes up makes the search for an explanation seem a particular kind of mistake.

Frazer, he asserts, merely makes the practice plausible to people who think as he does (1e), and what Frazer thinks is that the enactors of the practice are acting out an error, a mistaken theory. But, Wittgenstein responds, it is very remarkable that all these practices should be represented in the end as stupidities, for it never does become plausible that people behave so out of sheer stupidity (1). They may well have views about what they do (and these opinions may appear mistaken), but "where that practice and these views go together, the practice does not spring from the view, but both of them are just there" (2). Also, as he wrote in another manuscript (of 1945): "Why should we not say, These customs and laws are not *based* on the belief; they show *to what extent* (in what sense) such a belief exists" (in Rhees 1982: 97).

This is cogent as far as it goes, but then Wittgenstein proceeds to a more comprehensive statement about the explanation of ritual: "I think one reason that the attempt at an explanation is wrong is that we have only to put together in the right way what we *know*, without adding anything, and the satisfaction we are trying to get from the explanation comes of itself" (2); "We can only *describe* here and say: that is what human life is like" (3). These remarks can be subsumed under the notion, which was of fundamental importance to Wittgenstein (cf. 1967a, sec. 122), of a "perspicuous representation" (1979: 9). The tenor of this phrase has indeed been demonstrated repeatedly by Wittgenstein in connection with verbal concepts, but its application is not so clear when we are confronted with social facts such as the practices of ritual.

There are, in the event, considerable difficulties in construing Wittgenstein's statement about explanation. When he declares that we have only to put together in the right way what we know, his words seem to imply that "we" (*man*, one, in the German) is a constant, or at least a subject whose identity and capacities are tacitly given. But this is far from being the case, and in any case the criteria for "what we *know*" must be highly unsure (cf. 6). The first necessity in drawing on an ethnographic report, for instance, is not to presume that it represents objective knowledge but to try to assess it objectively as a representation. Ethnographic reports about alien concepts can hardly ever be accepted as they stand (cf. Needham 1972: 198), but they call instead for a deliberate interpretation which is intrinsically more complex than the apprehension of what is reported. Far from not adding anything, as Wittgenstein enjoins, we need to add all manner of circumstantial particulars if we are to make a reliable cognitive assessment of what the ethnographer relates.

Concomitantly, we cannot fall in directly with Wittgenstein's assertion that "we can only *describe* . . ." Clear description (cf. a "perspicuous representation") is a supreme art in the practice of ethnography, and the resultant account has to be assessed, moreover, in the light of the methodological principles and general concepts by which the ethnographer is guided. The observation of a symbolic act may need to be framed by notions, such as lateral values or complementarity or reversal, which are not given by observation but have to be adduced in a careful exercise of interpretation. Furthermore, such notions are ultimately scientific abstractions, and they are hence disputable. A critical apprehension of lateral values entails a resort to the relation of opposition, which is not a logical constant, and to that of analogy, which is puzzlingly obscure (Needham 1980, chap. 2); the concept of complementarity has no intrinsic logical form, but may possess a more or less adventitious use as a term of expository rhetoric; the idea of reversal is neither simple nor self-evident, but it can be decomposed into a number of more or less disparate modes (Needham 1983, chap. 5). All of these considerations, to cite no more, make it a hard matter to describe ritual, let alone to put together what we know in a definite arrangement that could be seen as the right way.

V

Another reason to think that Frazer's explanations are misleading, Wittgenstein writes, is that "we could very well imagine primitive practices for ourselves, and it would be an accident if they were not actually found somewhere" (5). This means, he continues, that the principle according to which these practices are ordered is much more general than Frazer takes it to be; it is present in our own minds, so that "we could think out all the possibilities for ourselves" (5).

For certain fields of social life this can indeed be done. Thus the great variety of descent systems, together with the recurrent resemblances among them, can be accounted for as realizations of elementary modes of descent; there are only six modes, and two of them are impracticable as operational rules of social organization (Needham 1974: 47). A similar isolation of principles can be made in the case of prescriptive systems, by reference to criteria of symmetry, transitivity, and other relations; it is then readily understandable that remarkably similar systems should be found in far-separated parts of the world, and also that the discovery of additional instances of prescriptive alliance should offer no surprises as to their principles of order. It may be thought not all that perplexing that we should be able to "think out all the possibilities" when we are dealing with systematic aspects of social forms, for in addition to logical or schematic constraints there are also practical exigencies that conduce to a relatively simple economy of systems. But it is more arresting when we find that very general principles can be discerned among the imaginative variegations of symbolic forms. Admittedly, it is hardly feasible in these cases to think out the possibilities from scratch, but a number of common or basic features can still be isolated, and these can then be employed as premises in understanding the elaborations. Thus if it is accepted that men attribute symbolic significance to space, it is an obvious task to go on to work out the contrasts of values that may define the individual dimensions such as right/left, above/below, and so on (cf. Needham

1973a). Inductively, also, a number of relational constants and transformations in systems of symbolic classification can be established (Needham 1979, chaps. 4 and 5), and these in their turn lend weight to the precept, expressed in phrases taken from Wittgenstein in another connection, that in comparativism "our investigation . . . is directed not towards phenomena, but, as one might say, towards the 'possibilities' of phenomena" (cf. Wittgenstein 1967a, sec. 90; Needham 1974: 71).

Wittgenstein's examples of thinking out possibilities of ritual conduct are not so comprehensive as this formulation, but they are telling enough. We can readily imagine, he says, that in a given tribe no one is allowed to see the king, but we can also imagine that everybody in the tribe is obliged to see him; and in the latter event it will certainly not be left more or less to chance, but he will be *displayed* to the people. Perhaps no one will be allowed to touch the king—but perhaps they will be *compelled* to do so (5). These examples make Wittgenstein's point, but then they are entirely overshadowed by another example that is one of the most enlightening paradigms in all that has been written about ritual and its purposes. This concerns the treatment of Schubert's manuscript scores.

After Schubert's death, Wittgenstein relates, his brother cut some of the scores into small pieces, of a few bars each, and gave them to the composer's favorite pupils. "This action, as a sign of piety, is *just* as comprehensible to us as would be that of keeping the scores undisturbed and accessible to no one. And if Schubert's brother had burnt the scores, this also would be comprehensible as a sign of piety" (5).

To this splendid paradigm Wittgenstein appends a gloss: "the ceremonial . . . as opposed to the haphazard, . . . characterizes piety." In other words, it would seem, the inner attitude is given expression through a formal outward observance. Here, then, we have a fine demonstration that even a given sentiment of piety, together with a deliberate purpose to fulfill the duty of commemoration, can be expressed equally comprehensibly through very contrasting forms of conduct. The premise, of course, is that the particular formality that happens to be enacted will be recognized as inspired by that sentiment, or as intended to symbolize [*sic*] it, and as directed by the concomitant intention. The ritual, as we may call it, thus has a patent meaning that may not be characteristic of traditional and collective formalities of the kind. Nevertheless, the arbitrary connection between meaning and form remains strikingly demonstrated. Moreover, the paradigm has an important converse; namely that we cannot infer from the form of a symbolic action what its meaning may be (or may previously have been), and hence cannot conclude that rituals with a common form will have any common meaning or purpose.

This outcome reinforces Wittgenstein's contention that "what makes the character of ritual action is not any view or opinion, either right or wrong, although an opinion—a belief—can itself also be ritual, can belong to the rite" (7).

VI

Nevertheless, it remains deeply perplexing that certain actions of a formal or symbolic kind, whether or not we should be justified in labeling them as ritual, seem to express something that we feel called upon to comprehend in a special way. We still need to explain them, in the literal sense; that is, to unfold them, smooth out their anfractuosities, and expose some plainer significance that will allay our curious sense of puzzlement. With the concept of "ritual," one is reminded of what Wittgenstein says about thought: it is like silver paper, and once crumpled it cannot ever be quite smoothed out again (1977a: 39).

If concomitant sentiments or opinions or purposes do not provide the key to what is enacted as ritual, perhaps the answer lies in a distant past, possibly in a period which saw the origin of the practice. Wittgenstein has a number of corrective observations to offer on this score. A historical explanation, as a hypothesis of development, is, he says, "only *one* kind of summary of the data—of their synopsis"; it is equally possible to see the data in their relations one to another and to fit them together into a general picture without putting this into the form of a hypothesis about chronological development (8). Certainly it is possible to conceive of facts of ritual as governed by some law, and to set out this law by means of a developmental (or evolutionary) hypothesis; but the idea can also be expressed just by arranging the factual materials in a perspicuous representation, and this makes possible the comprehension which consists simply in "seeing the connections" (8–9). Hence, Wittgenstein adds, the importance of finding intermediate links. But for him, he explains, a hypothetical link "is not meant to do anything except draw attention to the similarity, the connection, of the *facts*" (9). Then he makes the illuminating comparison: "As one might illustrate an internal relation of a circle to an ellipse by gradually transforming an ellipse into a circle; *but not in order to assert that a given ellipse in fact, historically, developed from a circle* . . . but only to sharpen our eye for a formal connection."

So also the hypothesis of development can be seen as nothing but one way of expressing a formal connection (9).

These considerations do not mean that rites have no beginnings, or undergo no historical changes, or that their development cannot ever be traced or reconstructed; the Eucharist alone would suffice to refute such inferences. But the remarks do imply that we should not assume the significance of a rite to reside in its origin alone, or that the original significance has survived only as an ineffectual relic of custom, or that the present performance of the rite provides an insufficient justification of its existence.

The historical example that Wittgenstein reflects upon is the Beltane custom as reported from western Perthshire toward the end of the eighteenth century and as recounted by Frazer. A feature of this practice was that special cakes were baked for the occasion and that these had small lumps in the form of nipples raised all over the surface. In the reported practice of the custom, whoever got a particular piece of the cake was seized by the other participants, who made a show of putting him into the fire, and for a time thereafter this person was spoken of as dead. Frazer offers the "conjecture" that this looks like the relics of a casting of lots. "And through this aspect," remarks Wittgenstein, "it suddenly gains depth" (15e). If we were to learn that the cake with knobs on had originally been baked in honor of a button-maker on his birthday, and that the practice had persisted in the district, it would in fact lose all "depth." (Unless, he adds, the depth should lie in the present form of the practice itself.) Suppose further, Wittgenstein continues, that nowadays the Beltane custom is performed only by children, who hold contests in baking cakes and decorating them with knobs. "Then the depth lies consequently only in the thought of that ancestry" (15). It is as though it were the historical hypothesis that first gives the affair depth— "its *connection* with the burning of a man" (14). The question, to Wittgenstein, is consequently: "does the sinister character of the Beltane Fire inhere in the usage itself, or only if the hypothesis of its origin is confirmed?" (14).

Wittgenstein's remarks about the "depth" of a ritual are clearly important to him; as he proceeds, the topic is more frequently mentioned. It is as though he were working toward the contention that what distinguishes ritual, its "peculiar character," lies in something deep in it. This depth is not simply that of historical antiquity; the celebration of a button-maker's birthday might be just as old as the ceremonial survival of human sacrifice. Why then does the Beltane custom lose all depth, in his eyes, if it commemorates a button-maker? Is it because making buttons is a priori less important than killing a man? Or because the button-maker himself, or in his social standing, was less important and memorable than a victim of ritual burning? These contrasts in evaluation are not self-evident, and in the nature of the case they do not repose on historical evidence. So either they are arbitrary premises or else they reflect moral and other estimations which, apposite though they may be today, need not have prevailed at the time of the inception of the practice. The conviction of depth therefore calls for some other justification. Certainly a historical reconstruction will not serve: Wittgenstein later suggests that "what is sinister, deep, does not lie in the fact that this is how the history of this practice went, for perhaps it did not go that way; nor in the fact that perhaps or probably it was like that, but in what it is that gives me grounds to assume so" (16). For that matter, he asks, what makes human sacrifice something deep and sinister anyway? Is it only the suffering of the victim that impresses us in this way? But all kinds of illnesses cause just as much suffering, yet do not make this impression. "This deep and sinister character does not become obvious when we just learn the history of the external action, but we derive it from an experience in our inner selves" (16).

It is possible to feel that we can sympathize with Wittgenstein in the way he seems to respond to the "deep" nature of a practice originating in human sacrifice, but from a more detached standpoint there are numerous obscurities in his account. The example he considers is gruesome, we might well say, but then so, in physical terms, was the Crucifixion, and this is not supposed to create an impression of a "sinister" depth. Evidently, too, the depth does not depend exclusively on a terrible character in what is commemorated. Suppose a symbolic action represents something sublime, such as the Ascension or the Enlightenment of the Buddha, then presumably this too will have "depth." So the particular evaluation placed on the prototypical event is not what confers depth, and neither does a particular emotional response derived from our inner experience. Nevertheless, Wittgenstein insists on the "terrible," and again in a way with which we can sympathize ("we" in this instance having had, let us assume, much the same moral and religious education as he had) but which analytically is hard to sustain. He says that in the casting of lots (to determine who shall be the victim) the fact that a cake is chosen has something particularly terrible about it, "almost like betrayal through a kiss"—clearly in reference to Judas identifying Jesus in the Garden by kissing him before the multitude who had come to lay hands on him. This fact, he asserts, "is of central importance for the investigation of such practices"; the impression he gains is "very deep and extremely serious" (15). Well, no doubt the Beltane cake can be seen as a terribly deceptive or mocking means of sending a man to his death, but compared with the ghastly outcome the form of the lottery is surely quite trivial in importance. Suppose an unlucky dip were held instead. Concealed in a container are various objects, such as a nut, a cork, and other things, and the victim is the man who gets a flint or a steel (for making fire). Here the lot is of the same kind as the fate of the victim thus selected, but this symbolic appositeness does not self-evidently make the proceedings any less terrible.

It is a general finding in the study of symbolism, moreover, that anything can be made to stand for anything else; whatever it may be, a thing can bear practically any meaning in the eyes of those who use it for a given purpose. But then how do we know what meaning the Beltane cake had in addition to its function in determining the victim? There is no prior reason to think that for those who took part in the practice there was anything terrible about it. To judge that possibility we should have to know a great deal about foodstuffs, dietary laws, alimentary symbolism, types of cake, and much else among the hypothetical originators of the practice. And even then it would need to be discovered that those people actually regarded burning a man alive as being in itself terrible. But, alas, there is abundant historical evidence from elsewhere that they might well not have done so—and there is no intrinsic necessity, in any case, that they should have found terrible what they regularly practiced.

So neither the method of the lottery nor the fate of the victim has inherently any character or meaning other than what is ascribed to the festival by the practitioners. If there is anything deep or sinister going on, it is they who must tell us so. Only what they will tell us is not in general going to stand in any determinate connection with the way the particular symbolic action came into being; and there is even less chance that their ideas and emotions will correspond to those of an alien inquirer. On the one hand, therefore, Wittgenstein has good reason to abjure an explanation by historical reconstruction; but on the other hand he has not supplied the grounds to accept that the character of a rite is to be elicited from our own experience. In particular, the character of "depth" has not been shown to belong in a vocabulary for the comparative analysis of ritual.

Wittgenstein says that what gives depth to the consideration of characteristic features of ritual is that which connects these with "our own feelings and thoughts" (13). In the concluding lines to the first publication of the "Bemerkungen" (1967b: 253), he alludes to the embarrassment that we feel by reason of our physical or aesthetic inferiority; "we" (*wir*) is what he writes, but he revealingly qualifies this pronoun by adding at once, "or at any rate many people (I) [*ich*]."

VII

At the end of his "Remarks," Wittgenstein turns to an alternative interpretation of the Beltane festival: the people cast lots in order to have the fun of threatening to throw someone in the fire. This would be disagreeable, like a practical joke, and might procure the same kind of satisfaction. But such an explanation would take away all "mystery" from the festival, were it not that it is different in action and in mood from familiar games (18). There is still something about the rite that the explanation does not touch.

In the same way, he continues, the fact that on certain days children burn a straw man could make us uneasy, even if no explanation were given for it. Strange that they should celebrate by burning a *man*! And then Wittgenstein makes a remark that attaches in general to the search for such explanations as Frazer proposed. The German goes, "Ich will sagen: die Lösung ist nicht beunruhigender als das Rätsel" (18; cf. 1967b: 251). The English translation has, quite correctly, "What I want to say is: the solution is not any more disquieting than the riddle" (18e). But this really does not fit as a conclusion to Wittgenstein's preceding remarks. It may be that he intended to write "nicht minder beunruhigend" but left out *minder*, less, though this slip would still leave the comparative adjective *beunruhigender* unaccounted for. Whatever may have happened, the expectable sense of the passage would read: "The solution is no less disquieting than the riddle." This is not only a contextual improvement, from a logical point of view, but it is worth special stress because of its far wider implications. The methodological point to be taken is that an explanation should explain. If we are disquieted by a problem, and an attempt to explain it leaves us no *less* disquieted, then the explanation has failed.

In the case of the Beltane festival, the ground of Wittgenstein's disquiet is apparently moral, not analytical; the explanation that originally a man was burnt alive, and that this is what is celebrated, is "sinister." Nevertheless, it could still be a correct explanation. But the methodological point obtains in more pertinent regards. To say that the reported practice, which mimicked the burning of a man, commemorated an earlier practice in which a man was really burnt, is no explanation at all. Even if it could be proved that this was what was originally done, and that the ceremony later became reduced to a mere simulation, still the custom would not be explained. What we want to know is why a man should have been burnt alive anyway. To say that this was an instance of "human sacrifice" would be no answer, and would fail in three distinct ways. First, it merely replaces a description by a label. Second, the label does not denote a class of events for which there already exists a proved explanation. Third, the particular motivation of the originators of the Beltane festival is inaccessible and cannot be adequately surmised; so just to be assured that they did sacrifice a man would still leave us knowing no more than that they burned him. We are left wondering, therefore, what would qualify as an explanation, not only in this case but in a very extensive range of cases of which the present one is typical.

Wittgenstein says that what we strive for through an explanation is "satisfaction" (*Befriedigung*); and he thinks this can be attained, even if the attempt to find an explanation is wrong (2e). Perhaps there is a clue here to his understanding of ritual. He later alludes to satisfaction in another connection (4):

> Burning in effigy. Kissing the picture of a person one loves. This is *obviously not* based on a belief that it will have a definite effect on the object represented by the picture. It aims at a satisfaction and it also achieves it. Or rather: it does not *aim* at anything; we act in this way and then feel satisfied [*befriedigt*]. —One could also kiss the name of the beloved, and here the substitution by means of the name would be clear.

Kissing a picture (for example, a photograph) is a recognizable and perhaps even normal thing to do among ourselves; that is, among people who are brought up to kiss as a sign of affection and who are familiar with the pictorial representation of individuals. But the point of the practice—to the uncertain extent that it may in fact be a practice rather than a sentimental convention—is a matter of empirical psychology which cannot be presumed, only discovered. Perhaps in the minds of some it really does have an effect on the person represented, rather as blessing or prayer is taken to confer grace or protection at a distance. In the minds of others it may not be inspired by such a pragmatic confidence, but may express a longing, a wish, a hope, or else unease or desperation or whatever other state of mind may accompany the action. The likelihood, at any rate, must be that only the vaguest of affectionate commitments will inhere in the practice, and that an extensive variety of inner states and more or less clear-cut intentions can be accommodated by it.

The action of kissing a picture may or may not be aimed at some effect; this also is a matter of fact, not inference. But then the consequences for the actor will be just as uncertain. Wittgenstein states that "we feel satisfied," but as a matter of fact this is highly disputable. It can easily be conceived that the actor might instead feel frustrated, for example, or resentful or despondent after kissing the picture. And even if someone did say that he himself felt satisfied after doing so, it would not be at all clear what state he was reporting. We should at least have to elicit from him what his motive was, and what expectations he had in view, for only in the light of these factors could we begin to assess wherein he was satisfied. This alone, however, would still not be enough, for the actor's own explication could not always be accepted at face value; and even if what he said were accepted as being entirely candid, there might nevertheless subsist other factors of a subconscious nature which, if uncovered, could tell a different story. Moreover, in even the best of cases we should thus be provided with no more than the grounds for interpreting the actor's report that in the end he did feel satisfied; we should not know, just from that epithet, what was the peculiar quality of the inner state in question. The verb "to satisfy" means, with reference to feelings or needs, "to meet or fulfill the wish or desire or expectation of"; to be satisfied is "to be content (with)," to find something "sufficient" (*Shorter Oxford English Dictionary*). Surely none of these conditions obtains, typically, when someone kisses a picture. Only if kissing the picture were all he wanted to do could he be satisfied by doing only that.

Wittgenstein arrives at this example via that of burning in effigy, in connection with the Beltane custom. Although kissing a picture is less dramatic than mimicking the burning of a man—indeed, while conventional it is essentially private—it poses the same questions and gets the same answers as does any instance of what is ordinarily typed as ritual. When we designate ritual as symbolic action, the implication is that the analysis of it will be as intricate as is that of any other institutionalized form of action; the main difference is that the "symbolic" aspect makes it all the more obscure and problematical. The intricacy and the obscurity together extend to purposes, means, effects, inner states, and reasons. What is enacted is not really carried out, but we are confronted with representations and substitutions; the explanations that we are offered do not explain; and the plausibility of metaphors that seem at first to answer to the case also dissipates under the intensity of analysis. For all the salutary changes of aspect under which Wittgenstein exposes new facets of ritual, or presents the familiar in inventive formulations, the topic is still recalcitrant to a theoretical explanation.

VIII

If we take stock of the problem of ritual, in positive terms, we find in Wittgenstein's remarks two propositions that are particularly worth dwelling upon.

The first is that we have to do with the "ceremonial" in contrast with the haphazard (5, 16). This reinforces the property of formality that we began by ascribing to ritual. Admittedly, the formality is not a specific feature, since, as we have seen, it is shared by many other forms of conduct that we should not wish to call ritual. Nevertheless, it is a characteristic feature (cf. Needham 1972: 120–21), and it suggests a shift of method. In other fields of investigation a useful precept, it has been found, is to concentrate not on types but on properties; once these are isolated, the task is to see what they are properties of (Needham 1978: 57, 60), and only then may it be helpful to circumscribe a type of social fact such as "ritual." In the present instance, the significant property is formality, and it is this property itself that might repay comparative examination. That would take us very far beyond ritual, however, and for our present purpose we need not try to foresee what the outcome of such a comparison might be. It is enough to remark the formality that is a characteristic feature of ritual, and to affirm that this property is well founded by empirical generalization. The generalization finds expression in Wittgenstein's remark that we might almost say that man is a "ceremonial animal" (7).

The other proposition to be retained from Wittgenstein's remarks, as a clue to what may be a significant property of ritual, responds to the question: What makes us unwilling to assume that the Beltane festival has always been celebrated in its present (or very recent) form? Wittgenstein replies, "We feel like saying: it is too meaningless to have been invented in this form" (17e). He compares the case with seeing a ruin and saying that it must have been a house once, for nobody would have set up hewn and irregular stones in such a pile as this. "And even where people really do build ruins, they give them the forms of tumbled-down houses" (17). Here the presumption is that the festival (rite) must once have had an intrinsic significance which, if it could be reconstructed, would constitute an explanation of the practice. But it is none the less a presumption, and the analogy with a ruined house is in fact crucially misleading. It may help us to see on what grounds people do tend to assume that there must once have been an intact and identifiable meaning to a rite, and that what we now observe are "ruins," relics, survivals that have lost their original form and significance. It does not, however, justify such an interpretation on the part of an analyst, who ought indeed to be sceptically on his guard against the temptations of precisely this kind of analogy. The comparison of a "meaningless" rite with a ruined house expresses a theory—and the theory is not proved by merely assuming the aptness of the analogy.

So a main question remains: Why should a supposedly original form of a rite have had any more clear and intrinsic a meaning than does the present form? After all, if a rite can be performed today by participants who ascribe disparate and even conflicting meanings to it, or if it can be properly performed even while appearing to be meaningless, why should its performance ever have been inspired by a clearer ascription of significance? What calls for examination is the very assumption that the rite must have had a clear meaning once.

In certain cases it may seem that an original meaning can be determined, and it may therefore appear that such rites exemplify a general rule which could explain other rites for which no such historical demonstration was possible. The Eucharist, again, is apparently such a case. But when Christ enjoined his disciples, "This do in remembrance of me," he was already drawing on a multifarious complex of meanings centered on the Passover and on Judaic dietary laws and commensual practices; and in these respects he was not inventing an integral significance that would constitute the unique explanation of the subsequent enactment of the rite. It could still be, of course, that some other rite would actually meet this condition, but in the normal run of things we have no means whatever of determining any earlier meanings, let alone a single original significance for any particular rite. This general fact takes us back, therefore, to the medley of interpretations by which participants in rites currently offer to explain what they are doing, and we have already seen that these provide no analytical explanation. If this situation can in some way be seen as comparable with a ruin, in that it lacks form or coherence or the fulfillment of a unifying intention, there are still no grounds on which to infer that it must at some former time have been any different.

The foregoing considerations stem from Wittgenstein's remark about our unwillingness to accept that a rite may be meaningless. The unwillingness may well be a fact, but that a rite must possess a meaning that is the explanation for its performance is not a fact. The question then is: Why can a rite *not* be meaningless? After all, if we cannot determine an original meaning, and if there is no unitary significance agreed to by its current participants, then we have already acceded to the very fact that in these regards there is no meaning. In that case, then, a rite can indeed be intrinsically meaningless.

Naturally, we could also say conversely that in the circumstances of the matter there can be a superabundance of meaning, in that a variety of opinions may be held about a rite and its origins and occasions, but this contention would not settle the point at issue. What we have been looking for is a meaning that will explain the rite, and in this respect it can well be that there is no such meaning to be established. More fundamentally, also, a rite could be meaningless in that even in the minds of the participants it was not regarded as having any significance beyond itself. It would be, in Waley's words, "customary" or "the thing to do" (1938: 58)—and this is precisely the kind of statement that ethnographers so frequently meet with. It is not at all a queer state of affairs, in other words, for it is something that is encountered all the time by professional investigators of formal symbolic behavior.

In that case, though, why do we not just accept what we already know? For it is a fact that ritual can indeed be meaningless in the sense required. It may well be that the purpose and meaning and effect of a rite will consist in no more than the performance of the rite itself. Ritual can be self-sufficient, self-sustaining, and self-justifying. Considered in its most characteristic features, it is a kind of activity—like speech or dancing—that man as a "ceremonial animal" happens naturally to perform.

REFERENCES

Augé, Marc. 1979. *Symbole, fonction, histoire*. Paris: Hachette.

Bouveresse, Jacques. 1977. "L'Animal cérémoniel: Wittgenstein et l'anthropologie." *Actes de la Recherche en Sciences Sociales* 16: 43–54.

Browne, Thomas. 1658. *Hydriotaphia: Urne-Buriall*. London: Printed for Hen. Brome at the Signe of the Gun at Ivy-lane.

Descartes, René. 1649. *Les Passions de l'âme*. Amsterdam: Elsevier.

Feeley-Harnik, Gillian. 1981. *The Lord's Table: Eucharist and Passover in Early Christianity*. Philadelphia: University of Pennsylvania Press.

Needham, Rodney. 1972. *Belief, Language, and Experience*. Oxford: Basil Blackwell; Chicago: University of Chicago Press.

———. 1973a. ed., *Right & Left: Essays on Dual Symbolic Classification*. Chicago: University of Chicago Press.

———. 1973b. "Prospects and Impediments." *The Times Literary Supplement*, July 6: 785–86.

———. 1974. *Remarks and Inventions: Skeptical Essays about Kinship*. London: Tavistock Publications; New York: Harper & Row.

———. 1975. "Polythetic Classification: Convergence and Consequences." *Man*, n.s., 10: 349–69. Reprinted in Needham (1983), chap. 3.

———. 1976. "Skulls and Causality." *Man*, n.s., 11: 71–88. Reprinted in Needham (1983), chap. 4.

———. 1978. *Primordial Characters*. Charlottesville: University Press of Virginia.

———. 1979. *Symbolic Classification*. Santa Monica, CA: Goodyear Publishing. Distributed by Random House, New York.

———. 1980. *Reconnaissances*. Toronto: University of Toronto Press.

———. 1981. *Circumstantial Deliveries*. Berkeley: University of California Press.

———. 1983. *Against the Tranquility of Axioms*. Berkeley: University of California Press.

Rhees, Rush. 1982. "Wittgenstein on Language and Ritual." In *Wittgenstein and His Times*, edited by Brian McGuinness, 69–107. Oxford: Basil Blackwell.

Rudich, Norman, and Manfred Stassen. 1971. "Wittgenstein's Implied Anthropology: Remarks on Wittgenstein's Notes on Frazer." *History and Theory* 10 (1): 84–89.

Waley, Arthur. 1938. *The Analects of Confucius*. London: George Allen & Unwin.

Wilson, Bryan R., ed. 1970. *Rationality*. Oxford: Basil Blackwell.

Wittgenstein, Ludwig. 1958. *The Blue and Brown Books*. Oxford: Basil Blackwell.

———. 1967a. *Philosophical Investigations*, 3rd ed. Translated by Elizabeth Anscombe. Oxford: Basil Blackwell.

———. 1967b. "Bemerkungen über Frazers *The Golden Bough*." *Synthese* 17: 233–53.

———. 1971. "Remarks on Frazer's 'The Golden Bough.'" Translated by A. C. Miles. Introductory note by Rush Rhees. *The Human World* 3: 18–41.

————. 1977a. *Vermischte Bermerkungen.* Edited by George Henrik von Wright in cooperation with Heikki Nyman. Oxford: Basil Blackwell.

————. 1977b. "Remarques sur le rameau d'or de Frazer." Translated by Jean Lacoste. *Actes de la Recherche en Sciences Sociales* 16 (September): 35–42.

————. 1979. *Remarks on Frazer's "Golden Bough"/Bemerkungen über Frazers "Golden Bough."* Edited by Rush Rhees. Translated by A. C. Miles. Reviewed by Rush Rhees. Retsford, Nottinghamshire: Brynmill Press.

Yarnold, Edward. 1971. *The Awe-Inspiring Rites of Initiation: Baptismal Homilies of the Fourth Century.* Slough: St. Paul Publications.

HAU Books is committed to publishing the most distinguished texts in classic and advanced anthropological theory. The titles aim to situate ethnography as the prime heuristic of anthropology, and return it to the forefront of conceptual developments in the discipline. HAU Books is sponsored by some of the world's most distinguished anthropology departments and research institutions, and releases its titles in both print editions and open-access formats.

www.haubooks.com